Income tax rates

	2010–11		
	%	%	%
Basic rate	20	20	20
Higher rate	40	40	40
Additional rate	50	0	0
Rate on non-dividend savings income	10/20/40/50[1]	10/20/40[2]	10/20/40[3]
Rate on dividend income	10/32.5/42.5[4]	10/32.5	10/32.5
Trust rate	50	40	40
Dividend trust rate	42.5	32.5	32.5
	£	£	£
Basic rate band	1–37,400	1–37,400	1–34,800
Maximum at basic rate	37,400	37,400	34,800
Higher rate band	37,401–150,000	n/a	n/a
Maximum at higher rate	112,600	n/a	n/a

Notes

[1] The rate of tax on non-dividend savings income is 10% up to £2,440, 20% for basic rate taxpayers, 40% for higher rate taxpayers and 50% for additional rate taxpayers.

[2] The rate of tax on non-dividend savings income is 10% up to £2,440, 20% for basic rate taxpayers, and 40% for higher rate taxpayers.

[3] The rate of tax on non-dividend savings income is 10% up to £2,320, 20% for basic rate taxpayers, and 40% for higher rate taxpayers.

[4] The dividend ordinary rate (up to basic rate limit) is 10%, the dividend higher rate (up to higher rate limit) is 32.5% and the dividend additional rate (above higher rate limit) is 42.5%.

Income tax reliefs

	2010–11 £	2009–10 £	2008–09 £	2007–08 £
Personal allowance	6,475	6,475	6,035	5,225
– age 65–74	9,490	9,490	9,030	7,550
– age 75 or over	9,640	9,640	9,180	7,690
Married couple's allowance				
– age less than 75 and born before 6 April 1935	[1]	[1]	6,535	6,285
– age 75 or over	6,965	6,965	6,625	6,365
Minimum amount of allowance	2,670	2,670	2,540	2,440
Maximum income before abatement of relief	22,900	22,900	21,800	20,900
Abatement income ceiling				
Single – age 65–74	28,930	28,930	27,790	25,550
– age 75 or over	29,230	29,230	28,090	25,830
Married – age 65–74	[1]	[1]	35,780	33,240
– age 75 or over	37,820	37,820	36,260	33,680
Blind person's allowance	1,890	1,890	1,800	1,730
'Rent-a-room' limit	4,250	4,250	4,250	4,250

Notes

[1] Not applicable.

National Insurance contributions

Class 1 primary (employee) contributions	2010–11	2009–10
Lower earnings limit (LEL)	£97 weekly	£95 weekly
Primary threshold	£110 weekly	£110 weekly
Upper earnings limit (UEL)	£844 weekly	£844 weekly
Upper accrual point (UAP)	£770 weekly	£770 weekly
Rate on earnings up to primary threshold	0%	0%
Not contracted-out rate	11% (£110.01–£844); 1% above £844	11% (£110.01–£844); 1% above £844
Contracted-out rate	9.4% (£110.01–£770); 11% (£770.01–£844); 1% above £844	9.4% (£110.01–£770); 11% (£770.01–£844); 1% above £844
Reduced rate	4.85% (£110.01–£844); 1% above £844	4.85% (£110.01–£844); 1% above £844

Class 1 secondary (employer) contributions 2010–11	
Secondary earnings threshold	£110 weekly £476 monthly £5,715 yearly
Not contracted-out rate	12.8% on earnings above threshold
Contracted-out rate	9.1% for salary-related (COSR) and 11.4% for money-purchase (COMP) schemes on earnings from secondary threshold to UAP (plus 3.7% and 1.4% rebates for earnings from LEL to secondary threshold), then 12.8% on earnings above UAP

Class 1 secondary (employer) contributions 2009–10	
Secondary earnings threshold	£110 weekly £476 monthly £5,715 yearly
Not contracted-out rate	12.8% on earnings above threshold
Contracted-out rate	9.1% for salary-related (COSR) and 11.4% for money-purchase (COMP) schemes on earnings from secondary threshold to UAP (plus 3.7% and 1.4% rebates for earnings from LEL to secondary threshold), then 12.8% on earnings above UAP

Class 2 – Self-employed	2010–11	2009–10	2008–09	2007–08
	£	£	£	£
Small earnings exemption limit (annual)	5,075	5,075	4,825	4,635
Weekly rate	2.40	2.40	2.30	2.20
Class 3 – Voluntary contributions	**2010–11**	**2009–10**	**2008–09**	**2007–08**
	£	£	£	£
Weekly rate	12.05	12.05	8.10	7.80
Class 4 – Self-employed	**2010–11**	**2009–10**	**2008–09**	**2007–08**
	£	£	£	£
Annual earnings limit – upper	43,875	43,875	40,040	34,840
– lower	5,715	5,715	5,435	5,225
Rate	8%	8%	8%	8%
	(£5,715–£43,875); 1% above £43,875	(£5,715–£43,875); 1% above £43,875	(£5,435–£40,040); 1% above £40,040	(£5,225–£34,840); 1% above £34,840

Taxation of capital gains

For gains of individuals arising on disposals occurring on or before 22 June 2010, the rate of tax is 18 per cent. Where disposals occur on or after 23 June 2010, the chargeable gains arising from those disposals are aggregated with the individual's taxable income and to the extent that the aggregate falls above the threshold of the income tax basic rate, capital gains tax is charged at 28 per cent (taking the chargeable gains as being the highest part of that aggregate). If the aggregate falls below the threshold, the capital gains tax rate remains at 18 per cent.

For gains of trustees or personal representatives arising on disposals occurring on or before 22 June 2010, the rate is 18 per cent. Where disposals occur on or after 23 June 2010, the rate is 28 per cent.

Exemptions and reliefs	2010–11	2009–10	2008–09	2007–08
	£	£	£	£
Annual exempt amount	10,100	10,100	9,600	9,200
Chattel exemption (max. sale proceeds)	6,000	6,000	6,000	6,000

Inheritance tax

	Gross rate of tax	
Gross cumulative transfer (on or after 6 April 2010)	Transfers on death	Lifetime transfers
	%	%
£1–£325,000	Nil	Nil
£325,000 upwards	40	20

Note
Estate on death taxed as top slice of cumulative transfers in the seven years before death. Most lifetime transfers (other than to discretionary trusts) are potentially exempt, only becoming chargeable where death occurs within seven years.

Annual exemption	£3,000
Small gift exemption	£250

Taxation of companies

Financial year	2010	2009	2008
Main rate	28%	28%	28%
Small companies' (SC) rate[1]	21%	21%	21%
Profit limit for SC rate	£300,000	£300,000	£300,000
Marginal relief fraction (SC rate)	7/400	7/400	7/400

Note
[1] The small companies' rate is not available to 'close investment-holding companies'.

VAT

Standard rate	
From 4 January 2011	20%
1 January 2010–3 January 2011	17.5%
1 December 2008–31 December 2009	15%
1 April 1991–30 November 2008	17.5%
Annual registration limit – taxable supplies (from 1 April 2010)	£70,000
De-registration limit – taxable supplies (from 1 April 2010)	£68,000
VAT fraction	
For standard rate of 15%	3/23
For standard rate of 17.5%	7/47
For standard rate of 20%	1/6

PREFACE

Now in its 35th edition, *Hardman's Tax Rates & Tables* contains the numerical and factual data in everyday use by the tax practitioner. The material is conveniently arranged in seventeen chapters:

- Principles of income tax
- Taxation of business profits
- Taxation of investment income
- Taxation of earnings
- Taxation of capital gains
- Inheritance tax
- Taxation of companies
- Capital allowances
- National Insurance contributions
- Tax credits
- State benefits and statutory payments
- General
- Stamp taxes
- Value added tax
- Insurance premium tax
- Landfill tax
- Aggregates levy

This Special Edition takes full account of the June 2010 Emergency Budget announcements which are likely to be contained in both the Finance (No. 2) Bill 2010 and the Finance Bill to be published as soon as possible after Parliament's 2010 summer recess. These provisions may be affected by amendments mades during the passage of the Bills through Parliament.

Cross-references to CCH's *Tax Reporter* and *VAT Reporter* are included.

Every effort has been taken to include, within the constraints of available space, the information of greatest use to the practitioner. A number of changes have been made in the light of suggestions received from users of previous years' editions. CCH welcomes further suggestions as to material which might be inserted in future editions.

Paul Robbins

July 2010

Note: the late Philip Hardman was the original editor of *Hardman's Tax Rates & Tables*. CCH gratefully acknowledges the considerable help and guidance that he provided.

Disclaimer

This publication is sold with the understanding that neither the publisher nor the authors, with regard to this publication, are engaged in rendering legal or professional services. The material contained in this publication neither purports, nor is intended to be, advice on any particular matter.

Although this publication incorporates a considerable degree of standardisation, subjective judgment by the user, based on individual circumstances, is indispensable. This publication is an aid and cannot be expected to replace such judgment.

Neither the publisher nor the authors can accept any responsibility or liability to any person, whether a purchaser of this publication or not, in respect of anything done or omitted to be done by any such person in reliance, whether sole or partial, upon the whole or any part of the contents of this publication.

Legislative and other material

While copyright in all statutory and other materials resides in the Crown or other relevant body, copyright in the remaining material in this publication is vested in the publisher.

The publisher advises that any statutory or other materials issued by the Crown or other relevant bodies and reproduced and quoted in this publication are not the authorized official versions of those statutory or other materials. In the preparation, however, the greatest care has been taken to ensure exact conformity with the law as enacted or other material as issued.

Crown copyright legislation is reproduced under the terms of Crown Copyright Policy Guidance issued by HMSO. Other Crown copyright material is reproduced with the permission of the controller of HMSO. European Communities Copyright material is reproduced with permission.

Telephone Helpline Disclaimer Notice

Where purchasers of this publication also have access to any Telephone Helpline Service operated by Wolters Kluwer (UK), then Wolters Kluwers total liability to contract, tort (including negligence, or breach of statutory duty) misrepresentation, restitution or otherwise with respect to any claim arising out of its acts or alleged omissions in the provision of the Helpline Service shall be limited to the yearly subscription fee paid by the Claimant.

Ownership of Trade Marks

The trade marks

a Wolters Kluwer business

are the property of Wolters Kluwer BV

ISBN: 978-1-84798-332-9
CCH Code: UP/TRTS-BI10001

British Library Cataloguing-in-Publication Data.

A catalogue record for this book is available from the British Library.

Printed and bound in the UK by Hobbs the Printers Ltd.

vii

About the Publisher

CCH is part of the Wolters Kluwer Group. Wolters Kluwer is the leading international publisher specialising in tax, business and law publishing throughout Europe, the US and the Asia Pacific region. The Group produces a wide range of information services in different media for the accounting and legal professions and for business.

All CCH publications are designed to be practical and authoritative reference works and guides and are written by our own highly qualified and experienced editorial team and specialist outside authors.

CCH publishes information packages including electronic products, loose-leaf reporting services, newsletters and books on UK and European legal topics for distribution world-wide. The UK operation also acts as distributor of the publications of the overseas affiliates.

CCH
145 London Road
Kingston-upon-Thames
Surrey
KT2 6SR
Telephone: 0844 561 8166
Facsimile: 0208 547 2638
Email: customerservices@cch.co.uk
Website: www.cch.co.uk

Part of the Wolters Kluwer Group

Acknowledgements

Certain material in this publication is Crown Copyright and is reproduced with the kind permission of the Controller of Her Majesty's Stationery Office.

CCH kindly acknowledges the endorsement of this publication by the Chartered Institute of Taxation and the Tax Faculty of the Institute of Chartered Accountants in England and Wales.

The Association of Taxation Technicians

PRINCIPLES OF INCOME TAX

[¶1-000]   Income tax rates

(ITA 2007, ss. 6–15)

(Tax Reporter: ¶148-075ff.)

2010–11

	Taxable income band £	Tax rate %	Tax on band £
Basic rate	1–37,400	20	7,480.00
Higher rate	37,400–150,000	40	45,040.00
Additional rate	Over 150,000	50	

Rate on non-dividend savings income	10% up to £2,440 20% up to basic rate limit 40% up to higher rate limit 50% thereafter
Dividend ordinary rate	10% up to basic rate limit
Dividend higher rate	32.5% up to higher rate limit
Dividend additional rate	42.5% above higher rate limit
Trust rate	50%
Dividend trust rate	42.5%

Note

It was announced in the emergency Budget of 22 June 2010 that for 2011–12 'the basic rate limit will be reduced by an amount to be confirmed once the RPI for September 2010 is known'. This is to ensure that higher rate taxpayers do not benefit from the increase in the personal allowance.

2009–10

	Taxable income band £	Tax rate %	Tax on band £
Basic rate	1–37,400	20	7,480.00
Higher rate	Over 37,400	40	

Rate on non-dividend savings income	10% up to £2,440 20% up to basic rate limit 40% thereafter
Dividend ordinary rate	10% up to basic rate limit
Dividend upper rate	32.5% above basic rate limit
Trust rate	40%
Dividend trust rate	32.5%

2008–09

	Taxable income band £	Tax rate %	Tax on band £
Basic rate	1–34,800	20	6,960.00
Higher rate	Over 34,800	40	

Rate on non-dividend savings income	10% up to £2,320 20% up to basic rate limit 40% thereafter
Dividend ordinary rate	10% up to basic rate limit
Dividend upper rate	32.5% above basic rate limit
Trust rate	40%
Dividend trust rate	32.5%

2007–08

	Taxable income band £	Tax rate %	Tax on band £
Starting rate	0– 2,230	10	223.00
Basic rate	2,231–34,600	22	7,121.40
Higher rate	Over 34,600	40	

Rate on non-dividend savings income	10% up to starting rate limit 20% up to basic rate limit 40% thereafter
Dividend ordinary rate	10% up to basic rate limit
Dividend upper rate	32.5% above basic rate limit
Trust rate	40%
Dividend trust rate	32.5%

2006–07

	Taxable income band £	Tax rate %	Tax on band £
Starting rate	0– 2,150	10	215.00
Basic rate	2,151–33,300	22	6,853.00
Higher rate	Over 33,300	40	

Rate on non-dividend savings income	10% up to starting rate limit 20% up to basic rate limit 40% thereafter
Dividend ordinary rate	10% up to basic rate limit
Dividend upper rate	32.5% above basic rate limit
Rate applicable to trusts	40%
Dividend trust rate	32.5%

[¶1-100] Personal allowances and reliefs

(ITA 2007, ss. 35–46)

(Tax Reporter: ¶155-000ff.)

Type of relief	2010–11 £	2009–10 £	2008–09 £	2007–08 £	2006–07 £
Personal allowance[(1), (2)]					
Age under 65	6,475	6,475	6,035	5,225	5,035
Age 65–74	9,490	9,490	9,030	7,550	7,280
Age 75 & over	9,640	9,640	9,180	7,690	7,420
Married couple's allowance[(3)]					
Born before 6 April 1935;					
Age up to 74	– [(4)]	– [(4)]	6,535	6,285	6,065
Born before 6 April 1935;					
Age 75 & over	6,965	6,965	6,625	6,365	6,135
Minimum amount of allowance	2,670	2,670	2,540	2,440	2,350
Maximum income before abatement of reliefs for older taxpayers:	22,900	22,900	21,800	20,900	20,100
Abatement income ceiling Personal allowance:					
Age 65–74	28,930	28,930	27,790	25,550	24,590
Age 75 & over	29,230	29,230	28,090	25,830	24,870
Married couples allowance					
Born before 6 April 1935;					
Age up to 74	–[(3)]	–[(3)]	35,780	33,240	32,020
Born before 6 April 1935;					
Age 75 & over	37,820	37,820	36,260	33,680	32,440
Blind person's allowance	1,890	1,890	1,800	1,730	1,660
Life assurance relief (policies issued before 14 March 1984)	12.5% of premiums	12.5% of premiums	12.5% of premiums	12.5% of premiums	12.5% of premiums
'Rent-a-room' limit	4,250	4,250	4,250	4,250	4,250

Notes

[(1)] It was announced in the emergency Budget of 22 June 2010 that for 2011–12 the personal allowance for those aged under 65 will be £7,475. Details of other allowances and thresholds are not yet available.

[(2)] From April 2010, the personal allowance is gradually withdrawn for income over £100,000 at a rate of £1 of allowance lost for every £2 over £100,000 until it is completely removed (FA 2009, s. 4).

[(3)] Relief is given at a rate of 10%.

[(4)] Claimants born before 6 April 1935 will have become 75 at some point during 2009-10 and therefore will be entitled to the higher amount of the allowance for that tax year and subsequent tax years, i.e. for those aged 75 or over.

[¶1-150]   Gifts of assets

Nature of asset	Legislation	Effect of relief
Stock manufactured or sold by trader that is given to charity, etc. (Tax Reporter: ¶226–650)	CTA 2009, s. 105; ITA 2007, s. 108	No amount is brought into account as trading receipt as result of the donation
Plant and machinery used by trader given to a charity, etc. (Tax Reporter: ¶238–235)	CAA 2001, s. 63	Disposal value is nil for capital allowances purposes
Stock manufactured or sold by trader that is given to a designated educational establishment and qualifies as plant or machinery in the donee's hands. (Tax Reporter: ¶238–235)	CTA 2009, s. 105; ITA 2007, s. 108	No amount is brought into account as a trading receipt as result of the donation
Plant or machinery used by trader that is given to a designated educational establishment and qualifies as plant and machinery in the donee's hands. (Tax Reporter: ¶238–235)	CAA 2001, s. 63	Disposal value is nil for capital allowances purposes
Listed shares and securities, unlisted shares and securities dealt with on a recognised stock exchange, units in unit trusts, etc., interests in land, that are given to a charity. (Tax Reporter: ¶115–575; ¶709–350)	CTA 2010, s. 203; ITA 2007, Pt. 8, Ch. 3	Full value of gift is deductible in calculating profits for IT or CT purposes
Property settled by gift on a UK trust which has a charity as a beneficiary and the settlor retains an interest (Tax Reporter:¶351-200)	ITTOIA 2005, s. 646A	The trust income allocated to the settlor is reduced by an amount equal to the income paid to the charity in the year

[¶1-250]   Submission dates for 2010–11 personal tax returns

(TMA 1970, s. 8)

(Tax Reporter: ¶180-050)

TMA 1970, s. 8 contains provisions concerning submission dates for returns issued on or after 6 April 2010 which relate to 2010–11, as follows:

- paper returns (whether or not HMRC is to calculate the tax liability) must be filed by 31 October 2011; and
- online returns must be filed by 31 January 2012.

There are the following exceptions:

Circumstances	Filing date
Return issued after 31 July 2011 but before 31 October 2011	3 months from the date of issue (paper returns); 31 January 2012 (online returns)
Return issued after 31 October 2011	Three months from date of issue
Taxpayer wishes underpayment (below £2,000) to be coded out under 2012–13 PAYE (paper returns)	31 October 2011
Taxpayer wishes underpayment (below £2,000) to be coded out under 2012–13 PAYE (online returns)	30 December 2011

[¶1-300]   Payment dates 2010–11

(TMA 1970, ss. 59A, 59B)

(Tax Reporter: ¶181-200 and ¶181-250)

Tax is paid on 31 January next following the year of assessment as a single sum covering capital gains tax and income tax on all sources. Interim payments on account may be required. No interim payments are required if:

- the tax paid by assessment was less than £1,000, or
- more than 80% of the tax due the previous year was collected at source

A payment on account can never exceed 50% of the net tax for the preceding year, even though it may already be clear, at the time the payments are made, that the actual liability for the year will exceed that for the preceding year. Net tax is the previous year's tax after taking off tax deducted at source and tax on dividends. For 2010–11, the following due dates apply:

First interim payment 31 January 2011
Second interim payment 31 July 2011
Final balancing payment 31 January 2012

Note

If a return is not issued until after 31 October 2010 and the tax payer has notified chargeability by 5 October 2010, the due date for the final payment becomes three months from the issue of the return (TMA 1970, s. 59B).

[¶1-350] Main penalty provisions 2010–11

Offence	Penalty[1][2]
Late return (TMA 1970, s. 93; Tax Reporter: ¶186–100)[3][4][5]:	
• if paper return not filed by 1 November 2011 or online return not filed by 1 February 2012	£100
• if paper return still not filed by 30 April 2012 or online return still not filed by 31 July 2012	£100
• for continuing delay	Up to £60 per day
• if paper return not filed after November 2012 or online return not filed after 1 February 2013	Tax geared
Failure to notify chargeability (TMA 1970, s. 7 and FA 2008, Sch. 41; Tax Reporter: ¶181–800)	
For failures **after** 1 April 2010	
• failure not deliberate	up to 30% of potential lost revenue
• failure deliberate but not concealed	up to 70% of potential lost revenue
• failure deliberate and concealed	up to 100% of potential lost revenue
For failures **before** 1 April 2010	Tax geared up to 100% of the tax, subject to mitigation
Inaccuracies in a return or document (FA 2007, Sch. 24; Tax Reporter: ¶186–225)[6][7]	
• careless inaccuracy	up to 30% of potential lost revenue
• where the inaccuracy is deliberate but not concealed	up to 70% of potential lost revenue
• where the inaccuracy is deliberate and concealed	up to 100% of the potential lost revenue
Failure to keep and retain tax records (TMA 1970, s. 12B; Tax Reporter: ¶180–250)	Up to £3,000 per year of assessment
False statements to reduce interim payments (TMA 1970, s. 59A(6); Tax Reporter: ¶181–200)	Up to the difference between the amount correctly due and the amount paid

Principles of Income Tax

8 ¶1-400

Offence	Penalty[(1)(2)]
Failure to produce documents required to check a person's tax position or obstructing an inspection (FA 2008, Sch. 36, para. 39 and 40; Tax Reporter: ¶184–900)	
• standard amount	£300
• continued failure	daily penalty of £60
Tax-related penalty where significant tax is at risk (FA 2008, Sch. 36, para. 50)	tax geared amount decided by Upper Tribunal

Notes

(1) Interest is charged on penalties not paid when due. The due date is 30 days after the notice of determination of the penalty is issued.

(2) A defence of 'reasonable excuse' may be available.

(3) Late return penalties are cumulative, e.g. for a return six or more months late there are two £100 penalties.

(4) The two fixed £100 penalties are reduced if the total tax payable by assessment is less than the penalty which would otherwise be chargeable.

(5) A new penalty regime for delay was introduced in FA 2009 but the appointed day for its commencement has not yet been announced.

(6) There are certain maximum reductions from the fixed penalties available which vary according to the level of the fixed penalty and whether a disclosure was prompted or unprompted (FA 2007, Sch. 24, para. 10). In determining how much of that reduction to allow HMRC will look at the quality of the disclosure and use weightings of 30% for telling, 40% for helping and 30% for giving access (*Compliance Handbook* CH82430).

(7) No penalty for inaccuracies that occur despite taking reasonable care.

[¶1-400] Surcharges 2010–11

(TMA 1970, s. 59C)

(Tax Reporter: ¶181-350)

Surcharges arise as follows:

Tax overdue	Surcharge
28 days	5% of tax overdue
6 months	further 5% of tax overdue

Notes

(1) Tax is not subject to a surcharge if it is taken into account for penalties for failure to notify – return over 12 months late or incorrect return. A surcharge will be repaid if one of these penalties is subsequently levied.

(2) A new penalty regime for late payments was introduced in FA 2009 but the appointed day for its commencement has not yet been announced except for PAYE. The new regime applies to PAYE for 2010–11 onwards.

Surcharges apply to:

• final tax payments on self-assessments (this includes any amounts due as interim payments which remain unpaid);

• tax on inspector's amendments to a self-assessment made during or as a result of an audit; and

• discovery assessments.

[¶1-450] Interest 2010–11

(TMA 1970, s. 86)

(Tax Reporter: ¶181-400)

Interest is payable from the 'relevant date':

Payment	Relevant date
First interim payment[1]	31 January 2011
Second interim payment	31 July 2011
Final payment	31 January 2012
Tax due on an amendment to a return	31 January 2012
Tax due on determination of appeal	31 January 2012

Notes

[1] Where the taxpayer has provided HMRC in good time with the information required to issue a statement of account ahead of the payment date of 31 January, but no statement is received before 1 January, interest on the tax to be paid will run from 30 days after the taxpayer is actually notified rather than from 31 January.

[2] Where notice to make a return is issued after 31 October 2010, then, provided there has been no failure to notify chargeability under TMA 1970, s. 7, the relevant date becomes the last day in the period of three months beginning with the day notice to make a return was given.

FA 2009, s. 101, 103 and 104 and Sch. 53 contain provisions to harmonise interest regimes across all HMRC taxes and duties.

[¶1-500] Rates of interest on overdue tax

(FA 1989, s. 178)

(Tax Reporter: ¶181-400)

The following table gives the rates of interest applicable in recent years.

Period of application	Rate %
From 29 September 2009	3.0
24 March 2009 to 28 September 2009	2.5
27 January 2009 to 23 March 2009	3.5
5 January 2009 to 26 January 2009	4.5
6 December 2008 to 5 January 2009	5.5
6 November 2008 to 5 December 2008	6.5
6 January 2008 to 5 November 2008	7.5
6 August 2007 to 5 January 2008	8.5
6 September 2006 to 5 August 2007	7.5
6 September 2005 to 5 September 2006	6.5
6 September 2004 to 5 September 2005	7.5
6 December 2003 to 5 September 2004	6.5
6 August 2003 to 5 December 2003	5.5
6 November 2001 to 5 August 2003	6.5
6 May 2001 to 5 November 2001	7.5

Period of application	Rate %
6 February 2000 to 5 May 2001	8.5
6 March 1999 to 5 February 2000	7.5
6 January 1999 to 5 March 1999	8.5
6 August 1997 to 5 January 1999	9.5
6 February 1997 to 5 August 1997	8.5

Notes

(1) Fixed by Treasury order under SI 1989/1297. From September 2009 interest charged on late payments of tax will be the Bank of England base rate plus 2.5%.

(2) Rates revised by HMRC (press release of 16 September 2009).

[¶1-550]   Rates of interest on tax repayments

(ICTA 1988, s. 824)

(Tax Reporter: ¶181-550)

Interest on tax repayments qualifying for repayment supplement is given at the following rates:

Period of application	Rate %
From 29 September 2009	0.50
From 27 January 2009 to 28 September 2009	0.00
5 January 2009 to 26 January 2009	0.75
6 December 2008 to 5 January 2009	1.50
6 November 2008 to 5 December 2008	2.25
6 January 2008 to 5 November 2008	3.00
6 August 2007 to 5 January 2008	4.00
6 September 2006 to 5 August 2007	3.00
6 September 2005 to 5 September 2006	2.25
6 September 2004 to 5 September 2005	3.00[1]
6 December 2003 to 5 September 2004	2.25[1]
6 August 2003 to 5 December 2003	1.50[1]
6 November 2001 to 5 August 2003	2.25[1]
6 May 2001 to 5 November 2001	3.00[1]
6 February 2000 to 5 May 2001	4.00[1]
6 March 1999 to 5 February 2000	3.00
6 January 1999 to 5 March 1999	4.00
6 August 1997 to 5 January 1999	4.75
6 February 1997 to 5 August 1997	4.00

Notes

(1) From September 2009 the interest rate on overpayments is the Bank of England base rate minus 1, subject to a minimum interest rate of 0.5% on repayments.

(2) Rates revised by HMRC (press release of 16 September 2009).

The qualifying period is as set out below:

> From the date of payment (deemed to be 31 January following the tax year in respect of tax deducted at source) to the date on which the order for the repayment is issued.

> For periods to self-assessment, the qualifying period was:

> Later of:

> (i)   due date; or

> (ii)   actual date of payment,

> until the end of the tax month in which the repayment order was issued.

[¶1-600]   Interest rates on certificates of tax deposit (CTD)

The interest rates that follow apply to CTDs issued under the Series 7 prospectus.

CTDs (Series 7) can be purchased to settle most tax liabilities, except PAYE, VAT and corporation tax falling due under Pay and File, or for subsequent encashment. (No CTDs are available for purchase for use against corporation tax liabilities since the start of the Pay and File regime.) A higher rate of interest is paid if the CTD is used in payment of tax. Interest is allowed/paid gross and is taxable.

Rates of interest vary according to the period for which the deposit is held. The rates in force at issue apply for one year; thereafter the rate applicable is that on the most recent anniversary of the date of issue.

Details of how to purchase a CTD and use it in payment of tax are contained in the Series 7 Prospectus which can be found on the HMRC website at http://www.hmrc.gov.uk/howtopay/cert_tax_deposit.htm.

Rates applicable over recent years have been as follows:

Certificates of tax deposit (Series 7): rates of interest

Deposits on or after	Deposits under £100,000		Deposits of £100,000 or more									
			Deposits held for under 1 month		Deposits held for 1 to under 3 months		Deposits held for 3 to under six months		Deposits held for 6 to under 9 months		Deposits held for 9–12 months	
	Applied in payment of tax %	Cash value %	Applied in payment of tax %	Cash value %	Applied in payment of tax %	Cash value %	Applied in payment of tax %	Cash value %	Applied in payment of tax %	Cash value %	Applied in payment of tax %	Cash value %
7 May 1997	2.75	1.50	2.75	1.50	5.50	2.75	5.25	2.75	5.50	2.75	5.25	2.75
9 June 1997	3	1.50	3	1.50	5.50	2.75	5.50	2.75	5.50	2.75	5.50	2.75
11 July 1997	3.25	1.75	3.25	1.75	6	3	5.75	3	5.75	3	6	3
8 Aug. 1997	4.50	2.25	4.50	2.25	6	3	6	3	6	3	5.75	3
7 Nov. 1997	4	2	4	2	6.50	3.25	6.50	3.25	6.25	3.25	6.25	3.25
5 June 1998	4	2	4	2	6.50	3.25	6.25	3.25	6.25	3.25	6	3
9 Oct. 1998	3.75	2	3.75	2	6.25	3.25	5.75	3	5.50	2.75	5.25	2.75
6 Nov. 1998	3.25	1.75	3.25	1.75	5.75	3	5.25	2.75	5	2.50	4.75	2.50
11 Dec. 1998	3	1.75	3	1.50	5.25	2.75	4.75	2.50	4.50	2.25	4.25	2.25
8 Jan. 1999	2.50	1.25	2.50	1.25	5	2.50	4.50	2.25	4	2	4	2
5 Feb. 1999	1.75	1	1.75	1	4.50	2.25	4	2	3.75	2	3.75	2
9 Apr. 1999	1.75	1	1.75	1	4.50	2.25	4	2	3.75	2	3.75	2
11 June 1999	1.50	.75	1.50	.75	4	2	4	2	4	2	4	2
9 Sept. 1999	1.75	1	1.75	1	4.50	2.25	4.50	2.25	4.50	2.25	4.50	2.25
4 Nov. 1999	2	1	2	1	5	2.50	4.75	2.50	4.75	2.50	4.75	2.50
14 Jan. 2000	2.25	1.25	2.25	1.25	5	2.50	5	2.50	5	2.75	5.25	2.75
11 Feb. 2000	2.50	1.25	2.50	1.25	5.25	2.75	5	2.50	5.25	2.75	5.25	2.75
9 Feb. 2001	2.25	1.25	2.25	1.25	4.75	2.50	4.25	2.25	4.25	2.25	4	2
6 Apr. 2001	2	1	2	1	4.25	2.25	4	2	3.75	2	3.50	1.75
11 May 2001	2	1	2	1	4	2	4	2	3.75	2	3.75	2
3 Aug. 2001	1.50	.75	1.50	.75	4	2	3.75	1.875	3.75	1.875	3.75	1.875
5 Oct. 2001	1	.50	1	.50	3.25	1.75	3	1.50	3	1.50	3	1.50
9 Nov. 2001	.50	.25	.50	.25	2.75	1.50	2.50	1.25	2.25	1.25	2.25	1.25
7 Feb. 2003	.25	Nil	.25	Nil	2.75	1.25	2.25	1.00	2.25	1.00	2.00	1.00
11 July 2003	Nil	Nil	Nil	Nil	2.50	1.25	2.25	1.00	2.00	1.00	2.00	1.00
7 Nov. 2003	.25	Nil	.25	Nil	3.00	1.50	3.00	1.50	3.00	1.50	3.00	1.50
6 Feb. 2004	.50	.25	.50	.25	3.00	1.50	3.00	1.50	3.00	1.50	3.00	1.50

Deposits on or after	Deposits under £100,000 Applied in payment of tax %	Cash value %	Deposits held for under 1 month Applied in payment of tax %	Cash value %	Deposits of £100,000 or more							
					Deposits held for 1 to under 3 months Applied in payment of tax %	Cash value %	Deposits held for 3 to under six months Applied in payment of tax %	Cash value %	Deposits held for 6 to under 9 months Applied in payment of tax %	Cash value %	Deposits held for 9–12 months Applied in payment of tax %	Cash value %
7 May 2004	.75	.25	.75	.25	3.25	1.50	3.25	1.50	3.25	1.50	3.25	1.50
11 June 2004	1.00	.50	1.00	.50	3.75	1.75	3.50	1.75	3.75	1.75	3.75	1.75
6 Aug. 2004	1.25	.50	1.25	.50	3.75	1.75	3.75	1.75	3.75	1.75	3.75	1.75
5 Aug. 2005	1.00	.50	1.00	.50	3.50	1.75	3.25	1.50	3.00	1.50	3.00	1.50
4 Aug. 2006	1.75	.75	1.75	.75	4.25	2.00	4.25	2.00	4.00	2.00	4.00	2.00
10 Nov. 2006	1.50	.75	1.50	.75	4.00	2.00	4.00	2.00	3.75	1.75	3.75	1.75
12 Jan. 2007	1.50	0.75	1.50	0.75	4.25	2.00	4.00	2.00	4.00	2.00	4.00	2.00
11 May 2007	2.00	1.00	2.00	1.00	4.75	2.25	4.50	2.25	4.50	2.25	4.50	2.25
6 July 2007	2.25	1.10	2.25	1.10	5.00	2.50	4.75	2.25	4.75	2.25	4.75	2.25
7 Dec. 2007	3.00	1.50	3.00	1.50	5.50	2.75	5.00	2.50	4.75	2.25	4.50	2.25
8 Feb. 2008	2.00	1.00	2.00	1.00	4.50	2.25	4.25	2.25	4.00	2.00	3.75	1.75
11 Apr. 2008	2.00	1.00	2.00	1.00	4.75	2.25	4.50	2.25	4.25	2.00	4.25	2.00
9 Oct. 2008	2.50	1.25	2.50	1.25	5.25	2.50	5.00	2.50	5.00	2.50	4.75	2.25
7 Nov. 2008	1.75	0.75	1.75	0.75	4.50	2.25	4.25	2.00	4.25	2.00	4.00	2.00
5 Dec. 2008	0.00	0.00	0.00	0.00	2.50	1.25	2.50	1.25	2.50	1.25	2.25	1.00
9 Jan. 2009	0.00	0.00	0.00	0.00	1.50	0.75	1.25	0.50	1.25	0.50	1.25	0.50
6 Feb. 2009	0.00	0.00	0.00	0.00	1.00	0.50	1.00	0.50	1.00	0.50	0.75	0.25
6 Mar. 2009	0.00	0.00	0.00	0.00	0.75	0.25	0.75	0.25	0.75	0.25	0.75	0.25

[¶1-650]   Remission of tax for official error

(ESC A19)

Arrears of income tax and capital gains tax may be given up if they result from HMRC's failure to make proper and timely use of information supplied by the taxpayer, or in certain circumstances by the taxpayer's employer or the Department for Work and Pensions.

The taxpayer must have reasonably believed that his or her affairs were in order. Tax will normally only be given up where there was a gap of 12 months or more between HMRC receiving the information that tax was due, and notifying the taxpayer of the arrears.

TAXATION OF BUSINESS PROFITS

[¶2-000] Relief for fluctuating profits (farming and market gardening; creative artists)

(ITTOIA 2005, s. 221ff)

(Tax Reporter: ¶272-300ff.; ¶268-300)

Full averaging

Full averaging applies where profits for either relevant tax year do not exceed 70 per cent of profits for the other year or are nil.

Marginal averaging

The amount of the adjustment to the profits of each relevant tax year, where lower profits are between 70 and 75 per cent of higher profits, is computed as follows:

$$(D \times 3) - (P \times 0.75)$$

where

D   is the difference between the relevant profits of the two years; and

P   is the relevant profits of the tax year of which those profits are higher.

[¶2-050] Car hire

(ITTOIA 2005, s. 48ff.)

(Tax Reporter: ¶212-025)

Rules applying from April 2009

The rules relating to restrictions on car hire charges changed from 1 or 6 April 2009 (for corporation tax and income tax respectively).

Leased cars, where the lease begins from 1 or 6 April 2009, suffer 15 per cent disallowance of relevant payments if CO_2 emissions exceed 160g/km; otherwise no disallowance. This applies to all cars (not just those costing more than £12,000).

Rules applying to 31 March / 5 April 2009

(ITTOIA 2005, s. 48ff.)

The restricted deduction for hire charges of motor cars with a retail price greater than £12,000 is as follows:

$$\text{Allowable amount} = \frac{£12,000 + \frac{1}{2}(\text{retail price} - £12,000)}{\text{retail price}} \times \text{hire charge}$$

Taxation of Business Profits

[¶2-100]   Time limits for elections and claims

(TMA 1970, s. 43(1))

(Tax Reporter: ¶183-100)

In the absence of any provision to the contrary, under self-assessment for the purposes of income tax, the normal rule is that claims are to be made within four years from the end of the tax year to which they relate. Before 1 April 2010, the time limit was generally five years from 31 January following the end of the tax year.

Other specific provisions are as below.

Provision	Time limit	Statutory reference
Averaging of profits of farmers or creative artists	first anniversary of the normal self-assessment filing date for the second tax year	ITTOIA 2005, s. 222
Stock transferred to a connected party on cessation of trade (or, from April 2009, profession or vocation) to be valued at higher of cost or sale price	first anniversary of the normal self-assessment filing date for the tax year of cessation	ITTOIA 2005, s. 178, CTA 2009, s. 167
Post-cessation expenses relieved against income and chargeable gains	first anniversary of the normal self-assessment filing date for the tax year	ITTOIA 2005, s. 257(4); ITA 2007, s. 96
Current and preceding year set-off of trading losses	first anniversary of the normal self-assessment filing date for the loss-making year	ITA 2007, s. 64
Three-year carry-back of trading losses in opening years of trade	first anniversary of the normal self-assessment filing date for the tax year in which the loss is made	ITA 2007, s. 72
Carry-forward of trading losses	normal rules apply (see above)	ITA 2007, s. 83ff.
Carry-back of terminal losses	normal rules apply (see above)	ITA 2007, s. 89

TAXATION OF INVESTMENT INCOME

[¶3-000]   Registered pension schemes: 2006–07 onwards

(FA 2004, Pt. 4, Ch. 1 to 7 and Sch. 28 to Sch. 36)

(BTR: ¶306-000ff.)

From 6 April 2006 ('A' day) a new, simplified set of rules apply to all forms of pension provision.

Individuals may obtain tax relief on any contributions made to a registered pension scheme, up to 100% of their relevant UK earnings for a tax year, or £3,600 per year if their relevant UK earnings are less than this amount. Employer's contributions do not count towards an individual's contributions. Greater amounts than these limits may be contributed to a registered scheme, without the benefit of tax relief for the individual, but see below for the effects on the scheme and individual. The normal minimum pension age is 50, but this may be higher for some schemes. For all registered schemes this age limit will rise to 55 years from 6 April 2010 (except for retirement on ill health grounds and some preserved, lower retirement ages; see below). Pension benefits must be taken by the age of 75, but in the June 2010 Budget it was announced that this requirement was to be reviewed and new provisions introduced from 6 April 2011. As an interim measure, effective from 23 June 2010, the age limit is to be raised to 77.

FA 2010 introduced legislation to be effective from 6 April 2011 relief which would have imposed a charge on those with 'gross incomes' over £150,000 to clawback relief which has been given at rates above the basic rate. In the June 2010 Budget, the Coalition Government announced its intention to revisit this issue. Powers would be introduced to allow the FA 2010 clawback provisions to be repealed by Statutory Instrument, That repeal would occur when the Government had decided on its approach. The anti-forestalling provisions which were included in FA 2009, Sch. 35 effective from 22 April 2009 (see BTR: ¶307-800) would remain in force. Theses are intended to counter the payment of abnormal contributions in 2009–10 and 2010–11 in respect of individuals with relevant incomes over £150,000. FA 2010 amended that limit to £130,000 with effect from 9 December 2009.

Annual and lifetime allowances

There are annual and lifetime limits on the value of contributions made to a registered scheme. Tax charges will be applied where these limits are exceeded.

Taxation of Investment Income

Year	Annual allowance[1]	Annual allowance charge[2]	Lifetime allowance[3]	Lifetime allowance charge[4]
2010–11	£255,000	40% on any annual increase in pension scheme value in excess of limit	£1.80 million	25% on excess if taken as pension 55% on excess if taken as a lump sum
2009–10	£245,000	40% on any annual increase in pension scheme value in excess of limit	£1.75 million	25% on excess if taken as pension 55% on excess if taken as a lump sum
2008–09	£235,000	40% on any annual increase in pension scheme value in excess of limit	£1.65 million	25% on excess if taken as pension 55% on excess if taken as a lump sum
2007–08	£225,000	40% on any annual increase in pension scheme value in excess of limit	£1.6 million	25% on excess if taken as pension 55% on excess if taken as a lump sum
2006–07	£215,000	40% on any annual increase in pension scheme value in excess of limit	£1.5 million	25% on excess if taken as pension 55% on excess if taken as a lump sum

Notes

[1] An individual's annual allowance (AA) applies to all of that individual's pension arrangements for a year. It measures the 'pension input amount' for a tax year. That is the increase in the pension savings in that tax year (including contributions made by the individual and employer); and/or the increase in the value of the individual's pension rights (depending on the type of scheme; i.e. money purchase, defined benefit etc.). If the 'pension input amount' for a year exceeds the AA for that year the excess is subject to the charge. For future years the AA will be fixed by Treasury Order. In the 2010 Budget it was announced that the allowance for the five years, 2011–12 to 2015–16, will be frozen at £255,000.

[2] An AA charge is the liability of the individual member of the scheme (or schemes where an individual is a member of more than one scheme) (FA 2004, s. 227 to 238).

[3] An individual's lifetime allowance (LTA) is a measure of the total value of an individual's pension savings at the time that pension benefits begin to be taken (or at the age of 75, if no pension benefits are taken prior to that age). For future years the AA (or LTA as appropriate) will be fixed by Treasury Order. In the 2010 Budget it was announced that the allowance for the five years, 2011–12 to 2015–16, will be frozen at £1.8 million.

[4] An LTA charge (55% on any excess over the LTA constituting a lump sum payment; and 25% on any excess over the LTA not used to pay a lump sum but to fund pension payments) is the joint and several liability of the individual and the pension scheme administrator (FA 2004, s. 214 to s. 226).

Other charges

If unauthorised payments are made out of a registered pension scheme the person receiving the payment(s) (i.e. the member, the employer or the recipient of any death benefits) is liable, for 2006–07 onwards, to a tax charge equal to 40% of the payment(s). A surcharge of 15%, in addition to the basic 40% charge, may be added to the unauthorised payment charge if a scheme pays out more than 25% of the schemes' fund in unauthorised payments (FA 2004, s. 208 to s. 213).

Where a registered scheme loses its registered status a 'deregistration charge' of 40% of the aggregate value of the pension scheme's assets is levied on and payable by the scheme administrator (FA 2004, s. 242).

A tax charge arises where a registered pension scheme repays tax-relieved pension contributions to a member who has completed less than two years service ('short service refund lump sums'). The rate is 20 per cent on the first £10,800 and 40 per cent thereafter. In the PBR 2009 it was announced that from 6 April 2010, the rates will be 20 per cent on the first £20,000 and 50 per cent thereafter.

Where an approved pension scheme existed prior to 6 April 2006 and its value exceeds the current LTA or it permits the payment of benefits in excess of those permitted under the post-6 April 2006 rules, it is possible to obtain protection from the limits and allowances applicable from that date by applying to HMRC, before April 2009, for Protection of Existing Rights (on form APSS200).

Judicial pension schemes (administered by the Lord Chancellor's Office) are not within the rules for Registered Pension Schemes and continue to be subject to modified versions of the previous rules.

Where it is necessary to determine the 'earnings cap' for 2006–07, for transitional purposes or for schemes still covered by the old rules (despite the effective repeal of the old rules for general purposes), the amount is to be taken as £108,600.

[¶3-150]   Early retirement ages: retirement annuity contracts and personal pension schemes

From 6 April 2006

(FA 2004. s. 279(1), Sch. 36, para. 23)

(BTR: ¶306-550)

Under the simplified pensions' rules applying from 6 April 2006 onwards early retirement ages (apart from on ill health grounds) are eliminated for all new schemes. The 'normal minimum pension age' is to be 55. Where arrangements for pre–6 April 2006 schemes permit retirement earlier than 55 the 'normal minimum pension age' will be 50, with effect from 6 April 2006; rising to 55, with effect from 6 April 2010.

It is possible for members of pre-6 April 2006 schemes that permit retirement earlier than the 'normal minimum pension age' to preserve their rights to early retirement in some circumstances . Members of retirement annuity contracts or personal pension schemes will be able to protect their right to take pension and lump sum benefits before the 'normal minimum pension age' (i.e. before 50 until 6 April 2010) by establishing their 'unqualified right', as at 6 April 2006, to a protected pension age that is lower than the 'normal minimum pension age'.

In order to exercise the right to a lower than normal pension age the member must:

- be or have been in one of the occupations prescribed in the list at *Registered Pension Schemes (Prescribed Schemes and Occupations) Regulations* 2005 (SI 2005/3451), Sch. 2, prior to 6 April 2006; and

- have had an 'unqualified right' to take a pension before the age of 50, prior to 6 April

Taxation of Investment Income

2006 (an 'unqualified right' is when the individual needs no other party to consent to their request to take an early pension before it becomes binding upon the scheme or contract holder).

The list below will continue to apply to retirement annuity contract holders and personal pension scheme members who are able to meet the conditions for a protected pension age lower than 50, as at 6 April 2006. All of the professions noted in the list below that have a retirement age of less than 50 are included in the list at SI 2005/3451, Sch. 2.

| | Retirement age[1] | |
| | Retirement annuity | Personal pension |
Profession or occupation	contracts	schemes
Air Pilots	55	–
Athletes (appearance and prize money)	35	35
Badminton Players	35	35
Boxers	35	35
Brass Instrumentalists	55	–
Cricketers	40	40
Croupiers	50	–
Cyclists	35	35
Dancers	35	35
Divers (Saturation, Deep Sea and Free Swimming)	40	40
Firemen (Part-time)	55	–
Fishermen (Inshore or Distant Water Trawlermen)	55	–
Footballers	35	35
Golfers (tournament earnings)	40	40
Interdealer Brokers	50	–
Jockeys – Flat Racing	45	45
– National Hunt	35	35
Martial Arts Instructors	50	–
Models	35	35
Moneybroker Dealers	50	–
Moneybroker Dealer Directors and Managers responsible for dealers	55	–
Motorcycle Riders (Motocross or Road Racing)	40	40
Motor Racing Drivers	40	40
Newscasters (ITV)	50	–
Nurses, Physiotherapists, Midwives or Health Visitors who are females	55	–
Off-Shore Riggers	50	–
Psychiatrists (who are also maximum part-time specialists employed within the National Health Services solely in the treatment of the mentally disordered)	55	–
Royal Naval Reservists	50	–
Royal Marine Reservists non-commissioned	45	45
Rugby League Players	35	35
Rugby League Referees	50	–

Profession or occupation	Retirement age[1] Retirement annuity contracts	Personal pension schemes
Skiers (Downhill)	–	30
Singers	55	–
Speedway Riders	40	40
Squash Players	35	35
Table Tennis Players	35	35
Tennis Players (including Real Tennis)	35	35
Territorial Army Members	50	–
Trapeze Artistes	40	40
Wrestlers	35	35

Notes

[1] The pension age shown applies only to pension arrangements funded by contributions paid in respect of the relevant earnings from the occupation or profession carrying that age. If an individual wishes to make pension provisions in respect of another source of relevant earnings to which the pension age shown above does not apply then a separate arrangement, with a pension age within the normal range, must be made.

In particular, the ages shown above for professional sportsmen apply only to arrangements made in respect of relevant earnings from activities as professional sportsmen e.g. tournament earnings, appearance and prize money. They do not apply to relevant earnings from sponsorship or coaching.

[¶3-200] State retirement pensions

	Weekly rates	
	Single person £	Married couple wife not a contributor £
From 5/4/10	97.65	156.15
7/4/09 to 4/4/10	95.25	152.30
7/4/08 to 6/4/09	90.70	145.05
10/4/07 to 6/4/08	87.30	139.60
10/4/06 to 8/4/07	84.25	134.75
11/4/05 to 9/4/06	82.05	131.20
12/4/04 to 10/4/05	79.60	127.25

[¶3-300] Gilt-edged securities held by non-residents

(ITA 2007, ss. 893-897; s. 1024)

(BTR: ¶371-150)

Interest on all gilt-edged securities is payable gross. Interest may be paid net, if the holder wishes, by notice to the Registrar of Government Stock. Payment gross does not of itself imply that the interest is exempt from tax.

Taxation of Investment Income

All gilt-edged securities are automatically be given FOTRA status (Free Of Tax for Residents Abroad), thereby guaranteeing exemption from tax for holders not ordinarily resident in the UK. Where income tax has been deducted from such gilts, a repayment claim (on Form A1(CNR)) may be submitted to HMRC, Centre for Non-Residents, Fitz Roy House, PO Box 46, Nottingham NG2 1BD.

[¶3-350]   Individual savings accounts (ISAs)

(ITTOIA 2005, s. 694–701; and the *Individual Savings Account Regulations* 1998 (SI 1998/1870)

(BTR: ¶321-500)

With effect from 6 April 2011, the annual ISA limits will increase annually in line with inflation, measured by reference to the Retail Prices Index at September of the previous year, and rounded up to the nearest multiple of £120. In the event that inflation is zero, the previous limits would be unchanged. The limit for a cash ISA will remain at one-half of the overall limit.

	Maximum investment per year 2010–11 (all taxpayers) £
Maximum	10,200
made up of:	
Stocks and shares	up to 5,100
Cash	up to 5,100

	Maximum investment per year 2008–09 (all taxpayers) and 2009–10 (for those aged below 50) £
Maximum	7,200
made up of:	
Stocks and shares	up to 7,200
Cash	up to 3,600

	Maximum investment per year 2009–10 (for those aged 50 and over) £
Maximum	10,200
made up of:	
Stocks and shares	up to 5,100
Cash	up to 5,100

	Maximum investment per year 2005–06 to 2007–08 £
Maxi ISA	7,000
made up of:	
Stocks and shares	up to 7,000
Cash	up to 3,000
Mini ISA types:	
Stocks and shares	4,000
Cash	3,000

	Maximum investment per year 1999–2000 to 2004–05 £
Maxi ISA	7,000
made up of:	
Stocks and shares	up to 7,000
Cash	up to 3,000
Life insurance	up to 1,000
Mini ISA types:	
Stocks and shares	3,000
Cash	3,000
Life insurance	1,000

Notes

- A Maxi ISA could include a stocks and shares component and a cash component (and up to 2004–05, a life insurance component) within a single ISA with one manager. Mini ISAs were separate ISAs, which could be with different managers, for stocks and shares, and for cash (and up to 2004–05; life insurance).

- Each year an individual can either start new ISAs or can put money into existing ISAs, but until 2007–08 only into one Maxi ISA, or one Mini ISA of each type, in any particular tax year.

- To open an ISA an individual has to be aged 18 or over (or over the age of 16 for cash ISAs, with effect from 6 April 2001) and resident and ordinarily resident in the UK for tax purposes.

- All income and gains derived from investments within the account are tax free and withdrawals from the account will not attract any tax charge.

- All personal equity plans (PEPs) held at 5 April 1999 could continue to be held as PEPs until 5 April 2008, but with the same tax advantages as ISAs. From 6 April 2008 they are treated as stocks and shares ISAs. TESSAs which were open at 5 April 1999 can continue to be paid into under existing rules for their full five-year life. After that date, capital from maturing TESSAs could be transferred into the cash component of an ISA. Neither the value of any TESSA held, nor the amount of any transfer on maturity, affected the amount which could otherwise be subscribed to an ISA.

Taxation of Investment Income

[¶3-400]   Enterprise investment scheme (EIS)

(ITA 2007, Pt. 5)

(BTR: ¶323-000ff.)

EIS relief superseded business expansion scheme (BES) relief for qualifying individuals who subscribe cash for the issue of qualifying shares issued, after 31 December 1993, by non-quoted trading companies (except those carrying on prohibited trades).

Qualifying EIS shares issued:	Maximum individual investment[3]	Rate of IT relief on investment	Disposal of qualifying EIS shares	Carry back of EIS relief to previous tax year[2]
On or after 6 April 2009	£500,000 per annum	20%	Capital gains not chargeable, losses allowable[2]	Entire investment (subject to not exceeding £500,000 for the earlier year).
6 April 2008 to 5 April 2009	£500,000 per annum	20%	Capital gains not chargeable, losses allowable[2]	Lower of: (i) 50% of relief; and (ii) £50,000
6 April 2006 to 5 April 2008	£400,000 per annum	20%	Capital gains not chargeable, losses allowable[2]	Lower of: (i) 50% of relief; and (ii) £50,000
6 April 2004 to 5 April 2006	£200,000 per annum	20%	Capital gains not chargeable, losses allowable[2]	Lower of: (i) 50% of relief; and (ii) £25,000
6 April 1998 to 5 April 2004	£150,000 per annum	20%	Capital gains not chargeable, losses allowable[2]	Lower of: (i) 50% of relief; and (ii) £25,000

Notes

[1] Losses allowable in respect of the first disposal of EIS shares are eligible for relief against income tax and capital gains tax. For chargeable gains accruing on or after 29 November 1994 a CGT deferral relief ('reinvestment relief') permits the postponement of a capital gain to be claimed where an investor subscribes for EIS shares within the period of one year prior to and three years after the gain accrues.

[2] Carry back of EIS relief was permitted for years to 2008–09, subject to the limits, where qualifying shares are subscribed for between 6 April and 5 October in a tax year. Those limits were removed for 2009–10 onwards.

[3] For an investment to qualify under EIS, the company must have raised no more than £2 million under any or all EIS, VCT or corporate venturing schemes in the 12 months ending on the date of the relevant investment.

[¶3-450]   Venture capital trusts (VCTs)

(ITA 2007, Pt. 6; TCGA 1992, s. 151A, 151B, ITTOIA 2005, s. 709)

(BTR: ¶326-400)

A VCT is a specialised form of investment trust, which has been approved by the Board of HMRC on or since 6 April 1995. Certain tax advantages are obtained by individuals who subscribe for eligible shares issued by a qualifying VCT for the purposes of raising money.

Qualifying VCT Shares issued:	Maximum individual investment	Rate of IT relief on investment	Dividends paid by VCT	Disposal of shares in VCT	Minimum holding period
On or after 6 April 2006	£200,000 per annum	30%	Exempt from IT in hands of investor	Exempt from CGT	5 years
6 April 2004 to 5 April 2006	£200,000 per annum	40%	Exempt from IT in hands of investor	Exempt from CGT	3 years
6 April 2000 to 5 April 2004	£100,000 per annum	20%	Exempt from IT in hands of investor	Exempt from CGT	3 years

An investment in qualifying VCT shares, issued prior to 6 April 2004, was eligible for a CGT deferral relief that enabled an investor to postpone the incidence of a capital gain arising on the disposal of a chargeable asset.

To obtain and retain HMRC's approval, a VCT must satisfy a number of detailed conditions. The main ones are as follows:

- it must be a non-close company whose shares are quoted on the stock exchange;
- its income must be wholly or mainly derived from investments in shares or securities;
- at least 70% (by value) of its total investments must comprise of 'qualifying holdings' (broadly, shares and securities in unquoted trading companies except those carrying on prohibited trades; from 6 April 2007 cash held will be treated as an 'investment' for the purposes of the percentage limits);
- for funds raised on or after 6 April 2006; the gross assets of the VCT may not exceed £7 million immediately before the issue of shares to investors and £8 million immediately afterwards (for funds raised prior to 6 April 2006 the limits are £15 million and £16 million respectively, even if such funds are applied after 6 April 2006).

For an investment to qualify under VCT, the company must have raised no more than £2 million under any or all EIS, VCT or corporate venturing schemes in the 12 months ending on the date of the relevant investment (ITA 2007, s. 292A).

Taxation of Investment Income

[¶3-500]   Lease premiums

(ITTOIA 2005, s. 277 and CTA 2009, s. 217)

(BTR: ¶300-120 and ¶711-375)

Where a short-term lease, (i.e. one not exceeding 50 years in duration) is granted, a proportion of any premium charged on the grant is assessable as property business profits . The amount of the premium to be treated as rental income, received at the time of the grant, is given by a formula:

$$P \times \frac{50 - Y}{50} = TP$$

Where:

- 'P' is total premium paid;

- 'Y' is duration of lease in complete years (ignoring the first year). Only whole years are counted, part years are ignored; and

- 'TP' is the amount of the premium taxed on the landlord as if it were rent.

Amount taken into account in calculating a chargeable gain will be the balance of the premium (TCGA 1992, s. 240 and Sch. 8, para. 5 and 7) for which the restriction of allowable expenditure is applicable:

Length of lease in complete years	Premium % chargeable as gain	Premium % chargeable as rent
Over 50	100	0
50	98	2
49	96	4
48	94	6
47	92	8
46	90	10
45	88	12
44	86	14
43	84	16
42	82	18
41	80	20
40	78	22
39	76	24
38	74	26
37	72	28
36	70	30
35	68	32
34	66	34
33	64	36
32	62	38
31	60	40
30	58	42

Length of lease in complete years	Premium % chargeable as gain	Premium % chargeable as rent
29	56	44
28	54	46
27	52	48
26	50	50
25	48	52
24	46	54
23	44	56
22	42	58
21	40	60
20	38	62
19	36	64
18	34	66
17	32	68
16	30	70
15	28	72
14	26	74
13	24	76
12	22	78
11	20	80
10	18	82
9	16	84
8	14	86
7	12	88
6	10	90
5	8	92
4	6	94
3	4	96
2	2	98
1 or less	0	100

The following arrangements relating to short leases may also cause amounts to be treated as rent paid to the landlord:

- the tenant carrying out work on the rented premises;
- the commutation of rent for some other type of payment;
- the payment of a lump sum from the surrender of a lease;
- the payment of a lump sum for the variation or waiver of a lease's terms; and
- the assignment of a lease which has been previously granted at undervalue.

Premiums paid by instalment

Where an amount of a premium is received by instalments any income tax or corporation tax due on the amount may be paid by instalments, at the taxpayer's request and by agreement with HMRC. The tax instalment period may not exceed eight years and must

Taxation of Investment Income

end on or before the time that the final instalment of the premium is due (ITTOIA 2005, s. 299 for income tax; and CTA 2009, s. 236(1)-(3) for corporation tax).

Relief for premiums paid

Where a tenant occupies land, under a short lease, for the purposes of a trade, profession or vocation and has paid a premium in respect of the lease; an amount of lease premium paid is allowed as a deduction in computing the business profits (ITTOIA 2005, s. 61 for income tax; and CTA 2009, s. 62 for corporation tax). The amount of the premium taxed as rent in the hands of the landlord (see above) is treated as if it were daily rent paid by the tenant over the course of the lease. The effective deduction for an accounting or basis period is therefore:

$$\frac{TP}{\text{Lease duration in days}} \times \text{No. of days in accounting or basis period} = DRP$$

Where:

- 'TP' is the amount of the premium taxed on the landlord as if it were rent; and

- 'DRP' is the amount of the deemed rent paid by the tenant.

Relief is also available, in respect of premiums paid, for the computation of property business profits where an intermediate landlord has paid a premium to the superior landlord for premises that are in turn sub-let to a tenant.

[¶3-525] Qualifying territories for the purposes of foreign dividends on substantial holdings

(ITTOIA 2005, s. 397AA(4))

Argentina	Hungary	Oman
Australia	Iceland	Pakistan
Austria	India	Papua New Guinea
Azerbaijan	Indonesia	Philippines
Bangladesh	Ireland	Poland
Barbados	Israel	Portugal
Belarus	Italy	Romania
Belgium	Ivory Coast	Russian Federation
Bolivia	Jamaica	Serbia
Bosnia-Herzegovina	Japan	Singapore
Botswana	Jordan	Slovak Republic
Bulgaria	Kazakhstan	Slovenia
Canada	Kenya	South Africa
Chile	Korea	Spain
China	Kuwait	Sri Lanka
Croatia	Latvia	Sudan
Cyprus	Lithuania	Swaziland
Czech Republic	Luxembourg	Switzerland
Denmark	Macedonia	Taiwan
Egypt	Malaysia	Thailand
Estonia	Malta	Trinidad & Tobago
Falkland Islands	Mauritius	Tunisia
Fiji	Mexico	Turkmenistan

Finland	Montenegro	Uganda
France	Morocco	Ukraine
Gambia	Myanmar	USA
Georgia	Namibia	Uzbekistan
Germany	Netherlands	Venezuela
Ghana	New Zealand	Vietnam
Greece	Nigeria	Zambia
Guyana	Norway	Zimbabwe

However, dividends from certain types of company which are excluded from one or more of the benefits of the double taxation agreement with the UK do not attract a tax credit. These 'excluded companies' are:

Barbados	Companies established under the International Business Companies Act(s).
Cyprus	Companies entitled to any special tax benefits under various Cyprus enactments.
Jamaica	Companies established under enactments relating to International Business Companies and International Finance Companies.
Luxembourg	Holding companies established under the Luxembourg 1929 and 1937 Acts
Malaysia	Companies carrying on offshore business activities under the Labaun Offshore Business Activity Act 1990
Malta	Companies entitled to special tax benefits under various enactments.

[¶3-550] Settlements on children

(ITTOIA 2005, s. 629(3))

(BTR: ¶355-600)

Income paid to or for the benefit of a minor child arising from capital provided by a parent is not treated as parents' income if it does not exceed £100 per tax year.

[¶3-600] National Savings Bank interest

(ITTOIA 2005, s. 691)

(BTR: ¶343-150)

Limit of income tax exemption is £70. The exemption is available in respect of separate accounts of husband and wife. The exemption is unavailable in respect of investment deposits.

Taxation of Investment Income

[¶3-650]   Community investment tax relief

(ITA 2007, Pt. 7; FA 2002, Sch. 16)

(BTR: ¶325-000ff.)

Tax relief is claimed on an annual basis, at the rate of five per cent of the 'invested amount' for the tax year (or accounting period for a corporate investor) in which the investment date falls and the four subsequent tax years (or accounting periods). If the investment is by way of a loan, the 'invested amount' is not necessarily the amount of the loan made available at the beginning of the five-year investment period. The tax relief cannot reduce the taxpayer's tax liability below zero for any single tax year (or accounting period).

[¶3-700]   Time limits for elections and claims

In the absence of any provision to the contrary, for the purposes of income tax, the normal rule is that claims are to be made within five years from 31 January next following the tax year to which they relate. However, with effect from 1 April 2010, the time limit becomes four years after the end of the tax year (TMA 1970, s. 43(1)).

In certain cases HMRC *may* permit an extension of the strict time limit in relation to certain elections and claims.

Provision	Time limit	Statutory reference
Averaging election for furnished holiday accommodation	12 months from 31 January following year to which claim applies	ITTOIA 2005, s. 326 (BTR: ¶303–150
Set-off of property business loss against income of current or next year	12 months from 31 January following year of set-off	ITA 2007, s. 124 (BTR: ¶300–090)
Property business post-cessation relief	12 months from 31 January following year in which deduction to be made	ITA 2007, s. 125 (BTR: ¶300–095)
Set-off of loss on disposal of shares in unquoted trading company against income	12 months from 31 January following year in which loss arose	ITA 2007, s. 132 (BTR: ¶321–000ff.)

TAXATION OF EARNINGS

Company cars

[¶4-000] Car benefits charges: normal rules

(ITEPA 2003, s. 139)

(Tax Reporter: ¶415-050ff.)

The benefit is calculated on a percentage of the list price of the car appropriate to the level of the car's CO_2 emissions, as follows:

* 15 per cent of the list price of cars emitting up to the lower threshold of emissions of carbon dioxide in grams per kilometre;
* increased by one per cent per 5 g/km over the lower threshold; but
* capped at 35 per cent of the list price.

The lower thresholds are as follows:

Tax year	Lower threshold (in g/km)
2011–12	125
2010–11	130
2009–10	135
2008–09	135
2007–08	140
2006–07	140

If the exact CO_2 emissions figure does not end in 0 or 5, it should be rounded *down* to the nearest 5g/km before applying the above figures.

From 6 April 2012, a new set of thresholds will apply: see ¶4-012.

[¶4-010] Car benefit charges: table of taxable percentages

(ITEPA 2003, s. 139)

(Tax Reporter: ¶415-720ff.)

This table provides the 'appropriate percentage' figures for calculating the taxable benefit of a company car, based on CO_2 emissions figures for petrol cars, for periods to 5 April 2012. See ¶4-012 for later years.

CO_2 emissions (See note 1)	2011–12 %	2010–11 %	2008–09 to 2009–10 %	2005–06 to 2007–08 %	2004–05 %	2003–04 %
120	See note 2	See note 2	See note 2			

CO_2 emissions (See note 1)	2011–12 %	2010–11 %	2008–09 to 2009–10 %	2005–06 to 2007–08 %	2004–05 %	2003–04 %
125	15	15	15	15	15	15
130	16	15	15	15	15	15
135	17	16	15	15	15	15
140	18	17	16	15	15	15
145	19	18	17	16	15	15
150	20	19	18	17	16	15
155	21	20	19	18	17	15
160	22	21	20	19	18	16
165	23	22	21	20	19	17
170	24	23	22	21	20	18
175	25	24	23	22	21	19
180	26	25	24	23	22	20
185	27	26	25	24	23	21
190	28	27	26	25	24	22
195	29	28	27	26	25	23
200	30	29	28	27	26	24
205	31	30	29	28	27	25
210	32	31	30	29	28	26
215	33	32	31	30	29	27
220	34	33	32	31	30	28
225	35	34	33	32	31	29
230	35	35	34	33	32	30
235	35	35	35	34	33	31
240	35	35	35	35	34	32
245	35	35	35	35	35	33
250	35	35	35	35	35	34
255	35	35	35	35	35	35

Notes

[1] The actual CO_2 emissions figure, if it is not a multiple of five, should be rounded down to the nearest multiple of five before applying this table, except that rounding does not apply to emissions of between 121 and 124 g/km.

[2] From 6 April 2012, a new set of thresholds will apply: see ¶4-012.

[3] Special rules apply to:

- diesel cars: see ¶4-015;

- qualifying low emissions cars (QUALECs): see ¶4-020;

- ultra-low emission cars: see ¶4-025; and

- cars using alternative fuels and technologies: see ¶4-030.

[¶4-012]   Car benefit charges: 2012–13 to 2014–15

Table of taxable percentages

(ITEPA 2003, s. 139; FA 2010, s. 58, 59)

(Tax Reporter: ¶415-720)

CO_2 emissions (g/km) not exceeding	Appropriate percentage
0	0
75	5
99	10
100	11
105	12
110	13
115	14
120	15
125	16
130	17
135	18
140	19
145	20
150	21
155	22
160	23
165	24
170	25
175	26

Taxation of Earnings

CO₂ emissions (g/km) not exceeding	Appropriate percentage
180	27
185	28
190	29
195	30
200	31
205	32
210	33
215	34
220	35

Notes

(1) The actual emissions figure, if not a multiple of five, should be rounded down to the nearest multiple of five before applying this table, except that rounding does not apply to cars with emissions below 100g/km.

(2) All diesel cars are subject to a three per cent loading, but not to take the maximum figure above 35 per cent.

[¶4-015] Diesel cars: loading of appropriate percentage

Most diesel cars have an appropriate percentage that is three points higher than an equivalent petrol car (but still subject to a 35 per cent overall cap). See ¶4-000 for details of the petrol figures.

Cars that do not meet the Euro IV emissions standard

These cars are subject to the three point loading in all cases.

Cars that do meet the Euro IV emissions standard

The following table shows whether or not a three per cent loading is needed for diesel cars meeting the Euro IV emissions standard:

Tax year	Car first registered by 31 December 2005	Car first registered from 1 January 2006
2011–12 onwards	3% loading applies	3% loading applies
2006–07 to 2010–11	No loading	3% loading applies

[¶4-020] Qualifying low emissions cars

(ITEPA 2003, s. 139(3A)); FA 2010, s. 59

(Tax Reporter: ¶415-750)

Since 6 April 2008, a lower tax charge has been made if the vehicle is a 'qualifying low emissions car' ('QUALEC') for the tax year in which it is provided as a company car.

A car is a QUALEC if its CO₂ emissions figure does not exceed the limit for the year: 120 g/km.

In such a case, the appropriate percentage will be 10 per cent for petrol cars (but with a three per cent penalty loading, so a figure of 13 per cent, for most diesel cars). However, a lower percentage applies to ultra-low emission cars from 6 April 2010: see ¶4-025

[¶4-025]   Ultra-low emission cars
(ITEPA 2003, s. 139; FA 2010, s. 59)

A reduced appropriate percentage of five per cent applies, from 6 April 2010 for five years, for company cars with an approved CO_2 emissions figure not exceeding 75g per kilometre.

[¶4-030]   Alternative fuel cars: current rules
(ITEPA 2003, s. 140)

(Tax Reporter: ¶415-760ff.)

Type of car	Discounted charge
Cars producing zero CO_2 emissions when driven (from 2010–11 to 2014–15)	Zero per cent
Battery electric cars (from 2006–07 to 2009–10)	15% of list price, less 6% discount – i.e. 9% of list price
Bi-fuel gas and petrol cars manufactured or converted before type approval	Appropriate percentage of list price, less 2% discount
Hybrid electric and petrol cars	Appropriate percentage of list price, less 3% discount
Cars capable of running on E85 fuel	Appropriate percentage of list price, less two per cent discount. (But NB discount applies only from 6 April 2008)

Notes

[1] The cost of conversion is ignored for bi-fuel gas and petrol cars converted after type approval, but no additional percentage discount is given.

[2] The reductions are to be abolished from 6 April 2011, except that cars producing no CO_2 emissions when driven will continue to be taxed at zero per cent until 6 April 2015.

Fuel for company cars

[¶4-140] Fuel benefit charges: current rules

(ITEPA 2003, s. 149)

(Tax Reporter: ¶416-000ff.)

The additional taxable benefit of free fuel provided for a company car is calculated using the same CO_2 percentages as are used for calculating the company car charge.

The CO_2 percentage figure is applied to a fixed amount in accordance with the following table:

2010–11	18,000
2009–10	16,900
2008–09	16,900
2007–08	14,400
2006–07	14,400
2005–06	14,400
2004–05	14,400

The fuel benefit is reduced to nil if the employee is required to make good the full cost of all fuel provided for private use, and does so.

A proportionate reduction is made where the company car is only available for part of the year, where car fuel ceases to be provided part-way through the year, or where the benefit of the company car is shared.

[¶4-160] Fuel types

Where there is a fuel benefit, employers must notify HMRC of the type of fuel (or other power) by entering the appropriate 'key letter' on the form P11D. The key letters are as follows:

Key letter	Fuel or power type description
P	Petrol
D	Diesel not meeting Euro IV standard
L	Diesel meeting Euro IV standard
E	Electric only
H	Hybrid electric
B	Gas only, or bi-fuel with approved CO_2 emissions figure for gas when first registered (which must be from 1 January 2000).
C	conversion, and all other bi-fuel cars with an approved CO_2 emissions figure for petrol only when first registered.

In *Employer's Bulletin 17*, the Revenue wrote that:

> 'we have been asked to make it clear that the key letter shown in the P11D (Guide) refers to the car, not to the fuel in isolation.'

From 6 April 2011, the number of letters used to describe cars will be reduced to three: E for electric-only cars (though it is likely that this will be amended to encompass all cars that produce zero emissions when driven), D for all diesel cars (current types D and L) and A for all other types (current types P, H, B, G, C).

[¶4-180] Advisory fuel rates for company cars

(Tax Reporter: ¶416-040)

HMRC publish rates that can be used by employers wishing to pay their employees the cost of fuel for business journeys in company cars (or, where the employer initially pays for all fuel, for reimbursement of private mileage by company car drivers to their employers). Passenger payments may be made for company cars as for private cars (see below).

In the past, HMRC would give approximately one month's warning, and employers could choose to implement the changes immediately or from the official start date (see alternative dates in tables below). HMRC caused confusion by announcing at the end of 2009 that they would no longer give a month's notice of changes, 'after discussions with the relevant trade bodies'. However, they have gone back on that change and the intention is that rate changes will in future apply from 1 June and 1 December, but employers will have up to a month from each of those dates in which to implement those changes.

Rates applying from 1 June 2010

Engine size	Petrol	Diesel	LPG
1400cc or less	12p	11p	8p
1401cc to 2000cc	15p	11p	10p
Over 2000cc	21p	16p	14p

Petrol hybrid cars are treated as petrol cars for this purpose.

Rates applying from 1 December 2009*

Engine size	Petrol	Diesel	LPG
1400cc or less	11p	11p	7p
1401cc to 2000cc	14p	11p	8p
Over 2000cc	20p	14p	12p

Petrol hybrid cars are treated as petrol cars for this purpose.

*The rates have effect for all journeys made from 1 December 2009.

Rates applying from 1 July 2009*

Engine size	Petrol	Diesel	LPG
1400cc or less	10p	10p	7p
1401cc to 2000cc	12p	10p	8p
Over 2000cc	18p	13p	12p

Petrol hybrid cars are treated as petrol cars for this purpose.

Taxation of Earnings

*The rates were announced on 1 June 2009, to have effect from 1 July 2009. However, HMRC then added the following comment:

'HMRC is content for the new rates to be implemented immediately where employers are able and wish to do so.'

Rates applying from 1 January 2009 (or 2 December 2008*)

Engine size	Petrol	Diesel	LPG
1400cc or less	10p	11p	7p
1401cc to 2000cc	12p	11p	9p
Over 2000cc	17p	14p	12p

Petrol hybrid cars are treated as petrol cars for this purpose.

*The rates were announced near the end of May to give the agreed one-month notice period before 1 July 2008. However, HMRC then added the following comment:

'However, the recent fuel price increases which justify these AFR changes have happened very rapidly. In these unusual circumstances we are mindful that an implementation date of 1 July might mean that drivers will be incurring higher fuel prices before the new rates become effective. Consequently, where employers are able to do so, HMRC is content for the new rates to be implemented immediately, ie form 1 June.'

Rates applying from 1 July (or June*) 2008

Engine size	Petrol	Diesel	LPG
1400cc or less	12p	13p	7p
1401cc to 2000cc	15p	13p	9p
Over 2000cc	21p	17p	13p

Petrol hybrid cars are treated as petrol cars for this purpose.

*The rates were announced near the end of May to give the agreed one-month notice period before 1 July 2008. However, HMRC then added the following comment:

'However, the recent fuel price increases which justify these AFR changes have happened very rapidly. In these unusual circumstances we are mindful that an implementation date of 1 July might mean that drivers will be incurring higher fuel prices before the new rates become effective. Consequently, where employers are able to do so, HMRC is content for the new rates to be implemented immediately, ie form 1 June.'

Rates applying from 1 January 2008

Engine size	Petrol	Diesel	LPG
1400cc or less	11p	11p	7p
1401cc to 2000cc	13p	11p	8p
Over 2000cc	19p	14p	11p

Petrol hybrid cars are treated as petrol cars for this purpose.

HMRC announced on 30 November 2007 that rates will now be reviewed twice a year. Any changes will take effect on 1 January and 1 July but will be published about one month in advance. HMRC will also consider changing the rates if fuel prices fluctuate by five per cent during the six-month period.

HMRC had previously commented:

'We aim to provide employers with as much certainty as possible by keeping the fuel rates unchanged where there are modest variations in fuel prices. In line with the commitment made when they were introduced, they will be reviewed during a tax year only in the event of a variation in fuel prices of greater than 10% from the prices used at that time.'

Rates applying from 1 August 2007

Engine size	Petrol	Diesel	LPG
1400cc or less	10p	10p	6p
1401cc to 2000cc	13p	10p	8p
Over 2000cc	18p	13p	10p

According to HMRC guidance, these rates apply to journeys undertaken from 1 August 2007 (and not, for example, to claims submitted from that date or to amounts reimbursed from that date).

Rates applying from 1 February 2007 (but see note below)

Engine size	Petrol	Diesel	LPG
1400cc or less	9p	9p	6p
1401cc to 2000cc	11p	9p	7p
Over 2000cc	16p	12p	10p

Note: having announced that the above rates would apply from 1 February 2007, HMRC subsequently posted the following paragraph on their website:

'Where employers have practical difficulties implementing the new lower rates they can continue to use the older higher rates for a further month, i.e. to 28 February 2007, without having to take account of the income tax, NIC and VAT implications of paying allowances at the higher rate. This will allow time for drivers and employers to adjust to the new rate.

This treatment will extend to those employers with dispensations for fuel rates which are linked, usually by a formula, to AFRs.

Employers can however use the new lower rate with effect from 1 February for employees with fuel cards who reimburse their employers for private fuel bought with a company fuel card.'

Rates applying from 1 July 2006 to 31 January 2007

Engine size	Petrol	Diesel	LPG
1400cc or less	11p	10p	7p
1401cc to 2000cc	13p	10p	8p
Over 2000cc	18p	14p	11p

HMRC have commented:

'We aim to provide employers with as much certainty as possible by keeping the fuel rates unchanged where there are modest variations in fuel prices. In line with the commitment made when they were introduced, they will be reviewed during a tax year only in the event of a variation in fuel prices of greater than 10% from the prices used at that time.'

Private vehicles

[¶4-200]   Mileage allowance payments
(ITEPA 2003, s. 230)

(Tax Reporter: ¶432-100ff.)

Statutory rates are set for mileage allowance payments. An employer may, of course, reimburse business mileage driven in a privately-owned car at more or less than the statutory rates but any excess is taxable. Any shortfall is tax deductible and the employee may claim relief accordingly. The rates below have applied since 6 April 2002 and continue to do so in 2010-11:

Kind of vehicle	Rate per mile
Car or van	40p for the first 10,000 miles 25p after that
Motorcycle	24p
Cycle	20p

[¶4-220]   Passenger payments
(ITEPA 2003, s. 233)

(Tax Reporter: ¶432-150)

No liability to income tax arises in respect of an approved passenger payment made to an employee for a car or a van, whether the vehicle is privately owned or provided by the employer. The approved amount is 5p per passenger mile.

Company vans

[¶4-300]   Rules applying from April 2007
(ITEPA 2003, s. 114)

(Tax Reporter: ¶416-200ff.)

	£
Van benefit	3,000

But nil if (1) the restricted private use conditions are met, (2) private use in the tax year is insignificant, or (3) (from 6 April 2010) the van cannot produce any CO_2 emissions under any circumstances by being driven (e.g., an electric van).

[¶4-320]   Rules applying for 2005–06 and 2006–07
(Tax Reporter: ¶416-475)

Age of van at end of tax year	Taxable benefit £
Less than four years	500
Four years or more	350

However, there is no taxable benefit if the restricted private use conditions are met, or if private use in the tax year is insignificant.

[¶4-345]   Fuel for company vans
(ITEPA 2003, s. 160ff.)
(Tax Reporter: ¶416-200ff.)

Tax Year	£
2010–11	550
2009–10	500
2008–09	500
2007–08	500

But nil if (1) the restricted private use conditions are met, (2) private use in the tax year is insignificant, or (3) the van cannot produce any CO_2 emissions by being driven.

There was no taxable benefit on the provision of fuel for private journeys in a company van before 6 April 2007.

Buses

[¶4-360]   Bus services
ITEPA 2003, s. 242 and 243
(Tax Reporter: ¶432-600ff.)

An exemption applies to:
(1)   works transport services, which must be a bus or minibus:
    (a)   available to employees generally;
    (b)   used mainly for qualifying journeys; and
    (c)   used substantially by employees or their children;
(2)   support for public bus services:
    (a)   available to employees generally;
    (b)   used for qualifying journeys by employees of one or more employers; and
    (c)   either:
        (i)   a local bus service; or
        (ii)   the bus must be provided to other passengers on terms that are as favourable as the terms on which the bus is provided to employees.

Official rates of interest

[¶4-400]   Official rate of interest

(ITEPA 2003, s. 181)

(Tax Reporter: ¶419-200)

The official rate of interest is used to calculate the cash equivalent of the benefit of an employment-related loan which is a taxable cheap loan. HMRC normally set a single rate in advance for the whole tax year and gave a commitment in January 2000, that (following announcement of the rate for any given tax year) the official rate may be reduced but will not be increased in the light of interest rate changes generally.

The official rate of interest was reduced with effect from 6 April 2010 and figures for recent periods have been as follows:

Date	Rate %	SI No.
From 6 April 2010	4.00	SI 2010/415
From 1 March 2009 to 5 April 2010	4.75	SI 2009/199
From 6 April 2007 to 28 February 2009	6.25	SI 2007/684
From 6 January 2002 to 5 April 2007	5.00	SI 2001/3860

The average official rates of interest are given below. These should be used if the loan was outstanding throughout the tax year and the normal averaging method of calculation is being used.

Year	Average official rate %
2009–10	4.75
2008–09	6.10
2007–08	6.25
2006–07	5.00

[¶4-420]   Official rate of interest: foreign currency loans

(ITEPA 2003, s. 181)

(Tax Reporter: ¶418-100)

The official rate of interest for certain employer-provided loans in Japanese yen or Swiss francs has been set as follows since 6 July 1994:

• Loans in Swiss francs: 5.5 per cent.
• Loans in Japanese yen: 3.9 per cent.

Travel and subsistence

[¶4-500]   Day subsistence rates

(Tax Reporter: ¶457-560)

The following 'day subsistence' rates may be used when applying for a dispensation for payments to employees away from home for work purposes:

Rate	Detail	£
Breakfast rate	Irregular early starters	5
One meal rate	Away for at least five hours	5
Two meal rate	Away for at least 10 hours	10
Late evening meal rate	Irregular late finishers	15

[¶4-520]   Accommodation and subsistence – overseas rates

(Tax Reporter: ¶457-570)

In March 2008, HMRC published for the first time benchmark scale rates that employers were to be allowed to use when paying for accommodation and subsistence costs for employees working abroad. Payments up to these rates did not require receipts and did not need to be shown on form P11D.

By July 2008, however, HMRC had changed their mind about the best approach. While the principle remains as planned earlier in the year, the table of rates has been removed. Instead, HMRC instruct employers to use the benchmark scale rates published by the Foreign and Commonwealth Office. These rates (as updated in January 2009) are available at www.hmrc.gov.uk/employers/wwsr-jan09.pdf.

The principles will change again from 6 April 2011: see ¶457-570.

[¶4-540]   Incidental overnight expenses and benefits

(ITEPA 2003, s. 240)

(Tax Reporter: ¶432-900)

Benefits, reimbursements and expenses provided by an employer for employees' minor, personal expenditure whilst on business-related activities requiring overnight accommodation away from home are not taxable provided that the total amount reimbursed, etc. does not exceed the relevant maximum amount(s) per night, multiplied by the number of nights' absence). If the limit is exceeded, the whole amount provided remains taxable.

From	Authorised maximum per night	
	In UK £	Overseas £
6 April 1995	5	10

Shares and share incentives

[¶4-600]   Share incentive plans
(ITEPA 2003, s. 488ff)
(Tax Reporter: ¶468-000ff.)

	Free shares	Partnership shares	Matching shares	Dividend shares
Employment before eligibility[(1)]	Up to 12 months employment	Up to 12 months employment	Only awarded to employees who buy partnership shares	Must be acquired with dividends from plan shares
Limits	Up to £3,000 per tax year	Up to £1,500 per tax year, capped at lower of: £125 per month and 10% of monthly salary	Up to 2 matching shares for each partnership share bought	Dividends from shares in the plan reinvested: – £500 in 1st year – £1,000 in 2nd year – £1,500 per year thereafter
Minimum amount if stated[(1)]	–	£10 per month	–	–
Performance measures[(1)]	Yes	No	No	No
Holding period	At least 3 years from award[(2)]	None	At least 3 years from award[(2)]	3 years from acquisition
Forfeiture on cessation of employment[(1)]	Yes	No	Yes	No
Tax on award	None	None – tax relief for salary used to buy shares	None	None

	Free shares	Partnership shares	Matching shares	Dividend shares
Tax on removal of shares from plan within 3 years of award[3]	On market value when taken out	On market value when taken out	On market value when taken out	Original dividend taxable but in year when shares taken out of plan.
Tax on removal between 3 and 5 years of award[2]	On lower of: – value at award; and – value on removal	On lower of: – salary used to buy shares; and – value on removal	On lower of: – value at award; and – value on removal	None
Tax on removal after 5 years	None	None	None	None
CGT on removal – any time	None	None	None	None

Notes

[1] These conditions can be included at the option of the company.

[2] The holding period may be up to 5 years at the option of the company.

[3] PAYE and NICs will be operated in relation to any income tax charge where the shares are readily convertible assets.

[¶4-620]   Enterprise management incentives (EMI)

(ITEPA 2003, Sch. 5)

(Tax Reporter: ¶466-000ff)

Qualifying company	Gross assets not exceeding £30m. In relation to options granted from 21 July 2008, company must have fewer than 250 employees (full time or equivalent).
Maximum options	For options granted on or after 6 April 2008: up to £120,000 per employee. Previously: up to £100,000.

[¶4-640]   SAYE bonus rates: multiple of monthly payments

(ITEPA 2003, Sch. 3)

(Tax Reporter: ¶470-000ff.)

From	3-year	5-year	7-year
14 May 2010	0.0	1.8	4.9
29 May 2009	0.3	2.2	5.2
17 February 2009	0.6	2.6	5.6

From	3-year	5-year	7-year
27 December 2008	1.5	4.8	9.3
1 September 2008	2.4	7.0	12.7
4 April 2008	1.6	5.1	9.8
1 September 2007	2.4	7.2	13.3
1 September 2006	1.8	5.5	10.3
1 September 2005	1.4	4.4	8.4

Notes

See ¶4-660 for details of the 'early leaver rate' applying for those who withdraw their funds after 12 monthly contributions, but before the three-year anniversary.

Employees receive the bonus rate for the relevant contract in force when they join the scheme, and are not affected by subsequent bonus rate changes.

[¶4-660]   SAYE 'early leaver rates'

(ITEPA 2003, Sch. 3)

(Tax Reporter: ¶470-000ff.)

The following 'early leaver rates' have applied for employees whose SAYE contracts are cancelled after 12 monthly contributions but before the maturity date:

Dates	Rates %
14 May 2010	0.00
29 May 2009	0.36
17 February 2009	0.5
1 September 2008	2.0
1 September 2007	3.0
1 September 2006	2.0
1 September 2005	1.5

Note: the relevant date is that on which the employee starts saving under the contract, not the date on which the contract is cancelled.

[¶4-680]   SAYE effective interest rates

(ITEPA 2003, Sch. 3)

(Tax Reporter: ¶470-000ff.)

From	3-year	5-year	7-year
14 May 2010	0.00	1.16	1.74
29 May 2009	0.54	1.42	1.84
17 February 2009	1.08	1.67	1.98
27 December 2008	2.67	3.04	3.20
1 September 2008	4.23	4.36	4.28
4 April 2008	2.84	3.22	3.36
1 September 2007	4.23	4.48	4.46
1 September 2006	3.19	3.46	3.52
1 September 2005	2.49	2.79	2.91

National minimum wage

[¶4-700]   National minimum wage

There are three minimum wage hourly rates, as follows (but see note re new rate for apprentices):

	Workers aged 22 plus £	Workers aged 18 to 21 £	Workers aged under 18 £	Apprentices £
From 01.10.10	5.93	4.92	3.64	2.50
01.10.09–30.09.10	5.80	4.83	3.57	–
01.10.08–30.09.09	5.73	4.77	3.53	–
01.10.07–30.09.08	5.52	4.60	3.40	–
01.10.06–30.09.07	5.35	4.45	3.30	–
01.10.05–30.09.06	5.05	4.25	3.00	–

Notes

(1)   The 'development rate' for workers aged 22 or more was abolished from 1 October 2006. All such workers now qualify for the main rate.

(2)   See ¶4-720 for a table of amounts that may be deducted in relation to the provision of living accommodation.

(3)   Tips paid through a tronc system do not count towards the national minimum wage, and the rules on this point were tightened from October 2009 (see Tax Reporter: ¶495-230).

(4)   The apprentice minimum wage is introduced from October 2010. It applies to apprentices aged 19 or more who are in the first year of their apprenticeship, and to all apprentices under 19.

[¶4-720]   National minimum wage: accommodation offset

The maximum permitted daily and weekly rates of accommodation offset in relation to the national minimum wage are as follows:

Period	Daily offset £	Weekly offset £
From 01.10.10	4.61	32.27
01.10.09 – 30.09.10	4.51	31.57
01.10.08 – 30.09.09	4.46	31.22
01.10.07 – 30.09.08	4.30	30.10
01.10.06 – 30.09.07	4.15	29.05
01.10.05 – 30.09.06	3.90	27.30

Flat rate expenses

[¶4-750]   Fixed sum deductions for repairing and maintaining equipment

(ITEPA 2003, s. 367)

(Tax Reporter: ¶457-500)

A tax deduction is given for certain amounts 'representing the average annual expenses incurred by employees of the class to which the employee belongs in respect of the repair and maintenance of work equipment'. The term 'flat rate expenses' is often used for these figures. The following table is from EIM 32712, though the industry codes in the left hand column are based on a former appendix to ESC A1:

Manual and certain other employees: flat rate expenses deduction for tools and special clothing

Industry code	Industry	Occupation	Deduction for 2008–09 onwards £	Deduction for 2004–05 to 2007–08 £
10	Agriculture	All workers	100	70
100	Aluminium	a. Continual casting operators, process operators, de-dimplers, driers, drill punchers, dross unloaders, firemen, furnace operators and their helpers, leaders, mouldmen, pourers, remelt department labourers, roll flatteners	140	130
		b. Cable hands, case makers, labourers, mates, truck drivers and measurers, storekeepers	80	60
		c. Apprentices	60	45
		d. All other workers	120	100
330	Banks	Uniformed bank employees	60	45
90	Brass and copper	All workers	120	100
270	Building	a. Joiners and carpenters	140	105
		b. Cement works and roofing (asphalt) labourers	80	55
		c. Labourers and navvies	60	45
		d. All other workers	120	85
250	Building materials	a. Stone-masons	140	85
		b. Tilemakers and labourers	60	45
		c. All other workers	80	55
190	Clothing	a. Lacemakers, hosiery bleachers, dyers, scourers and knitters, knitwear bleachers and dyers	60	45
		b. All other workers	60	45
150	Constructional Engineering	a. Blacksmiths and their strikers, burners, caulkers, chippers, drillers, erectors, fitters, holders up, markers off, platers, riggers, riveters, rivet heaters, scaffolders, sheeters, template workers, turners, welders	140	115
		b. Banksmen labourers, shop-helpers, slewers, straighteners	80	60

Industry code	Industry	Occupation	Deduction for 2008–09 onwards £	Deduction for 2004–05 to 2007–08 £
		c. Apprentices and storekeepers	60	45
		d. All other workers	100	75
170	Electrical and Electricity supply	a. Those workers incurring laundry costs only (generally CEGB employees)	60	45
		b. All other workers	120	90
110	Engineering	a. Pattern makers	140	120
		b. Labourers, supervisory and unskilled workers	80	60
		c. Apprentices and storekeepers	60	45
		d. Motor mechanics in garage repair shops	120	100
		e. All other workers	120	100
40	Fire service	Uniformed fire fighters & fire officers	80	60
220	Food	All workers	60	45
20	Forestry	All workers	100	70
240	Glass	All workers	80	60
80	Healthcare	a. Ambulance staff on active service (i.e. excluding staff who take telephone calls or provide clerical support)	140	110
		b. Nurses and midwives, chiropodists, dental nurses, occupational speech physios and therapists, phlebotomists, radiographers	100	70
		c. Plaster room orderlies, hospital porters, ward clerks, sterile supply workers, hospital domestics, hospital catering staff	100	60
		d. Laboratory staff, pharmacists, pharmacy assistants	60	45
		e. Uniformed ancillary staff – maintenance workers, grounds staff, drivers, parking attendants and security guards, receptionists and other uniformed staff	60	45
280	Heating	a. Pipe fitters and plumbers	120	100
		b. Coverers, laggers, domestic glaziers, heating engineers and their mates	120	90
		c. All gas workers, all other workers	100	70

Taxation of Earnings

Industry code	Industry	Occupation	Deduction for 2008–09 onwards £	Deduction for 2004–05 to 2007–08 £
50	Iron Mining	a. Fillers, miners and underground workers	120	100
		b. All other workers	100	75
70	Iron and Steel	a. Day labourers, general labourers, stockmen, time-keepers, warehouse staff and weighmen	80	60
		b. Apprentices	60	45
		c. All other workers	140	120
210	Leather	a. Curriers (wet workers), fellmongering workers, tanning operatives (wet)	80	55
		b. All other workers	60	45
140	Particular Engineering	a. Pattern makers	140	120
		b. All chainmakers; cleaners, galvanisers, tinners and wire drawers in the wire drawing industry; tool-makers in the lock making industry	120	100
		c. Apprentices and storekeepers	60	45
		d. All other workers	80	60
355	Police Force	Police officers (ranks up to and including Chief Inspector)	140	55 (but £110 for 2007–08)
160	Precious Metals	All workers	100	70
230	Printing	a. *Letterpress Section*: Electrical engineers (rotary presses), electrotypers, ink and roller makers, machine minders (rotary), maintenance engineers (rotary presses) and stereotypers	140	105
		b. Bench hands (P & B), compositors (lp), readers (lp), T & E Section wireroom operators, warehousemen (Ppr box)	60	45
		c. All other workers	100	70
320	Prisons	Uniformed prison officers	80	55
300	Public Service	a. *Dock and inland waterways* – Dockers, dredger drivers, hopper steerers	80	55
		– All other workers	60	45
		b. *Public transport* – Garage hands (including cleaners and mechanics)	80	55
		– Conductors and drivers	60	45

Industry code	Industry	Occupation	Deduction for 2008–09 onwards £	Deduction for 2004–05 to 2007–08 £
60	Quarrying	All workers	100	70
290	Railways	(See the appropriate category for craftsmen, e.g. engineers, vehicle builders etc.)		
		All other workers	100	70
30	Seamen	a. Carpenters (Seamen) Passenger liners	165	165
		b. Carpenters (Seamen) Cargo vessels, tankers, coasters and ferries	140	130
120	Shipyards	a. Blacksmiths and their strikers, boilermakers, burners, carpenters, caulkers, drillers, furnacemen (platers), holders up, fitters, platers, plumbers, riveters, sheet iron workers, shipwrights, tubers, welders	140	115
		b. Labourers	80	60
		c. Apprentices and storekeepers	60	45
		d. All other workers	100	75
180	Textiles and Textile Printing	a. Carders, carding engineers, overlookers and technicians in spinning mills	120	85
		b. All other workers	80	60
130	Vehicles	a. Builders, railway wagon etc. repairers and railway wagon lifters	140	105
		b. Railway vehicle painters and letterers, railway wagon etc. builders' and repairers' assistants	80	60
		c. All other workers	60	45
260	Wood & Furniture (formerly Wood)	a. Carpenters, cabinet makers, joiners, wood carvers and woodcutting machinists	140	115
		b. Artificial limb makers (other than in wood), organ builders and packaging case makers	120	90
		c. Coopers not providing own tools, labourers, polishers and upholsterers	60	45
		d. All other workers	100	75

Notes

Industry codes are HMRC computer identification numbers.

'Workers' and 'all other workers' are references to manual workers or to workers who have to pay for the upkeep of tools and special clothing.

'Firemen' means persons engaged to light and maintain furnaces.

'Constructional engineering' means engineering undertaken on a construction site, including buildings, shipyards, bridges, roads and other similar operations.

'Particular engineering' means engineering undertaken on a commercial basis in a factory or workshop for the purposes of producing components such as wire, springs, nails and locks.

Miscellaneous

[¶4-800] Mobile phones
(ITEPA 2003, s. 319)

(Tax Reporter: ¶437-700)

Rules applying from 6 April 2006

No tax charge on an employer-provided mobile phones but exemption restricted to one phone per employee, with no exemption for phones provided for family members. Limited exemption for vouchers supplied for mobile phone use. The right of the employee to surrender the phone for additional pay does not trigger a tax charge.

[¶4-810] Childcare vouchers
(ITEPA 2003, s. 318A)

(Tax Reporter: ¶437-670)

Year	Weekly limit	Monthly limit
2010–11	£55	£243
2009–10	£55	£243
2008–09	£55	£243
2007–08	£55	£243
2006–07	£55	£243

[¶4-820] Computer equipment
(ITEPA 2003, s. 316, s. 320)

(Tax Reporter: ¶437-715ff.)

Rules applying from 6 April 2006

No special treatment so private use of a computer triggers a tax charge on normal principles. HMRC have indicated, though, that no tax charge will normally arise in practice if the computer is provided for work purposes.

This is subject to transitional rules, however. A press release issued on 24 March 2006 stated:

> 'Following the Chancellor's budget announcement abolishing the tax exemption on the provision by employers of computer equipment for private use with effect from 6 April 2006, in response to a number of enquiries, HMRC confirm that anybody who has had a computer made available for private use before 6 April 2006 will **not** be affected by the change. If an employee entered into a home computer initiative (HCI) scheme arrangement with their employer before 6 April 2006, and under that arrangement the employer is committed to provide a computer to the employee, but for reasons beyond their control the employee cannot take physical possession of the computer until 6 April or later, HMRC accepts that the computer exemption will apply to the provision of that computer.'

[¶4-830]   Relocation allowance

(ITEPA 2003, s. 287)

(Tax Reporter: ¶433-850)

Tax relief for relocation expenses in relation to payments made or expenses provided in connection with an employee's change of residence where the employee's job or place of work is changed is generally subject to a statutory maximum of £8,000.

[¶4-840]   Payments on loss of office and employment

(ITEPA 2003, Pt. 6, Ch. 3)

(Tax Reporter: ¶437-000ff.)

Period	Relief
From 1998–99	£30,000 exempt

Notes

The exemption is not available for any payment or other benefit chargeable to income tax under other legislation (ITEPA 2003, s. 401(3)).

There is therefore no exemption for any amounts already taxable as earnings (e.g. payments made under a contract of employment).

[¶4-850] Scholarships and sandwich courses

(SP 4/86)

(Tax Reporter: ¶419-200)

Subject to conditions, employers may make tax-free payments up to a specified figure to employees who are attending certain educational courses. The specified amount for recent years has been as follows:

Period	Specified amount
From 1 September 2007	£15,480
From 1 September 2005 to 31 August 2007	£15,000
Before 1 September 2005	£7,000 but different principles also then applied

PAYE

[¶4-900] PAYE thresholds

(SI 2003/2682)

(Tax Reporter: ¶493-250ff.)

Tax year	Amount	
	Weekly £	Monthly £
2010–11	125.00	540.00
2009–10	125.00	540.00
2008–09	116.00	503.00
2007–08	100.00	435.00
2006–07	97.00	420.00

Notes

Under normal circumstances, employers need not deduct tax from employees who earn less than the above amounts.

The PAYE monthly and weekly thresholds are calculated arithmetically from the personal allowance (SI 2003/2682, reg. 9(8)).

[¶4-920] PAYE codes

The PAYE code enables an employer or payer of pension to give the employee or pensioner the approved amount of tax-free pay.

L   tax code with basic personal allowance;

P   tax code with full personal allowance for those aged 65–74;

Y   tax code with full personal allowance for those aged 75 or over;

T   tax code used where HMRC reviewing other items in tax code. Also used where HMRC asked not to use other codes;

K   total allowances are less than total deductions.

Other codes

The codes BR, DO, OT and NT are generally used where there is a second source of income and all allowances have been included in tax code which is applied to first or main source of income.

Code V has been obsolete since April 2009 (as all individuals born before 6 April 1935 and qualifying for Married Couple's allowance (MCA) are aged 75 and over during the tax year ended 5 April 2010. MCA is therefore due at the higher rate.)

[¶4-940] PAYE returns

(Tax Reporter: ¶497-600)

PAYE returns: deadlines

Forms	Date	Provision	Penalty provisions
P14, P35, P38 and P38A	19 May following tax year	*Income Tax (Pay As You Earn) Regulations 2003 (SI 2003/2682), reg. 73 and 74*	TMA 1970, s. 98A
P60 (to employee)	31 May following tax year	*Income Tax (Pay As You Earn) Regulations 2003 (SI 2003/2682), reg. 67*	TMA 1970, s. 98A
P9D and P11D	6 July following tax year	*Income Tax (Pay As You Earn) Regulations 2003 (SI 2003/2682), reg. 85*	TMA 1970, s. 98
P46 (Car)	3 May, 2 August, 2 November, 2 February	*Income Tax (Pay As You Earn) Regulations 2003 (SI 2003/2682), reg. 90*	TMA 1970, s. 98

PAYE returns: penalties

Returns for the purposes of the PAYE regulations (from 1 April 2009)

The maximum penalty for an incorrect return is 100 per cent of the potential lost revenue (deliberate and concealed action), 70 per cent (deliberate but not concealed) or 30 per cent (careless action) (FA 2007, Sch. 24, para 1 and 4).

Earlier periods

Penalties (fixed, but see ESC B46) imposed for delays (TMA 1970, s. 98A)

Forms	First 12 months	Thereafter
P14, P35, P38 and P38A	£100 per 50 employees per month	Additional penalty not exceeding 100% of the tax and NIC payable for the year but remaining unpaid by 19 April following end of tax year

Penalties (mitigable) that may be imposed for delays (TMA 1970, s. 98)

Forms	Initial	Continuing
P9D and P11D	£300 per return	£60 per day

Penalties that may be imposed for incorrect returns (returns due before 1 April 2009)

Forms	Provision TMA 1970	Penalty
P14, P35, P38 and P38A	s. 98A(4)	Maximum of 100% of tax underpaid
P9D and P11D	s. 98(2)	Maximum penalty £3,000

Interest on certain PAYE paid late

Where an employer has not paid the net tax deductible by him under PAYE to the collector within 14 days of the end of the tax year, the unpaid tax carries interest at the prescribed rate from the reckonable date until the date of payment. Certain repayments of tax also attract interest.

[¶4-950] Student loan deductions

(SI 2000/944, reg. 29)

Year	Percentage	Threshold
2010–11	9%	£15,000
2009–10	9%	£15,000
2008–09	9%	£15,000
2007–08	9%	£15,000
2006–07	9%	£15,000
2005–06	9%	£15,000

[¶4-960] Specified dates (electronic filing)

(SI 2003/2682, reg. 190(1), 198A(3))

(Tax Reporter: ¶497-250)

It is necessary to determine whether an employer is small, medium-sized or large. This then governs the question of both incentives and penalties for the making of year-end returns. From 2011-12 onwards, the specified date is set permanently at 31 October of the year preceding the tax year in question. For earlier years, the specified dates were as follows:

> 2010–11 – 18 October 2009 (see *www.hmrc.gov.uk/paye/paye-boards-direction.pdf*)
>
> 2009–10 – 19 October 2008 (see *www.hmrc.gov.uk/ebu/direction.pdf*)
>
> 2008–09 – 28 October 2007 (see *www.hmrc.gov.uk/ebu/dir-si2682.pdf*)
>
> 2007–08 – 29 October 2006 (see *www.hmrc.gov.uk/ebu/direction-regs.pdf*)
>
> 2006–07 – 30 October 2005 (see *www.hmrc.gov.uk/ebu/directions-300905.pdf*)

[¶4-965] PAYE electronic communications: penalties (reg. 205 failures)

Penalties for tax year 2010–11 and later years

(SI 2003/2682, reg. 210AA)

(Tax Reporter: ¶497-250ff)

Table 9ZA

Number of employees (note 1)	Penalty
1–5	£100
6–49	£300
50–249	£600
250–399	£900
400–499	£1,200
500–599	£1,500
600–699	£1,800
700–799	£2,100
800–899	£2,400
900–999	£2,700
1,000 or more	£3,000

Note
(1) Number of employees for whom particulars should have been included with the relevant annual return.

Penalties for tax year 2009–10

(SI 2003/2682, reg. 210A)

(Tax Reporter: ¶497-250ff)

Table 9

Number of employees (note 1)	Penalty
1–5	£0
6–49	£100
50–249	£600
250–399	£900
400–499	£1,200
500–599	£1,500
600–699	£1,800
700–799	£2,100
800–899	£2,400
900–999	£2,700
1,000 or more	£3,000

Note
(1) Number of employees for whom particulars should have been included with the relevant annual return.

Penalties for tax years 2004–05 to 2008–09

(SI 2003/2682, reg. 210A)

(Tax Reporter: ¶497-250ff)

Former table 9

Number of employees (note 1)	Penalty
1–49	£0
50–249	£600 (but see note 2)
250–399	£900
400–499	£1,200
500–599	£1,500

Number of employees (note 1)	Penalty
600–699	£1,800
700–799	£2,100
800–899	£2,400
900–999	£2,700
1,000 or more	£3,000

Note
[1] Number of employees for whom particulars should have been included with the specified information.
[2] But nil for tax year 2004-05 only (50-249 employees).

[¶4-968]   PAYE electronic communications: penalties (reg. 205A failures)

Penalties for tax quarter ending 5 April 2010 and for tax year 2010–11

(SI 2003/2682, reg. 210B)

(Tax Reporter: ¶497-250ff)

Table 9A

Number of items (note 1)	Penalty
1–5	£0
6–49	£100
50–149	£300
150–299	£600
300–399	£900
400–499	£1,200
500–599	£1,500
600–699	£1,800
700–799	£2,100
800–899	£2,400
900–999	£2,700
1,000 or more	£3,000

Note
[1] Number of items of specified information the employer has failed to deliver in the tax quarter. (Each item mentioned in reg. 207(1) paras. (a) to (d) counts as a separate item of specified information.)

[¶4-970]   PAYE surcharges

(SI 2003/2682, reg. 203)

(Tax Reporter: ¶497-660)

Specified percentage for each default in a surcharge period	
Default number (within the surcharge period)	Specified percentage %
1	0.00
2	0.00
3	0.17
4	0.17
5	0.17
6	0.33
7	0.33
8	0.33
9	0.58
10	0.58
11	0.58
12 and more defaults	0.83

[¶4-975]   PAYE monthly accounting periods

(SI 2003/2682, reg. 69)

(Tax Reporter: ¶493-850)

Period	Month no.	Payment due (electronic)	Payment due (other)
6 Apr to 5 May	1	22 May	19 May
6 May to 5 June	2	22 June	19 June
6 June to 5 July	3	22 July	19 July
6 July to 5 Aug	4	22 August	19 August
6 Aug to 5 Sept	5	22 September	19 September
6 Sept to 5 Oct	6	22 October	19 October
6 Oct to 5 Nov	7	22 November	19 November
6 Nov to 5 Dec	8	22 December	19 December

Period	Month no.	Payment due (electronic)	Payment due (other)
6 Dec to 5 Jan	9	22 January	19 January
6 Jan to 5 Feb	10	22 February	19 February
6 Feb to 5 Mar	11	22 March	19 March
6 Mar to 5 Apr	12	22 April	19 April

[¶4-976]   PAYE quarterly accounting periods

(SI 2003/2682, reg. 70)

(Tax Reporter: ¶493-850)

Period	Month no.	Payment due (electronic)	Payment due (other)
6 Apr to 5 July	1–3	22 July	19 July
6 July to 5 Oct	4–6	22 October	19 October
6 Oct to 5 Jan	7–9	22 January	19 January
6 Jan to 5 Apr	10–12	22 April	19 April

[¶4-980]   Payroll giving scheme

(ITEPA 2003, s. 713)

(Tax Reporter: ¶457-500)

Employees whose remuneration is subject to deduction of tax at source under PAYE can make unlimited tax-deductible donations to charity by requesting that their employers deduct the donations from their pay.

TAXATION OF CAPITAL GAINS

[¶5-000]   Rates, annual exemption, chattel exemption
(TCGA 1992, s. 4; s. 3 and s. 262)

(BTR: ¶500-250, ¶535-100, ¶535-200)

Tax year	Annual exempt amount		Chattel exemption (max sale proceeds)[3] £	Rate	
	Individuals, PRs[1], trusts for mentally disabled £	Other trusts[2] £		Individuals %	Trustees and PRs %
2010–11	10,100	5,050	6,000	18/28[4]	18/28[5]
2009–10	10,100	5,050	6,000	18	18
2008–09	9,600	4,800	6,000	18	18
2007–08	9,200	4,600	6,000	10/20/40[6]	40
2006–07	8,800	4,400	6,000	10/20/40[6]	40

Notes

[1] For year of death and next two years in the case of personal representatives (PRs) of deceased persons.

[2] Multiple trusts created by the same settlor; each attracts relief equal to the annual amount divided by the number of such trusts (subject to a minimum of 10% of the full amount).

[3] Where disposal proceeds exceed the exemption limit, marginal relief restricts any chargeable gain to $5/3$ of the excess. Where there is a loss and the proceeds are less than £6,000 the proceeds are deemed to be £6,000.

[4] For gains arising on disposals occurring on or before 22 June 2010, the rate is 18 per cent. Where disposals occur on or after 23 June 2010, the chargeable gains arising from those disposals are aggregated with the individual's taxable income and to the extent that the aggregate falls above the threshold of the income tax basic rate, capital gains tax is charged at 28 per cent (taking the chargeable gains as being the highest part of that aggregate). If the aggregate falls below the threshold, the capital gains tax rate remains at 18 per cent.

[5] For gains arising on disposals occurring on or before 22 June 2010, the rate is 18 per cent. Where disposals occur on or after 23 June 2010, the rate is 28 per cent.

[6] For 2004–05 to 2007–08, capital gains were taxed as top slice of income at:

- starting rate to the extent to the starting rate limit;

- lower rate to the extent above the starting rate limit but to the basic rate limit; and

- higher rate to the extent above the basic rate limit.

[¶5-050] Other exemptions and reliefs

Entrepreneurs' relief (from 6 April 2008 onwards)

(TCGA 1992, s. 169H-169S)

(BTR: ¶572-800ff.)

Chargeable gains arising on disposals of qualifying business assets in the period from 6 April 2008 to 22 June 2010 are to be reduced by 4/9ths before being charged to tax at the flat rate of 18 per cent. Eligible gains arising on or after 23 June 2010 are charged to tax at 10 per cent.

The qualifying gains eligible for this reduction are limited to a cap of;

- £1m for disposals in the period 6 April 2008 to 5 April 2010
- £2m for disposals in the period 6 April 2010 to 22 June 2010, and
- £5m for disposals on or after 23 June 2010.

Transitional provisions allow relief to be claimed in certain circumstances where gains deferred from disposals made on or before 5 April 2008 subsequently become chargeable.

Taper relief (to 5 April 2008)

(applies to individuals, trustees and personal representatives, NOT companies)

(TCGA 1992, s. 2A and Sch. A1, prior to repeal)

(BTR: ¶521-050)

Introduced for gains realised on or after 6 April 1998 and before 6 April 2008. Indexation allowance to 5 April 1998 (see below) may also be available.

The chargeable gain is reduced according to how long the asset has been held or treated as held after 5 April 1998. Non-business assets acquired prior to 17 March 1998 qualify for an addition of one year to the period for which they are treated as held after 5 April 1998.

The taper is generally applied to the net chargeable gain for the year after deduction of any losses of the same tax year and of any losses carried forward from earlier years.

The amount of taper relief depends on:

(a) the number of whole years in the qualifying holding period; and

(b) the amounts of the chargeable gain treated as:

  (i) a gain on the disposal of a business asset; and

  (ii) a gain on the disposal of a non-business asset.

The tables below show the percentage of chargeable gain that is subject to capital gains tax; i.e., after taper relief. Hence, if the percentage of gain chargeable is 100 per cent, then taper relief is 0 per cent; if the percentage of gain chargeable is 95 per cent, then taper relief is 5 per cent, and so on.

Business assets

Number of complete years after 5.4.98 for which asset held	Percentage of gains chargeable	
	All years from 2002–03 to 2007–08	2001–02
0	100	100
1	50	87.5
2	25	75
3	25	50
4 or more	25	25

Non-business assets

Number of complete years after 5.4.98 for which asset held	Percentage of gains chargeable (all years from 2001–02 to 2007–08)
0	100
1	100
2	100
3	95
4	90
5	85
6	80
7	75
8	70
9	65
10 or more	60

Indexation allowance up to 5 April 1998

(TCGA 1992, s. 53 and 54 as in force prior to 6 April 2008)

(BTR: ¶523-250)

Indexation allowance in respect of changes shown by the retail prices indices for months after April 1998 is allowed only for the purposes of corporation tax. For disposals made by individuals, trustees and personal representatives after April 1998 and before 6 April 2008, indexation allowance up to 5 April 1998 and taper relief (see above) could be obtained.

The table at ¶11-050 sets out the figure that is determined by the formula of (RD − RI)/RI where RD is the Retail Prices Index for April 1998 and RI is the Retail Prices Index for the later of March 1982 and the date that the item of relevant allowable expenditure was incurred. The indexation allowance is the aggregate of the indexed rise in each item of relevant allowable expenditure. In relation to each item of expenditure, the indexed rise is a sum produced by multiplying the amount of that item of expenditure by the appropriate figure in that table (for a fuller table applying for corporation tax purposes, see ¶11-000ff).

Taxation of Capital Gains

Rollover relief

(TCGA 1992, s. 152)

(BTR: ¶570-100)

To qualify for rollover relief, an asset must fall within one of the 'relevant classes of assets' and the reinvestment must generally take place within the period from 12 months before to three years after the disposal of the old asset. Classes of assets qualifying for relief are as follows, but see TCGA 1992, s. 156ZB for the interaction of this section with the corporation tax rules for gains and losses on intangible fixed assets:

- land and buildings occupied and used exclusively for the purposes of a trade;
- fixed plant or machinery (not forming part of a building);
- ships, aircraft, hovercraft;
- satellites, space stations and spacecraft (including launch vehicles);
- goodwill;
- milk quotas and fish quotas; and
- Lloyd's members' syndicate rights and assets treated as acquired by members.

Private residence relief

(TCGA 1992, s. 222)

(BTR: ¶540-000)

Relief is given on the dwelling house and on land enjoyed with the garden or grounds up to the permitted area of half a hectare, or more if required for the reasonable enjoyment of the property.

Time apportion as appropriate but last 36 months allowed in any event, as long as the property was at some time the only or main residence.

Up to £40,000 relief available where residence is partly let.

Enterprise investment scheme

(TCGA 1992, s. 150A and Sch. 5B and Sch. 5BA)

(BTR: ¶564-400ff. and ¶568-000)

The first disposal of shares on which relief has not been withdrawn is exempt from capital gains tax; losses arising from the first disposal of shares are eligible for relief against either income tax or capital gains tax.

Reinvestment relief is available for gains on assets where the disposal proceeds are reinvested in new EIS shares.

See ¶3-400 for EIS income tax relief.

Charities

(ICTA 1988, s. 505 and 506, TCGA 1992, s. 256(1), ITA 2007, 518ff)

(BTR: ¶589-100)

The gains of charities are not taxable provided they are applicable, and applied, for charitable purposes only. The legislation is designed to charge charities to tax on the amount of their income and gains that has not been invested, lent or spent in an approved way.

A charge to capital gains tax arises if a charity ceases to be a charity, when there is a deemed sale and reacquisition of the trust property by the trustees at market value.

[¶5-100] Leases which are wasting assets

Restrictions of allowable expenditure

(TCGA 1992, s. 240 and Sch. 8, para. 1)

(BTR: ¶509-600ff.)

Fraction equal to $\dfrac{P(1) - P(3)}{P(1)}$ excluded from expenditure of TCGA 1992, s. 38(1)(a),

and fraction equal to $\dfrac{P(2) - P(3)}{P(2)}$ excluded from expenditure of TCGA 1992, s. 38(1)(b), where:

P(1) = table percentage for duration of lease at time of acquisition (or 31 March 1982 where applicable);

P(2) = table percentage for duration of lease at time expenditure incurred; and

P(3) = table percentage for duration of lease at time of disposal.

Years	%	Monthly[1] increment
50 or more	100	–
49	99.657	.029
48	99.289	.031
47	98.902	.032
46	98.490	.034
45	98.059	.036
44	97.595	.039
43	97.107	.041
42	96.593	.043
41	96.041	.046
40	95.457	.049
39	94.842	.051
38	94.189	.054
37	93.497	.058
36	92.761	.061
35	91.981	.065
34	91.156	.069
33	90.280	.073
32	89.354	.077

Taxation of Capital Gains

Years	%	Monthly[1] increment
31	88.371	.082
30	87.330	.087
29	86.226	.092
28	85.053	.098
27	83.816	.103
26	82.496	.110
25	81.100	.116
24	79.622	.123
23	78.055	.131
22	76.399	.138
21	74.635	.147
20	72.770	.155
19	70.791	.165
18	68.697	.175
17	66.470	.186
16	64.116	.196
15	61.617	.208
14	58.971	.221
13	56.167	.234
12	53.191	.247
11	50.038	.263
10	46.695	.279
9	43.154	.295
8	39.399	.313
7	35.414	.332
6	31.195	.352
5	26.722	.373
4	21.983	.395
3	16.959	.419
2	11.629	.444
1	5.983	.470
0	0	.499

Notes

[1] Where duration is *not* an *exact* number of years, the table percentage for the whole number of years is increased by $1/12$ of the difference between that and the next highest percentage for each odd month. Fourteen odd days or more are rounded up and treated as a month; less than 14 odd days are ignored.

[¶5-150]   Premiums for short leases: CGT/IT charge

(ITTOIA 2005, s. 277)

(BTR: ¶509-950)

The chart at ¶3-500 shows the proportion of any premium received in respect of a lease of less than 50 years which is chargeable to capital gains tax and that which is chargeable to income tax as property business profits.

[¶5-200]   CGT exempt gilt-edged securities

(TCGA 1992, s. 16(2) and 115(1))

(BTR: ¶559-000)

Gains on the following securities are not chargeable gains and any losses are not allowable losses.

Stocks and bonds charged on the National Loans Funds

$2^{1}/_{2}$%	Annuities 1905 or after
$2^{3}/_{4}$%	Annuities 1905 or after
$2^{1}/_{2}$%	Consolidated Stock 1923 or after
$3^{1}/_{2}$%	War Loan 1952 or after
4%	Consolidated Loan 1957 or after
$3^{1}/_{2}$%	Conversion Loan 1961 or after
3%	Treasury Stock 1966 or after
$2^{1}/_{2}$%	Treasury Stock 1975 or after
$12^{3}/_{4}$%	Treasury Loan 1992
8%	Treasury Loan 1992
10%	Treasury Stock 1992
3%	Treasury Stock 1992
$12^{1}/_{4}$%	Exchequer Stock 1992
$13^{1}/_{2}$%	Exchequer Stock 1992
$10^{1}/_{2}$%	Treasury Convertible Stock 1992
2%	Index-Linked Treasury Stock 1992
$12^{1}/_{2}$%	Treasury Loan 1993
6%	Funding Loan 1993
$13^{3}/_{4}$%	Treasury Loan 1993
10%	Treasury Loan 1993
$8^{1}/_{4}$%	Treasury Stock 1993
$14^{1}/_{2}$%	Treasury Loan 1994
$12^{1}/_{2}$%	Exchequer Stock 1994
9%	Treasury Loan 1994
10%	Treasury Loan 1994
$13^{1}/_{2}$%	Exchequer Stock 1994
$8^{1}/_{2}$%	Treasury Stock 1994

Taxation of Capital Gains

Stocks and bonds charged on the National Loans Funds – cont'd

$8^1/_2$%	Treasury Stock 1994 'A'
2%	Index-Linked Treasury Stock 1994
3%	Exchequer Gas Stock 1990–95
12%	Treasury Stock 1995
$10^1/_4$%	Exchequer Stock 1995
$12^3/_4$%	Treasury Loan 1995
9%	Treasury Loan 1992–96
$15^1/_4$%	Treasury Loan 1996
$13^1/_4$%	Exchequer Loan 1996
14%	Treasury Stock 1996
2%	Index-Linked Treasury Stock 1996
10%	Conversion Stock 1996
10%	Conversion Stock 1996 'A'
10%	Conversion Stock 1996 'B'
$13^1/_4$%	Treasury Loan 1997
$10^1/_2$%	Exchequer Stock 1997
$8^3/_4$%	Treasury Loan 1997
$8^3/_4$%	Treasury Loan 1997 'B'
$8^3/_4$%	Treasury Loan 1997 'C'
$8^3/_4$%	Treasury Loan 1997 'D'
$8^3/_4$%	Treasury Loan 1997 'E'
15%	Exchequer Stock 1997
7%	Treasury Convertible Stock 1997
$6^3/_4$%	Treasury Loan 1995–98
$15^1/_2$%	Treasury Loan 1998
12%	Exchequer Stock 1998
12%	Exchequer Stock 1998 'A'
$9^3/_4$%	Exchequer Stock 1998
$9^3/_4$%	Exchequer Stock 1998 'A'
$7^1/_4$%	Treasury Stock 1998 'A'
$7^1/_4$%	Treasury Stock 1998 'B'
12%	Exchequer Stock 1998 'B'
$4^5/_8$%	Index-Linked Treasury Stock 1998
$7^1/_4$%	Treasury Stock 1998
$9^1/_2$%	Treasury Loan 1999
$10^1/_2$%	Treasury Stock 1999
$12^1/_4$%	Exchequer Stock 1999
$12^1/_4$%	Exchequer Stock 1999 'A'
$12^1/_4$%	Exchequer Stock 1999 'B'
$2^1/_2$%	Index-Linked Treasury Convertible Stock 1999
$10^1/_4$%	Conversion Stock 1999
6%	Treasury Stock 1999
	Floating Rate Treasury Stock 1999
9%	Conversion Stock 2000

Stocks and bonds charged on the National Loans Funds – cont'd

9%	Conversion Stock 2000 'A'
9%	Conversion Stock 2000 'B'
9%	Conversion Stock 2000 'C'
8$^{1}/_{2}$%	Treasury Loan 2000
8%	Treasury Stock 2000
8%	Treasury Stock 2000 'A'
13%	Treasury Stock 2000
13%	Treasury Stock 2000 'A'
7%	Treasury Stock 2001
7%	Treasury Stock 2001 'A'
14%	Treasury Stock 1998–2001
2$^{1}/_{2}$%	Index-Linked Treasury Stock 2001
9$^{3}/_{4}$%	Conversion Stock 2001
10%	Treasury Stock 2001
9$^{1}/_{2}$%	Conversion Loan 2001
10%	Treasury Stock 2001 'A'
10%	Treasury Stock 2001 'B'
	Floating Rate Treasury Stock
12%	Exchequer Stock 1999–2002
12%	Exchequer Stock 1999–2002 'A'
9$^{1}/_{2}$%	Conversion Stock 2002
10%	Conversion Stock 2002
9%	Exchequer Stock 2002
7%	Treasury Stock 2002
9$^{3}/_{4}$%	Treasury Stock 2002
9$^{3}/_{4}$%	Treasury Stock 2002 'A'
9$^{3}/_{4}$%	Treasury Stock 2002 'B'
9$^{3}/_{4}$%	Treasury Stock 2002 'C'
13$^{3}/_{4}$%	Treasury Stock 2000–2003
13$^{3}/_{4}$%	Treasury Stock 2000–2003 'A'
2$^{1}/_{2}$%	Index-Linked Treasury Stock 2003
9$^{3}/_{4}$%	Conversion Loan 2003
6$^{1}/_{2}$%	Treasury Stock 2003
8%	Treasury Stock 2003
8%	Treasury Stock 2003 'A'
10%	Treasury Stock 2003
10%	Treasury Stock 2003 'A'
10%	Treasury Stock 2003 'B'
3$^{1}/_{2}$%	Funding Stock 1999–2004
11$^{1}/_{2}$%	Treasury Stock 2001–2004
9$^{1}/_{2}$%	Conversion Stock 2004
10%	Treasury Stock 2004
6$^{3}/_{4}$%	Treasury Stock 2004
5%	Treasury Stock 2004

Taxation of Capital Gains

Stocks and bonds charged on the National Loans Funds – cont'd

$6^3/_4$%	Treasury Stock 2004 'A'
$4^3/_8$%	Index-Linked Treasury Stock 2004
$9^1/_2$%	Conversion Stock 2004 'A'
$12^1/_2$%	Treasury Stock 2003–2005
$12^1/_2$%	Treasury Stock 2003–2005 'A'
$10^1/_2$%	Exchequer Stock 2005
$9^1/_2$%	Conversion Stock 2005
$9^1/_2$%	Conversion Stock 2005 'A'
$8^1/_2$%	Treasury Stock 2005
8%	Treasury Loan 2002–2006
8%	Treasury Loan 2002–2006 'A'
2%	Index-Linked Treasury Stock 2006
$9^3/_4$%	Conversion Stock 2006
$7^1/_2$%	Treasury Stock 2006
$7^3/_4$%	Treasury Stock 2006
$11^3/_4$%	Treasury Stock 2003–2007
$11^3/_4$%	Treasury Stock 2003–2007 'A'
$7^1/_4$%	Treasury Stock 2007
$4^1/_2$%	Treasury Stock 2007
$8^1/_2$%	Treasury Loan 2007
$8^1/_2$%	Treasury Loan 2007 'A'
$8^1/_2$%	Treasury Loan 2007 'B'
$8^1/_2$%	Treasury Loan 2007 'C'
$13^1/_2$%	Treasury Stock 2004–2008
9%	Treasury Loan 2008
9%	Treasury Loan 2008 'A'
9%	Treasury Loan 2008 'B'
9%	Treasury Loan 2008 'C'
9%	Treasury Loan 2008 'D'
5%	Treasury Stock 2008
$2^1/_2$%	Index-Linked Treasury Stock 2009
$5^3/_4$%	Treasury Stock 2009
8%	Treasury Stock 2009
4%	Treasury Stock 2009
8%	Treasury Stock 2009 'A'
$6^1/_4$%	Treasury Stock 2010
$4^3/_4$%	Treasury Stock 2010
$2^1/_4$%	Treasury Gilt 2011
$3^1/_4$%	Treasury Gilt 2011
$4^1/_2$%	Index-Linked Treasury Stock 2011
9%	Conversion Loan 2011
9%	Conversion Loan 2011 'A'
9%	Conversion Loan 2011 'B'
9%	Conversion Loan 2011 'C'

Stocks and bonds charged on the National Loans Funds – cont'd

9%	Conversion Loan 2011 'D'
5$^1/_2$%	Treasury Stock 2008–2012
9%	Treasury Stock 2012
9%	Treasury Stock 2012 'A'
5%	Treasury Stock 2012
5$^1/_4$%	Treasury Gilt 2012
2$^1/_2$%	Index-Linked Treasury Stock 2013
8%	Treasury Stock 2013
4$^1/_2$%	Treasury Gilt 2013
5%	Treasury Stock 2014
2$^1/_4$%	Treasury Gilt 2014
7$^3/_4$%	Treasury Loan 2012–2015
4$^3/_4$%	Treasury Stock 2015
2$^3/_4$%	Treasury Gilt 2015
8%	Treasury Stock 2015
8%	Treasury Stock 2015 'A'
2$^1/_2$%	Treasury Stock 1986–2016
2$^1/_2$%	Index-Linked Treasury Stock 2016
2$^1/_2$%	Index-Linked Treasury Stock 2016 'A'
4%	Treasury Gilt 2016
12%	Exchequer Stock 2013–2017
1$^1/_4$%	Index-Linked Treasury Gilt 2017
8$^3/_4$%	Treasury Stock 2017
8$^3/_4$%	Treasury Stock 2017 'A'
5%	Treasury Gilt 2018
4$^1/_2$%	Treasury Gilt 2019
3$^3/_4$%	Treasury Gilt 2019
2$^1/_2$%	Index-Linked Treasury Stock 2020
4$^3/_4$%	Treasury Stock 2020
8%	Treasury Stock 2021
4%	Treasury Gilt 2022
1$^7/_8$%	Index-Linked Treasury Gilt 2022
2$^1/_2$%	Index-Linked Treasury Stock 2024
5%	Treasury Stock 2025
1$^1/_4$%	Index-Linked Treasury Gilt 2027
4$^1/_4$%	Treasury Gilt 2027
6%	Treasury Stock 2028
4$^1/_8$%	Index-Linked Treasury Stock 2030
4$^3/_4$%	Treasury Gilt 2030
4$^1/_2$%	Treasury Stock 2032
1$^1/_4$%	Index-linked Treasury Gilt 2032
4$^1/_2$%	Treasury Gilt 2034
2%	Index-Linked Treasury Stock 2035
4$^1/_4$%	Treasury Stock 2036

Taxation of Capital Gains

Stocks and bonds charged on the National Loans Funds – cont'd

$1\frac{1}{8}\%$	Index-Linked Treasury Gilt 2037
$4\frac{3}{4}\%$	Treasury Stock 2038
$4\frac{1}{4}\%$	Treasury Gilt 2039
$0\frac{5}{8}\%$	Index-linked Treasury Gilt 2040
$4\frac{1}{2}\%$	Treasury Gilt 2042
$0\frac{5}{8}\%$	Index-linked Treasury Gilt 2042
$4\frac{1}{4}\%$	Treasury Gilt 2046
$0\frac{3}{4}\%$	Index-Linked Treasury Gilt 2047
$4\frac{1}{4}\%$	Treasury Gilt 2049
$0\frac{1}{2}\%$	Index-linked Treasury Gilt 2050
$1\frac{1}{4}\%$	Indexed-linked Treasury Gilt 2055
$4\frac{1}{4}\%$	Treasury Gilt 2055
4%	Treasury Gilt 2060
$0\frac{1}{2}\%$	Index-linked Treasury Gilt 2060

Securities issued by certain public corporations and guaranteed by the Treasury

3%   North of Scotland Electricity Stock 1989–92

[¶5-250]   Securities of negligible value

(TCGA 1992, s. 24(2))

(BTR: ¶515-150)

The HMRC website contains a list, constantly updated, of 'shares or securities formerly quoted (largely) on the London Stock Exchange which have been officially declared of negligible value for the purposes of a claim under .' A summary of principles, together with a link to the current list, may be found at *http://www.hmrc.gov.uk/cgt/negligible_list.htm*.

The time limit for a claim is two years from the end of the tax year (or accounting period of a company) in which the deemed disposal and reacquisition take place.

[¶5-300]   Identification of securities

(TCGA 1992, s. 104-109)

(BTR: ¶556-525ff.)

Disposals by individuals and trustees: 2008–09 onwards

Disposals on or after 6 April 2008 are to be identified with acquisitions in the following order:

(1)   same-day acquisitions, but subject to an election under s. 105A (see below)

(2)   acquisitions within the following 30 days on the basis of earlier acquisitions in that period, rather than later ones (a FIFO basis)

(3)   securities within the expanded s. 104 holding, which specifically does not include acquisitions under (1) and (2) above.

Where the number of securities which comprise the disposal exceed those identified under the above rules, that excess is identified with subsequent acquisitions beyond the 30-day period referred to above.

Disposals by individuals and trustees: years to 2007–08

Pooling for capital gains tax ceased for acquisitions made on or after 6 April 1998.

Disposals made on or after 6 April 1998 are identified with acquisitions in the following order:

(1)   shares acquired on the same day as the disposal, but subject to the effect of an election under s. 105A (see below);

(2)   shares acquired within 30 days following the disposal, on a FIFO (First In First Out) basis;

(3)   shares acquired after 5 April 1998, on a LIFO (Last In First Out) basis;

(4)   shares in a 'section 104' holding;

(5)   shares in a 1982 holding; and

(6)   shares acquired before 6 April 1965.

An election under s. 105A could be made for approved-scheme shares, as defined in that section, to be treated as a separate holding from that of the other shares acquired on the same day as the disposal. Where the election was made, the holding of the approved-scheme shares was identified, with the disposal, after the holding of the other shares acquired on the same day.

Disposals by companies

The order of identification is:

(1)   any acquisition on the same day

(2)   acquisitions within the previous 10 days

(3)   acquisitions since 6 April 1985, 'the s. 104 holding', previously termed 'the new holding';

(4)   acquisitions in the period 6 April 1965 to 5 April 1982, 'the 1982 holding', and

(5)   those held on 6 April 1965, in respect of which no election has been made to include them in the pre-1982 pool; these will be identified on a last-in, first-out (LIFO) basis

In respect of disposals before 5 December 2005, where a company or group of companies held at least two per cent of the shares or securities of that class, acquisitions and disposals within one month (for most quoted shares or securities) or six months (for most other shares or securities) could be matched .

Taxation of Capital Gains

[¶5-350]   Expenses incurred by personal representatives

(SP 2/04)

(BTR: ¶585-500)

In respect of deaths after 5 April 2004, the scale of expenses allowable in computing the gains or losses of personal representatives on the sale of assets in a deceased person's estate is as follows:

Gross value of estate	Allowable expenditure
Up to £50,000	1.8% of probate value of assets sold by personal representatives
£50,001–£90,000	£900, divided among all assets in the estate in proportion to their probate values and allowed in those proportions on assets sold by personal representatives
£90,001–£400,000	1% of probate value of assets sold
£400,001–£500,000	£4,000, divided as above
£500,001–£1,000,000	0.8% of probate value of assets sold
£1,000,001–£5,000,000	£8,000, divided as above
Over £5,000,000	0.16% of the probate value of the assets sold, subject to a maximum of £10,000

Note

Computations based either on the above scale or on actual expenditure incurred are accepted.

In respect of deaths before 6 April 2004, under SP 8/94 the scale of expenses allowable in computing the gains or losses of personal representatives on the sale of assets in a deceased person's estate is as follows:

Gross value of estate	Allowable expenditure
Up to £40,000	1.75% of probate value of assets sold by personal representatives
£40,001–£70,000	£700, divided among all assets in the estate in proportion to their probate values and allowed in those proportions on assets sold by personal representatives
£70,001–£300,000	1% of probate value of assets sold
£300,001–£400,000	£3,000, divided as above
£400,001–£750,000	0.75% of probate value of assets sold
Over £750,000	Negotiated with the inspector

Note

Computations based either on the above scale or on actual expenditure incurred are accepted.

[¶5-500]   Submission dates for 2010–11 personal tax returns
(TMA 1970, s. 8)

(BTR: ¶595-750)

For summary of the main provisions which relate both to capital gains tax and income tax, see ¶1-250.

[¶5-550]   Payment dates 2010–11
(TMA 1970, s. 59B)

(BTR: ¶597-200)

For summary of the main provisions which relate both to capital gains tax and income tax, see ¶1-300.

[¶5-600]   Main penalty provisions
For summary of the main penalty provisions which relate both to capital gains tax and income tax, see ¶1-350.

[¶5-650]   Interest 2010–11
(TMA 1970, s. 86)

Interest is payable from the 'relevant date' of 31 January 2011.

[¶5-700]   Surcharges 2010–11
Surcharges will arise on unpaid capital gains tax in the same way as for income tax, see ¶1-450.

[¶5-750]   Rates of interest on overdue tax
See ¶1-500.

[¶5-800]   Rates of interest on tax repayments
See ¶1-550.

[¶5-850]   Interest rates on certificates of tax deposit (CTD)
See ¶1-600.

Taxation of Capital Gains

[¶5-900]   Remission of tax for official error
See ¶1-650.

[¶5-950]   Time limits for elections and claims

For periods up to 31 March 2010, in the absence of any specific provision to the contrary, under self-assessment the normal rule is that claims by individuals and trustees are to be made within five years from 31 January next following the year to which they relate. For companies the limit is six years from the end of the relevant chargeable period. However with effect from 1 April 2010, the time limits in all cases become four years from the end of the chargeable year or period (TMA 1970, s. 43(1)).

In certain cases HMRC *may* permit an extension of the strict time limit in relation to certain elections and claims.

Provision	Time limit	References
Post-cessation expenses relieved against gains	12 months from 31 January next following the tax year in which expenses paid	TCGA 1992, s. 261D(6)(BTR: ¶524–125)
Trading losses relieved against gains	12 months from 31 January next following the tax year loss arose	TCGA 1992, s. 261B(8) (BTR: ¶524–100)
Value of asset negligible	2 years from end of tax year (or accounting period if a company) in which deemed disposal/ reacquisition takes place	TCGA 1992, s. 24(2)(BTR: ¶515–150)
Re-basing of all assets to 31 March 1982 values (pre 06/04/08 disposals)	Within 12 months from 31 January next following the tax year of disposal (or 2 years from end of accounting period of disposal if a company)	TCGA 1992, s. 35(6), prior to repeal (BTR: ¶520–350)
50% relief if deferred charge on gains before 31 March 1982 (pre 06/04/08 disposals)	Within 12 months from 31 January next following the tax year of disposal (or 2 years from end of accounting period of disposal if a company)	TCGA 1992, s. 36 and Sch. 4, para. 9(1), prior to repeal. (BTR: ¶520–600)
Variation within 2 years of death not to have CGT effect	6 months from date of variation (election not necessary for variations on or after 1 August 2002)	TCGA 1992, s. 62(7) (BTR: ¶586–500ff.)
Specifying which "same day" share acquisitions (through employee share schemes) should be treated as disposed of first	Date of earliest disposal	TCGA 1992, s. 105A (BTR: ¶556–650)

Provision	Time limit	References
Replacement of business assets (roll-over relief)	5 years from 31 January next following the tax year (or 6 years from the end of the accounting period if a company), but, from 1 April 2010, 4 years from the end of the tax year/accounting period in all cases. Replacement asset to be purchased between 12 months before and 3 years after disposal of old asset	TCGA 1992, s. 152(1) (BTR: ¶570–250)
Disapplication of incorporation relief under TCGA 1992, s. 162	2 years from 31 January following the end of the year of assessment in which the business is transferred	TCGA 1992, s. 162A (BTR: ¶574–125)
Hold-over of gain on gift of business asset	5 years from 31 January next following the tax year, but, from 1 April 2010, 4 years from the end of the tax year.	TCGA 1992, s. 165(1) (BTR: ¶574–550)
Determination of main residence	2 years from acquisition of second property (see ESC D21)	TCGA 1992, s. 222(5) (BTR: ¶545–950)
Irrecoverable loan to a trader	5 years from 31 January next following the tax year (or 6 years from the end of the accounting period in the case of companies), but, from 1 April 2010, 4 years from the end of the tax year/ accounting period in all cases.	TCGA 1992, s. 253(4A) (BTR: ¶511–150)
Deemed disposal/reacquisition on expiry of mineral lease	6 years from the relevant event, but 4 years from 1 April 2010	TCGA 1992, s. 203(2)
Delayed remittances of foreign gains	5 years from 31 January next following the tax year (or 6 years from the end of the accounting period in the case of companies), but, from 1 April 2010, 4 years from the end of the tax year/ accounting period in all cases.	TCGA 1992, s. 279(5)

Taxation of Capital Gains

INHERITANCE TAX

[¶6-000] Lifetime transfers
(IHTA 1984, s. 7 and Sch. 1)

(Tax Reporter: ¶600-300)

Lifetime transfers from 15 March 1988 to 5 April 2011

FA 2010, s. 8 freezes the inheritance tax nil rate band at £325,000 for tax years 2011–12 to 2014–15.

Gross cumulative total £	Gross rate of tax %	Net cumulative total £	Tax on each £ *over* net cumulative total for grossing up
6 April 2010–5 April 2011			
325,000	Nil	325,000	$^1/_4$
Over 325,000	20	–	–
6 April 2009–5 April 2010			
325,000	Nil	325,000	$^1/_4$
Over 325,000	20	–	–
6 April 2008–5 April 2009			
312,000	Nil	312,000	$^1/_4$
Over 312,000	20	–	–
6 April 2007–5 April 2008			
300,000	Nil	300,000	$^1/_4$
Over 300,000	20	–	–
6 April 2006–5 April 2007			
285,000	Nil	285,000	$^1/_4$
Over 285,000	20	–	–
6 April 2005–5 April 2006			
275,000	Nil	275,000	$^1/_4$
Over 275,000	20	–	–
6 April 2004–5 April 2005			
263,000	Nil	263,000	$^1/_4$
Over 263,000	20	–	–
6 April 2003–5 April 2004			
255,000	Nil	255,000	$^1/_4$
Over 255,000	20	–	–

Inheritance Tax

Gross cumulative total £	Gross rate of tax %	Net cumulative total £	Tax on each £ *over* net cumulative total for grossing up
6 April 2002–5 April 2003			
250,000	Nil	250,000	$^1/_4$
Over 250,000	20	–	–
6 April 2001–5 April 2002			
242,000	Nil	242,000	$^1/_4$
Over 242,000	20	–	–
6 April 2000–5 April 2001			
234,000	Nil	234,000	$^1/_4$
Over 234,000	20	–	–
6 April 1999–5 April 2000			
231,000	Nil	231,000	$^1/_4$
Over 231,000	20	–	–
6 April 1998–5 April 1999			
223,000	Nil	223,000	$^1/_4$
Over 223,000	20	–	–
6 April 1997–5 April 1998			
215,000	Nil	215,000	$^1/_4$
Over 215,000	20	–	–
6 April 1996–5 April 1997			
200,000	Nil	200,000	$^1/_4$
Over 200,000	20	–	–
6 April 1995–5 April 1996			
154,000	Nil	154,000	$^1/_4$
Over 154,000	20	–	–
10 March 1992–5 April 1995			
150,000	Nil	150,000	$^1/_4$
Over 150,000	20	–	–
6 April 1991–9 March 1992			
140,000	Nil	140,000	$^1/_4$
Over 140,000	20	–	–
6 April 1990–5 April 1991			
128,000	Nil	128,000	$^1/_4$
Over 128,000	20	–	–
6 April 1989–5 April 1990			
118,000	Nil	118,000	$^1/_4$
Over 118,000	20	–	–

Gross cumulative total £	Gross rate of tax %	Net cumulative total £	Tax on each £ *over* net cumulative total for grossing up
15 March 1988–5 April 1989			
110,000	Nil	110,000	$^1/_4$
Over 110,000	20	–	–

Lifetime transfers from 17 March 1987 to 14 March 1988

Portion of value		Rate of tax %
Lower limit £	Upper limit £	
0	90,000	Nil
90,001	140,000	15
140,001	220,000	20
220,001	330,000	25
330,001	upwards	30

Grossing up table

Gross cumulative total £	Gross rate of tax %	Inheritance tax on band £	Cumulative inheritance tax payable £	Net cumulative total £	Tax on each £ over net cumulative total for grossing up
90,000	Nil	Nil	Nil	90,000	$^3/_{17}$
140,000	15	7,500	7,500	132,500	$^1/_4$
220,000	20	16,000	23,500	196,500	$^1/_3$
330,000	25	27,500	51,000	279,000	$^3/_7$
Over 330,000	30	–	–	–	–

Inheritance Tax

Lifetime transfers from 18 March 1986 to 16 March 1987

(FA 1986, Sch. 19, para. 36)

Portion of value		Rate of tax %
Lower limit £	Upper limit £	
0	71,000	Nil
71,000	95,000	15
95,000	129,000	17$^{1}/_{2}$
129,000	164,000	20
164,000	206,000	22$^{1}/_{2}$
206,000	257,000	25
257,000	317,000	27$^{1}/_{2}$
317,000	upwards	30

Grossing up table

Gross cumulative total £	Gross rate of tax %	Inheritance tax on band £	Cumulative inheritance tax payable £	Net cumulative total £	Tax on each £ over net cumulative total for grossing up
71,000	Nil	Nil	Nil	71,000	$^{3}/_{17}$
95,000	15	3,600	3,600	91,400	$^{7}/_{33}$
129,000	17$^{1}/_{2}$	5,950	9,550	119,450	$^{1}/_{4}$
164,000	20	7,000	16,550	147,450	$^{9}/_{31}$
206,000	22$^{1}/_{2}$	9,450	26,000	180,000	$^{1}/_{3}$
257,000	25	12,750	38,750	218,250	$^{11}/_{29}$
317,000	27$^{1}/_{2}$	16,500	55,250	261,750	$^{3}/_{7}$
Over 317,000	30	–	–	–	–

[¶6-050] Transfers on death or within seven years before death

(IHTA 1984, s. 7 and Sch. 1)

(Tax Reporter: ¶600-300)

Where a person dies on or after 18 March 1986, his or her estate and all chargeable transfers made within seven years before death are subject to inheritance tax at the rates set out below. There is a tapered reduction in the tax payable on transfers between seven and three years before death.

FA 2008, s. 10 and Sch. 4 allow a claim to be made to transfer any unused nil-rate band of the first deceased spouse or civil partner to the estate of their surviving spouse or civil partner who dies on or after 9 October 2007.

FA 2010, s. 8 freezes the inheritance tax nil rate band at £325,000 for the tax years 2011–12 to 2014–15.

Transfers from 15 March 1988 to 5 April 2011

Gross cumulative total £	Gross rate of tax %	Net cumulative total £	Tax on each £ *over* net cumulative total for grossing up
6 April 2010–5 April 2011			
325,000	Nil	325,000	$^2/_3$
Over 325,000	40	–	–
6 April 2009–5 April 2010			
325,000	Nil	325,000	$^2/_3$
Over 325,000	40	–	–
6 April 2008–5 April 2009			
312,000	Nil	312,000	$^2/_3$
Over 312,000	40	–	–
6 April 2007–5 April 2008			
300,000	Nil	300,000	$^2/_3$
Over 300,000	40	–	–
6 April 2006–5 April 2007			
285,000	Nil	285,000	$^2/_3$
Over 285,000	40	–	–
6 April 2005–5 April 2006			
275,000	Nil	275,000	$^2/_3$
Over 275,000	40	–	–
6 April 2004–5 April 2005			
263,000	Nil	263,000	$^2/_3$
Over 263,000	40	–	–
6 April 2003–5 April 2004			
255,000	Nil	255,000	$^2/_3$
Over 255,000	40	–	–
6 April 2002–5 April 2003			
250,000	Nil	250,000	$^2/_3$
Over 250,000	40	–	–
6 April 2001–5 April 2002			
242,000	Nil	242,000	$^2/_3$
Over 242,000	40	–	–

Inheritance Tax

Gross cumulative total £	Gross rate of tax %	Net cumulative total £	Tax on each £ *over* net cumulative total for grossing up
6 April 2000–5 April 2001			
234,000	Nil	234,000	$^2/_3$
Over 234,000	40	–	–
6 April 1999–5 April 2000			
231,000	Nil	231,000	$^2/_3$
Over 231,000	40	–	–
6 April 1998–5 April 1999			
223,000	Nil	223,000	$^2/_3$
Over 223,000	40	–	–
6 April 1997–5 April 1998			
215,000	Nil	215,000	$^2/_3$
Over 215,000	40	–	–
6 April 1996–5 April 1997			
200,000	Nil	200,000	$^2/_3$
Over 200,000	40	–	–
6 April 1995–5 April 1996			
154,000	Nil	154,000	$^2/_3$
Over 154,000	40	–	–
10 March 1992–5 April 1995			
150,000	Nil	150,000	$^2/_3$
Over 150,000	40	–	–
6 April 1991–9 March 1992			
140,000	Nil	140,000	$^2/_3$
Over 140,000	40	–	–
6 April 1990–5 April 1991			
128,000	Nil	128,000	$^2/_3$
Over 128,000	40	–	–
6 April 1989–5 April 1990			
118,000	Nil	118,000	$^2/_3$
Over 118,000	40	–	–
15 March 1988–5 April 1989			
110,000	Nil	110,000	$^2/_3$
Over 110,000	40	–	–

Transfers from 17 March 1987 to 14 March 1988

Portion of value		Rate of tax %
Lower limit £	Upper limit £	
0	90,000	Nil
90,000	140,000	30
140,000	220,000	40
220,000	330,000	50
330,000	upwards	60

Grossing up table

Gross cumulative total £	Gross rate of tax %	Inheritance tax on band £	Cumulative inheritance tax payable £	Net cumulative total £	Tax on each £ over net cumulative total for grossing up
90,000	Nil	Nil	Nil	90,000	$3/7$
140,000	30	15,000	15,000	125,000	$2/3$
220,000	40	32,000	47,000	173,000	1
330,000	50	55,000	102,000	228,000	$1\frac{1}{2}$
Over 330,000	60	–	–	–	–

Transfers from 18 March 1986 to 16 March 1987

(FA 1986, Sch. 19, para. 36)

Portion of value		Rate of tax %
Lower limit £	Upper limit £	
0	71,000	Nil
71,000	95,000	30
95,000	129,000	35
129,000	164,000	40
164,000	206,000	45
206,000	257,000	50
257,000	317,000	55
317,000	–	60

Inheritance Tax

Grossing up table

Gross cumulative total £	Gross rate of tax %	Inheritance tax on band £	Cumulative inheritance tax payable £	Net cumulative total £	Tax on each £ over net cumulative total for grossing up
71,000	Nil	Nil	Nil	71,000	$3/7$
95,000	30	7,200	7,200	87,800	$7/13$
129,000	35	11,900	19,100	109,900	$2/3$
164,000	40	14,000	33,100	130,900	$9/11$
206,000	45	18,900	52,000	154,000	1
257,000	50	25,500	77,500	179,500	$1 2/9$
317,000	55	33,000	110,500	206,500	$1 1/2$
Over 317,000	60	–	–	–	–

[¶6-100]   Nil rate band for capital transfer tax from 13 March 1975 to 17 March 1986

From	To	nil rate band
13.03.1975	26.10.1977	£15,000
27.10.1977	25.03.1980	£25,000
26.03.1980	08.03.1982	£50,000
09.03.1982	14.03.1983	£55,000
15.03.1983	12.03.1984	£60,000
13.03.1984	05.04.1985	£64,000
06.04.1985	17.03.1986	£67,000

[¶6-150]   Nil rate band for estate duty from 16 August 1914 to 12 March 1975

From	To	nil rate band
16.08.1914	09.04.1946	£100
10.04.1946	29.07.1954	£2,000
30.07.1954	08.04.1962	£3,000
09.04.1962	03.04.1963	£4,000
04.04.1963	15.04.1969	£5,000
16.04.1969	30.03.1971	£10,000
31.03.1971	21.03.1972	£12,500
22.03.1972	12.03.1975	£15,000

[¶6-200]   Annual and small gift exemption

(IHTA 1984, s. 19 and 20)

(Tax Reporter: ¶643-200 and ¶643-700)

	On or after 6 April 1981 £	6 April 1980 to 5 April 1981 £	6 April 1976 to 5 April 1980 £
Annual	3,000	2,000	2,000
Small gift	250	250	100

[¶6-250]   Gifts in consideration of marriage/civil partnership

(IHTA 1984, s. 22)

(Tax Reporter: ¶664-450)

Donor	Exemption limit £
Parent of party to the marriage/civil partnership	5,000
Remote ancestor of party to the marriage/civil partnership	2,500
Party to the marriage/civil partnership	2,500
Any other person	1,000

[¶6-300]   Gift by UK-domiciled spouse/civil partner to non-UK domiciled spouse/civil partner

(IHTA 1984, s. 18)

(Tax Reporter: ¶644-900)

Transfer on or after	Exemption limit £
9 March 1982	55,000

[¶6-400]   Agricultural and business property relief

(IHTA 1984, s. 103ff. and 115ff.)

(Tax Reporter: ¶664-000 and ¶658-000)

Type of relief	Rate of relief for disposals			
	on or after 6/4/96 %	1/9/95– 5/4/96 %	10/3/92– 31/8/95 %	before 10/3/92 %
Agricultural property[1][2]				
Vacant possession or right to obtain it within 12 months	100	100	100	50
Tenanted land with vacant a possession value	100	100	100	50
Entitled to 50% relief at 9 March 1981 and not since able to obtain vacant possession	100	100	100	50
Agricultural land let on or after 1 September 1995	100	100	N/A	N/A
Other circumstances	50	50	50	30
Business property				
Nature of property				
Business or interest in business	100	100	100	50
Controlling shareholding in quoted company	50	50	50	50
Controlling shareholding in unquoted[3] company	100	100	100	50
Settled property used in life tenant's business	100/50[4]	100/50[4]	100/50[4]	50/30[4]
Shareholding in unquoted[3] company: more than 25% interest	100	100	100	50[5]
Minority shareholding in unquoted[3] company: 25% or less	100	50	50	30[6]
Land, buildings, machinery or plant used by transferor's company or partnership	50	50	50	30

Notes

[1] FA 2009, s. 122 extends agricultural property relief to property in the European Economic Area. IHT due or paid on or after 23 April 2003 in relation to agricultural property located in a qualifying EEA state at the time of the chargeable event will become eligible for relief.

[2] From 6 April 1995, short rotation coppice is regarded as agricultural property.

[3] With effect from 10 March 1992 'unquoted' means shares not quoted on a recognised stock exchange and therefore includes shares dealt in on the Unlisted Securities Market (USM) or Alternative Investment Market (AIM).

[4] The higher rate applies if the settled property is transferred along with business itself.

[5] 30% if a minority interest transferred before 17 March 1987, or if transferor had not held at least 25% interest throughout preceding two years.

[6] The relief was 20% for transfers after 26 October 1977 but before 15 March 1983.

[¶6-450]   Quick succession relief
(IHTA 1984, s. 141)

(Tax Reporter: ¶627-400)

Years between transfers		Percentage applied to formula below
More than	Not more than	
0	1	100
1	2	80
2	3	60
3	4	40
4	5	20

Formula
Tax charge on earlier transfer $\times \dfrac{\text{Increase in transferee's estate}}{\text{Diminution in transferor's estate}}$

[¶6-475]   Intestate rules

Surviving family

Beneficiaries[1]

Spouse or civil partner and issue

Spouse or civil partner takes personal chattels (e.g. furniture, pictures, clothing, jewellery, etc.); £125,000 absolutely (or the entire estate where this is less); life interest in one half of the residue (if any)

Issue receive one half of residue (if any) on statutory trusts plus the other half of residue on statutory trusts upon the death of the spouse.

Spouse or civil partner, no issue but parent or brother or sister, or nephew or niece

Spouse or civil partner takes personal chattels plus £200,000 absolutely (or the entire estate where this is less); one half share of residue (if any) absolutely.

Remainder distributable to parent(s), failing a parent then on trust for the deceased's brothers and sisters, (nephews and nieces step into their parent's shoes if the latter is dead).

No spouse or civil partner

Everything is taken by:
Issue, but if none:
Parent(s), but if none:
Brothers and sisters (nephews and nieces step into their parent's shoes), but if none:
Grandparents, uncles and aunts and the issue of any deceased uncle or aunt, but if none:
The Crown.

Notes

[1] For deaths on or after 1 February 2008 under the *Administration of Estates Act* 1925, s. 49(1)(a); not applicable in Scotland.

Inheritance Tax

[¶6-500] Instalment option
(IHTA 1984, s. 227)

(Tax Reporter: ¶695-650)

Interest-free:

* Controlling shareholdings.
* Holdings of 10% or more of unquoted shares with value over £20,000.
* Certain other death transfers of unquoted shares.
* Business or interest in business.
* Agricultural value of agricultural property.
* Woodlands.

Not interest-free:

* Land, wherever situated, other than within categories above.
* Shareholdings in certain land investment and security dealing companies, or market makers or discount houses.

[¶6-550] Fall in value relief
(IHTA 1984, s. 179 and s. 191)

(Tax Reporter: ¶627-900)

Type of property	Period after death
Quoted securities sold	One year
Qualifying investments cancelled or whose quotations suspended – deaths after 15 March 1992	One year
Interests in land – deaths after 15 March 1990	Four years
Interests in land – deaths before 16 March 1990	Three years

[¶6-600] Taper relief
(IHTA 1984, s. 7(4))

(Tax Reporter: ¶611-400)

Years between gift and death More than	Not more than	Percentage of full tax charge at death – rates actually due %
3	4	80
4	5	60
5	6	40
6	7	20

[¶6-650]   Pre-owned assets

(FA 2004, s. 84 and Sch. 15)

(Tax Reporter: ¶614-800)

A freestanding income tax charge where individuals continue to enjoy property previously owned by them with effect from 6 April 2005. The charge to tax arises under three main heads, relating to:

- land;
- chattels; and
- intangible property in settlor interested trusts.

In determining whether charges arise in respect of land or chattels, certain transactions are excluded and there are a number of exemptions.

Land

The chargeable amount in the case of land or any interest in land is the 'appropriate rental value' less an amount paid under any legal obligation in respect of the occupation of the land. The appropriate rental value is:

$R \times DV/V$ where:

R is the 'rental value' of the relevant land for the 'taxable period';

DV is the value at the 'valuation date' of the interest in the relevant land that was disposed of by the chargeable person or, where the disposal was a non-exempt sale, the appropriate proportion of that value; and

V is the value of the relevant land at the valuation date.

The 'taxable period' is the year of assessment, or part of the year of assessment, during which the relevant conditions are met.

The 'rental value' is based on the assumption of a letting from year to year where the tenant pays the taxes, rates and charges and the landlord is responsible for repair and insurance. Land may be valued on a five-yearly rather than an annual valuation (SI 2005/724).

Chattels

In respect of chattels, the chargeable amount is the 'appropriate amount' less an amount paid under a legal obligation to the owner of the chattel. The 'appropriate amount' is:

$N \times DV/V$ where:

N is the notional interest for the taxable period, at the prescribed rate, on the value of the chattel at the valuation date;

DV is the value at the valuation date of the interest in the relevant chattel that was disposed of by the chargeable person or, where the disposal was a non-exempt sale, the appropriate proportion of that asset; and

V is the value of the chattel at the valuation date.

Intangible property in settlor interested trusts

The chargeable amount in relation to the relevant property is N minus T where:

Inheritance Tax

N is the notional amount of interest for the taxable period, at the prescribed rate, on the value of the property at the valuation date, and

T is the amount of income tax or capital gains tax payable by the chargeable person in the taxable period as gains from contracts of life assurance, income where settlor retains an interest, transfer of assets abroad, charge on settlor with interest in settlement and attribution of gains to settlors with interest in non- resident or dual resident settlements.

Where the aggregate amount attributable to a chargeable person in respect of land, chattels and intangibles does not exceed £5,000, there is no income tax payable. If benefits exceed £5,000, the charge is on the full amount including the first £5,000.

Limited reliefs prevent double charges to tax. Special rules apply to individuals not resident or not domiciled in the UK. Provisions allow for opting out of the pre-owned assets charge arising in respect of any property, with inheritance tax consequences.

[¶6-700]   Delivery of accounts

(IHTA 1984, s. 216)

(Tax Reporter: ¶693-800)

Nature of transfer	Due Date
Chargeable lifetime transfer	Later of: – 12 months after end of month in which transfer occurred – 3 months after person became liable
Potentially exempt transfers which have become chargeable	12 months after end of month in which death of transferor occurred
Transfers on death	Later of: – 12 months after end of month in which death occurred – 3 months after personal representatives first act or have reason to believe an account is required
Gifts subject to reservation included in donor's estate at death	12 months after end of month in which death occurred
National heritage property	6 months after end of month in which chargeable event occurred

Values below which no account required

(The *Inheritance Tax (Delivery of Accounts) (Excepted Transfers and Excepted Terminations) Regulations* 2008 (SI 2008/605), IHTA 1984, s. 256)

(Tax Reporter: ¶693-850)

Excepted lifetime chargeable transfers on or after 6 April 2007	£
Where the property given away, or in which the interest subsists, is wholly attributable to cash or quoted stocks and securities, the cumulative total of all chargeable transfers made by the transfer in the seven years before the transfer must not exceed the nil rate band.	
Where the property given away, or in which the interest subsists, is wholly or partly attributable to property other than cash or quoted stocks and securities: (1) the value transferred by the chargeable transfer together with the cumulative total of all chargeable transfers made by the transferor in the seven years before the transfer must not exceed 80 per cent of the relevant IHT nil rate band; (2) the value transferred must not exceed the nil rate band that is available to the transferor at the time the disposal takes place.	
Excepted lifetime chargeable transfers from 1 April 1981 to 5 April 2007	
Transfer in question, together with all other chargeable transfers in same 12-month period ending on 5 April	10,000
Transfer in question, together with all previous chargeable transfers during preceding ten years	40,000

Inheritance Tax

Excepted estates

(IHTA 1984, s. 256, the *Inheritance Tax (Delivery of Accounts) (Excepted Estates) Regulations* 2004 (SI 2004/2543), as amended by SI 2005/3230 and SI 2006/2141)

(Tax Reporter: ¶693-950)

Domiciled in the United Kingdom

Deaths on and after	But before	Total gross value[1] £	Total gross value of property outside UK £	Total value of settled property £	Aggregate value of 'specified transfers' £
6 April 2010	5 April 2011	325,000[1], [2]	100,000	150,000	150,000
6 April 2009	5 April 2010	325,000[1], [2]	100,000	150,000	150,000
6 April 2008	5 April 2009	312,000[1], [2]	100,000	150,000	150,000
6 April 2007	5 April 2008	300,000[1], [2]	100,000	150,000	150,000
6 April 2006	5 April 2007	285,000[1], [2]	100,000	150,000	150,000
6 April 2005	5 April 2006	275,000[1], [2]	100,000	150,000	150,000
6 April 2004	5 April 2005	263,000[1], [2]	100,000	150,000	150,000
6 April 2003	5 April 2004	240,000	75,000	100,000	100,000
6 April 2002	6 April 2003	220,000	75,000	100,000	100,000
6 April 2000	6 April 2002	210,000	50,000	–	75,000
6 April 1998	5 April 2000	180,000	30,000	–	50,000
6 April 1996	5 April 1998	180,000	30,000	–	50,000
6 April 1995	5 April 1996	145,000	15,000	–	–
1 April 1991	6 April 1995	125,000	15,000	–	–
1 April 1990	1 April 1991	115,000	15,000	–	–
1 April 1989	1 April 1990	100,000	15,000	–	–
1 April 1987	1 April 1989	70,000	10,000	–	–

Notes

[1] The aggregate of the gross value of that person's estate, the value transferred by any specified transfers made by that person, and the value transferred by any specified exempt transfers made by that person, must not exceed the IHT threshold. (Where the deceased dies after 5 April and before 6 August and application for probate or confirmation is made before 6 August in the same year as death, the inheritance tax threshold used is that for the preceding tax year.)

[2] An estate will qualify as an excepted estate where the gross value of the estate, plus the chargeable value of any transfers in the seven years to death, does not exceed £1,000,000 and the net chargeable estate after deduction of spouse or civil partner and/ or charity exemption **only** is less than the IHT threshold.

[3] For deaths on or after 6 April 2002, the limit applies to the aggregate of the gross value of the estate *plus* the value of 'specified transfers' which is extended and includes chargeable transfers, within seven years prior to death, of cash, quoted shares or securities, **or an interest in land and furnishings and chattels disposed of at the same time to the same person** (excluding property transferred subject to a reservation or property which becomes settled property).

For deaths on or after 6 April 1996 but before 6 April 2002, this limit applies to the total gross value of the estate *plus* the value of any transfers of cash or of quoted shares or securities made within seven years before death.

[4] If any of the sections dealing with alternatively secured pension funds apply by reason of an individual's death, that individual's estate does not qualify as an excepted estate (SI 2006/2141).

[¶6-750]   Due dates for payment

(IHTA 1984, s. 226)

(Tax Reporter: ¶695-600)

Transfer	Due Date
Chargeable lifetime transfers between 6 April and 30 September	30 April in following year
Chargeable lifetime transfers between 1 October and 5 April	6 months after end of month in which transfer made
Potentially exempt transfers which become chargeable	6 months after end of month in which death occurred
Transfers on death; extra tax payable on chargeable lifetime transfers within seven years before death	6 months after end of month in which death occurred

[¶6-800]   Penalties for failure in relation to obligations falling due after 22 July 2004

(IHTA 1984, s. 216, s. 217, s. 218, s. 218, s. 219, s. 219A, s. 247, FA 2007, Sch. 24, as added by FA 2008, Sch. 40).

(Tax Reporter: ¶696-700)

Failure to deliver an IHT account (IHTA 1984, s. 216)	Account outstanding at end of statutory period	Fixed penalty of £100 (but not exceeding tax due)[1]
	Daily penalty after failure declared by a court or the tribunal	Up to £60 a day
	Penalty after six months from end of statutory period, if proceedings for declaring the failure not started before then	Fixed penalty of £200 (but not exceeding tax due)[1]
	Penalty after twelve months from end of statutory period where tax is payable	Up to £3,000[2]
Failure by professional person to deliver a return of a settlement by a UK-domiciled person but with non-resident trustees (IHTA 1984, s. 218)	Account outstanding at end of statutory period (three months from making of settlement)	Up to £300

Inheritance Tax

Failure to report a deed of variation which increases the IHT liability (IHTA 1984, s. 218A)	Penalty for failure to report within 18 months of deed of variation being executed	Up to £3,000[3]
	Daily penalty after failure declared by a court or the tribunal	Up to £60 a day
Failure to comply with a notice requiring information (IHTA 1984, s. 219)	Penalty	Up to £300
	Daily penalty after failure declared by a court or the tribunal	Up to £60 a day
Failure to comply with a notice requiring documents, accounts or particulars (IHTA 1984, s. 219A)	Penalty	Up to £50
	Daily penalty after failure declared by a court or the tribunal	Up to £30 a day
Incorrect information provided by others (IHTA 1984, s. 247(3))	Fraud or negligence	Up to £3,000[4]
Person assisting in providing incorrect information etc. (IHTA 1984, s. 247(4))	Penalty	Up to £3,000
Failure to take reasonable care with an IHT account or return (FA 2007, Sch. 24, para. 1)[5]	standard amount (careless behaviour)	30% of potential revenue lost
	where the inaccuracy is deliberate but not concealed	70% of potential lost revenue
	where the inaccuracy is deliberate and concealed	100% of the potential lost revenue
Error in taxpayer's document attributable to another person (FA 2007, Sch. 24, para. 1A)[6]	Penalty	Tax geared

Notes

[1] The change took effect on 23 January 2005.

[2] The change applies where the due date for delivery of an account expires after 22 July 2004. Where the due date has expired before 22 July 2004, the penalty does not apply until 23 July 2005. The penalty is subject to the defence of reasonable excuse.

(3) The change applies where the due date for notification expires after 22 July 2004. Where the due date has expired before 22 July 2004, the penalty does not apply until 23 July 2005.

(4) These changes take effect for accounts, information and documents delivered after 22 July 2004.

(5) FA 2008, Sch. 40 extended the new penalty regime in FA 2007, Sch. 24 to inheritance tax from 1 April 2009 where documents are due to be filed on or after 1 April 2010.

There are certain maximum reductions from the fixed penalties available which vary according to the level of the fixed penalty and whether a disclosure was prompted or unprompted (FA 2007, Sch. 24, para. 10).

(6) FA 2007, Sch. 24, para. 1A as added by FA 2008, Sch. 40 allows a penalty to be charged where an inaccuracy in the liable person's document was attributable to another person. Where it can be shown that the other person deliberately withheld information or supplied false information to the liable person, with the intention that the account or return would contain an inaccuracy, a penalty may be charged on that other person. But that will not necessarily mean that the personal representative themselves may not also be chargeable to a penalty. If the withheld or false information gave rise to inconsistencies in the information they had received about the estate and they did not question those inconsistencies; the liable person may still be charged a penalty for failing to take reasonable care as well.

[¶6-850] Prescribed rates of interest

(IHTA 1984, s. 233)

(Tax Reporter: ¶695-900)

Interest is charged at the following rates on late payments or repayments of inheritance tax or capital transfer tax.

Dates at which rates applicable	Chargeable transfers made on death %	Chargeable transfers not made on death %	Source
From 29 September 2009 onwards (late payments)	3	3	(1)
From 29 September 2009 onwards (overpayments)	0.5	0.5	(2)
24 March 2009 to 28 September 2009	0	0	(1)
27 January 2009 to 23 March 2009	1	1	(1)
6 January 2009 to 26 January 2009	2	2	(1)
6 November 2008 to 5 January 2009	3	3	(1)
6 January 2008 to 5 November 2008	4	4	(1)

Inheritance Tax

Dates at which rates applicable	Chargeable transfers made on death %	Chargeable transfers not made on death %	Source
6 August 2007 to 5 January 2008	5	5	(1)
6 September 2006 to 5 August 2007	4	4	(1)
6 September 2005 to 5 September 2006	3	3	(1)
6 September 2004 to 5 September 2005	4	4	(1)
6 December 2003 to 5 September 2004	3	3	(1)
6 August 2003 to 5 December 2003	2	2	(1)
6 November 2001 to 5 August 2003	3	3	(1)
6 May 2001 to 5 November 2001	4	4	(1)
6 February 2000 to 5 May 2001	5	5	(1)
6 March 1999 to 5 February 2000	4	4	(1)

Note

(1) Fixed by Treasury order under the *Taxes (Interest Rate) Regulations* 1989 (SI 1989/1297). From September 2009 interest charged on late payments of tax will be the Bank of England base rate plus 2.5%.

(2) Fixed by Treasury order under SI 1989/1297. From September 2009 the interest rate on overpayments is the Bank of England rate minus 1, subject to a minimum rate of 0.5% on repayments.

(3) Rates revised by HMRC (press release 16 September 2009).

TAXATION OF COMPANIES

[¶7-000] Rates of corporation tax

(Tax Reporter: ¶704-000ff.)

Financial year	Main rate %	Small profits rate %	Limit for small profits rate (lower limit)	Limit for marginal relief (upper limit)	Standard fraction for marginal relief	Starting rate %	Limit for starting rate marginal relief (lower limit)	Limit for starting rate marginal relief (upper limit)	Marginal relief fraction for starting rate
2010	28	21	300,000	1,500,000	7/400	(4)	(4)	(4)	(4)
2009	28	21	300,000	1,500,000	7/400	(4)	(4)	(4)	(4)
2008	28	21	300,000	1,500,000	7/400	(4)	(4)	(4)	(4)
2007	30	20	300,000	1,500,000	1/40	(4)	(4)	(4)	(4)
2006	30	19	300,000	1,500,000	11/400	(4)	(4)	(4)	(4)

Notes

(1) It was announced in the Emergency Budget 2010 that the main and small profits rates for financial year 2011 will be 27 per cent and 20 per cent respectively (see note (3) for companies with ring fence profits). The lower and upper profit limits are expected to remain at £300,000 and £1,500,000 and the standard fraction applying for marginal relief purposes is expected to remain at 7/400. It was also announced that the main rate would fall by a further 1 per cent each year with the main rate for financial year 2014 expected to be 24 per cent.

(2) The lower and upper limits for the small profits rate and marginal relief are reduced proportionally:

- for accounting periods of less than 12 months, and

- in the case of associated companies, by dividing the limits by the total number of non-dormant associated companies (CTA 2010, s. 24).

(3) 'Close investment holding companies' do not receive the benefit of the small profits rate and so are taxable entirely at the main rate regardless of the level of their profits (CTA 2010, s. 18). Special rules also apply to companies in liquidation and administration (CTA 2010, s. 628 and s. 630).

For companies with ring fence profits, the rates are as above except that:

- for financial years 2007 to 2010 the small profits' rate of tax is 19 per cent and the standard fraction is 11/400; and

- for financial years 2008 to 2010 the main rate is 30 per cent.

It was announced during the Emergency Budget report that for companies with ring fence profits the main and small profits rates for financial year 2011 will be 30 per cent and 19 per cent respectively. The lower and upper profit limits are expected to remain at £300,000 and £1,500,000 and the standard fraction applying for marginal relief purposes is expected to be unchanged at 11/400.

For open-ended investment companies and authorised unit trusts, the rate of corporation tax for a financial year is the rate at which income tax at the basic rate is charged for that year of assessment which begins on 6 April in that financial year (CTA 2010, s. 614 and s. 618).

Effective marginal rates

For marginal relief and marginal starting rate relief, there is an effective rate of tax in the margin, i.e. between the lower and upper limits given for each in the preceding table, which *exceeds* the main rate. These marginal rates are not prescribed by statute, but are derived from the appropriate corporation tax rates and fractions. The applicable rates are as follows.

Financial year	Marginal rate %	Marginal starting rate %
2010	29.75	(2)
2009	29.75	(2)
2008	29.75	(2)
2007	32.5	(2)
2006	32.75	(2)

Notes

(1) For financial year 2011, the effective marginal rate is expected to be 28.75 per cent (see note (1) above).

Marginal relief

(CTA 2010, s. 19)

(Tax Reporter: ¶704-200)

$$\text{Deduction} = (\text{Upper Limit} - \text{Augmented Profits}) \times \frac{\text{Taxable Total Profits}}{\text{Augmented Profits}} \times \text{Standard Fraction}$$

'**Augmented Profits**' (formerly 'Profits') means a company's taxable total profits *plus* franked investment income *excluding* franked investment income received from companies in the same group (CTA 2010, s. 32). Distributions are treated as coming from within the group if they are received from a company which is a 51 per cent subsidiary or a consortium company, the recipient being a member of the consortium. For distributions received on or after 1 July 2009, the reference to franked investment income (and the exclusion for franked investment income received from group companies) includes distributions that are exempt from tax under the new broad exemptions for distributions.

'**Taxable Total Profits**' (formerly 'Basic Profits') means profits as finally computed for corporation tax purposes (also known as 'profits chargeable to corporation tax') (CTA 2010, s. 4(2)).

Similar provisions apply for calculating marginal relief for the starting rate effective from 1 April 2000 to 31 March 2006.

Charge on loan to participators

(CTA 2010, s. 455)

(Tax Reporter: ¶776-900ff.)

The rate of charge is fixed at 25 per cent of the amount of the loan or advance until further notice.

The charge itself is separate from other liabilities, being treated as if it were an amount of corporation tax chargeable on the company.

Banks

(FA 2010, s. 22 and Sch. 1)

(Tax Reporter: ¶807-000ff.)

A bank payroll tax was introduced by the *Finance Act* 2010. The tax, set at 50 per cent, is payable by banks on bonuses awarded to banking employees to the extent that the bonuses exceed £25,000. The tax applies to all discretionary and contractual bonuses awarded between 9 December 2009 and 5 April 2010, with the exception of contractual obligations existing before 9 December 2009 where the payer had no discretion as to the amount of the bonus. The tax is to be paid on 31 August 2010.

It was announced in the Emergency Budget 2010 that a levy would be introduced on banks' balance sheets from 1 January 2011.

[¶7-400]   Filing deadlines

(FA 1998, Sch. 18, para. 14)

(Tax Reporter: ¶811-600ff.)

The filing date for a return of profits (CT600, or approved substitute) is generally the later of the three dates outlined below. Note that only the first two of these are relevant unless the company is making a return in respect of an accounting period forming part of a period of account which is greater than 12 months in length.

- 12 months from the end of the return period.

- Three months after the issue of a notice to deliver a corporation tax return.

- If a period of account is greater than 12 months in length, it will be divided into two or more accounting periods.

  If such a period of account is no longer than 18 months, the filing date for both accounting periods is 12 months from the end of the period of account.

  If such a period of account is greater than 18 months, the filing date is 30 months from the start of the period of account.

Notes

Obligation to file a return is not automatic but is imposed by notice issued by the inspector.

Every company which is chargeable to corporation tax in respect of any accounting period, and which has not made a return of its profits for that period, nor received a notice to make such a return, is under a duty to give notice to the inspector that it is so chargeable. The notice must be given not later than 12 months after the end of that accounting period.

For accounting periods beginning on or after 22 July 2004, a company must notify HMRC that its first accounting period has begun within 3 months of the accounting period beginning. This also applies to dormant companies which cease to be dormant.

An amended return under self assessment may not be made later than 12 months after the filing date stipulated above.

[¶7-450] Due and payable dates

(Tax Reporter: ¶811-000ff.)

Liability	Due date
Mainstream tax (TMA 1970, s. 59D)	Nine months and one day after end of an accounting period[1]
Mainstream tax in instalments[2]:	The 14th day of the seventh, tenth, 13th and 16th months after start of a 12 month accounting period.
Income tax on interest, annual payments etc.	14 days after end of return period.[3]
Charge on loans to participators (CTA 2010, s. 455)	Nine months and one day after the end of the accounting period in which the loan was advanced.

Notes

[1] FA 2009, s. 111 provides for companies to enter into voluntary payment plans with HMRC under which corporation tax liabilities can be paid in instalments spread equally before and after the due date. It should be noted that only corporation tax payable in accordance with TMA 1970, s. 59D (i.e. tax payable nine months and one day after the end of the accounting period) can be the subject of a managed payment plan. This excludes corporation tax payable by large companies in accordance with the quarterly instalment payment scheme. In addition, companies which have entered into a group payment arrangement can not enter into a managed payment plan. The payment plans will be launched in April 2011.

[2] TMA 1970, s. 59E and SI 1998/3175 provide for the payment of corporation tax by 'large' companies (defined in accordance with the small profits marginal relief upper limit) in instalments.

Companies which are 'large' because of the number of associated companies or because of substantial dividend income will not have to pay by instalments if their corporation tax liabilities are less than £10,000. Companies which become 'large' in an accounting period, having previously had profits below the upper limit, may be exempt from instalment arrangements in certain circumstances. Groups containing 'large' companies are able to pay corporation tax on a group-wide basis.

For accounting periods ending after 30 June 2005, corporation tax and the supplementary charge payable by oil companies on ring fence profits are payable in three equal instalments. Corporation tax due on other profits (i.e. non-ring fence) continues to be payable in quarterly instalments as above.

The payment dates for the three instalments once the transitional period (see below) has passed are as follows:

(1)   one-third payable six months and 13 days from the start of the accounting period (unless the date for instalment (3) is earlier);

(2)   one-third payable three months from the first instalment due date (unless (3) is earlier); and

(3)   the balance payable 14 days from the end of the accounting period (regardless of the length of the period). Transitional arrangements apply for the first accounting period affected. These arrangements leave the first two quarterly instalments unchanged (at one-quarter each of the estimated liability for the period) but then require payment of the remainder of the estimated liability on ring fence profits for that accounting period to be paid on the new third instalment date.

[3] Return periods end on 31 March, 30 June, 30 September, 31 December and at the end of an accounting period. The requirement for companies to deduct and account for income tax on certain payments is removed with effect for payments after 31 March 2001 of:

•   interest, royalties, annuities and other annual payments made to companies within the charge to UK corporation tax on that income; and

•   interest on quoted Eurobonds paid to non-residents.

[¶7-500] Penalties

(Tax Reporter: ¶812-050)

Infringement penalised	Maximum penalty	Provision	
		TMA 1970	Other
Failure to notify chargeability[1]	*Standard amount*		FA 2008, Sch. 41, para. 1, 6
• deliberate and concealed act or failure	100 per cent of potential lost revenue		
• deliberate but not concealed act or failure	70 per cent of potential lost revenue		
• any other case	30 per cent of potential lost revenue		
Failure to make return[2]	*Fixed rate penalty*[3]	s. 94(1), (5)	FA 1998, Sch. 18, para. 17(2), (3)
• up to 3 months after filing date	£100 (persistent failure, £500)		
• more than 3 months after filing date	£200 (persistent failure, £1,000)		
	Tax-geared penalty[4]	s. 94(6)	FA 1998, Sch. 18, para. 18
• at least 18 months but less than 24 months after end of return period	10% of tax unpaid at 18 months after end of return period		
• 24 months or more after end of return period	20% of tax unpaid at 18 months after end of return period		
Failure to take reasonable care with a return		–	FA 2007, Sch. 24, para. 4
• standard amount	30% of potential lost revenue		
• where the inaccuracy is deliberate but not concealed	70% of potential lost revenue		
• where the inaccuracy is deliberate and concealed	100% of potential lost revenue		
Failure to keep and preserve records (subject to specific exceptions)	Up to £3,000	–	FA 1998, Sch. 18, para. 23
Failure to produce documents required in connection with an enquiry[5]		–	FA 2008, Sch. 36, para. 39 and 40
• standard amount	£300		
• continued failure	daily penalty of £60		

Infringement penalised	Maximum penalty	Provision	
		TMA 1970	Other
Failure to notify commencement of trade within 3 months of first accounting period	standard amount of £300 plus £60 per day for continued failure	–	FA 2004, s. 55

Notes

(1) FA 2008, Sch. 41 applies with effect from 1 April 2010. Prior to that date, a penalty was provided for by FA 1998, Sch. 18, para. 2(3) and (4). The standard penalty imposed by FA 2008, Sch. 41 can be reduced where disclosure is made or where there are special circumstances.

(2) From a date yet to be announced, *Finance Act* 2009 introduced a new flat rate and tax-geared penalty regime for the late filing of corporation tax returns (FA 2009, Sch. 55).

(3) Fixed rate penalty does not apply if return filed by date allowed by Registrar of Companies.

(4) Tax geared penalty is charged in addition to fixed penalty. Where more than one tax–geared penalty is incurred the total penalty shall not exceed the largest individual penalty on that part.

(5) An additional tax-related penalty can be imposed under FA 2008, Sch. 36, para. 50.

(6) From a date yet to be announced, *Finance Act* 2009 introduced a new penalty regime for late payment of corporation tax (FA 2009, Sch. 56).

(7) For financial years beginning on or after 21 July 2009, the senior accounting officer of a qualifying company is obliged to ensure that the company establishes and maintains appropriate tax accounting arrangements, and to provide a certificate to HMRC indicating whether or not this was the case for each financial year (FA 2009, Sch. 46). Qualifying companies are obliged to provide details of their senior accounting officer to HMRC. Failure to comply with these requirements will make the senior accounting officer and/or the company liable to a penalty.

[¶7-550] Interest on overdue tax

(Tax Reporter: ¶811-350)

Interest on	Interest runs from	Provision in TMA 1970
Overdue corporation tax	Date tax due and payable (nine months and one day after end of accounting period)(1)	s. 87A
Corporation tax payable in instalments	Date instalment is due to be paid	s. 87A(2)
Overdue income tax deducted from certain payments	14 days after end of return period	s. 87
Overdue tax due on loans to participators	Date tax due and payable	s. 109

Notes

(1) Where one group company is liable to interest and another group company with the same accounting period is due a repayment of corporation tax an election may be made for the overpayment to be surrendered so as to reduce the interest liability of the first company which will be treated as having paid tax at the same time as the surrendering company (FA 1989, s. 102).

(2) As modified by SI 1998/3175, reg. 7.

(3) *Finance Act* 2009 contained provisions to harmonise interest regimes across all HMRC taxes and duties except corporation tax (CT) and petroleum revenue tax (PRT). Legislation to apply the harmonised interest regime to CT and PRT is expected to be included in a Finance Bill to be introduced later in 2010.

[¶7-600] Rates of interest on overdue tax

With effect for **interest** periods commencing on 6 February 1997, the rates of interest for the purposes of late paid or unpaid corporation tax are different from those for other taxes. From that date, the rate of interest on late paid or unpaid corporation tax will depend on the accounting period for which the tax is due and, under self assessment, the nature of the tax due:

Self assessment

For accounting periods within the self assessment regime (or CTSA – APs ending on or after 1 July 1999), these rates are distinct from those for periods before the start of self assessment because the interest is an allowable deduction for tax purposes (see below).

In addition, there are separate provisions for:

- overpaid instalments of corporation tax (which benefit from a more favourable rate – for details of payment by instalments, see 7-450); and
- other liabilities such as the final liability due on the date specified in accordance with the table below.

Pre-self assessment

For accounting periods before the start of self assessment, there are two rates of interest applicable to all unpaid/late paid tax depending on whether the accounting period is within the Pay and File regime (APs ending after 30 September 1993) or not (i.e. periods ending before 1 October 1993).

CTSA (APs ending on or after 1 July 1999)

1. Unpaid CT (other than underpaid instalments)

Period of application	Rate %
From 29 September 2009	3.0
24 March 2009 to 28 September 2009	2.5
27 January 2009 to 23 March 2009	3.5
6 January 2009 to 26 January 2009	4.5
6 December 2008 to 5 January 2009	5.5
6 November 2008 to 5 December 2008	6.5
6 January 2008 to 5 November 2008	7.5
6 August 2007 to 5 January 2008	8.5

Period of application	Rate %
6 September 2006 to 5 August 2007	7.5
6 September 2005 to 5 September 2006	6.5
6 September 2004 to 5 September 2005	7.5
6 December 2003 to 5 September 2004	6.5
6 August 2003 to 5 December 2003	5.5
6 November 2001 to 5 August 2003	6.5
6 May 2001 to 5 November 2001	7.5
6 February 2000 to 5 May 2001	8.5
6 March 1999 to 5 February 2000	7.5
6 January 1999 to 5 March 1999	8.5

2. Underpaid instalments

Period of application	Rate %
From 16 March 2009	1.50
16 February 2009 to 15 March 2009	2.00
19 January 2009 to 15 February 2009	2.50
15 December 2008 to 18 January 2009	3.00
17 November 2008 to 14 December 2008	4.00
20 October 2008 to 16 November 2008	5.50
21 April 2008 to 19 October 2008	6.00
18 February 2008 to 20 April 2008	6.25
17 December 2007 to 17 February 2008	6.50
16 July 2007 to 16 December 2007	6.75
21 May 2007 to 15 July 2007	6.50
22 January 2007 to 20 May 2007	6.25
20 November 2006 to 21 January 2007	6.00
14 August 2006 to 19 November 2006	5.75
15 August 2005 to 13 August 2006	5.50

Period of application	Rate %
16 August 2004 to 14 August 2005	5.75
21 June 2004 to 15 August 2004	5.50
17 May 2004 to 20 June 2004	5.25
16 February 2004 to 16 May 2004	5.00
17 November 2003 to 15 February 2004	4.75
21 July 2003 to 16 November 2003	4.5
17 February 2003 to 20 July 2003	4.75
19 November 2001 to 16 February 2003	5.00
15 October 2001 to 18 November 2001	5.5
1 October 2001 to 14 October 2001	5.75
13 August 2001 to 30 September 2001	6.00
21 May 2001 to 12 August 2001	6.25
16 April 2001 to 20 May 2001	6.5
19 February 2001 to 15 April 2001	6.75
20 April 2000 to 18 February 2001	7.00
21 February 2000 to 19 April 2000	8.00
24 January 2000 to 20 February 2000	7.75
15 November 1999 to 23 January 2000	7.5
20 September 1999 to 14 November 1999	7.25
21 June 1999 to 19 September 1999	7.00
19 April 1999 to 20 June 1999	7.25
15 February 1999 to 18 April 1999	7.5
18 January 1999 to 14 February 1999	8.00
Before 18 January 1999	8.25

Taxation of Companies

Pre-CTSA

Period of application	Rate % pre-Pay and File	Rate % post-Pay and File
From 29 September 2009	3.00	3.00
24 March 2009 to 28 September 2009	2.00	1.75
27 January 2009 to 23 March 2009	2.75	2.75
6 January 2009 to 26 January 2009	3.50	3.50
6 December 2008 to 5 January 2009	4.25	4.25
6 November 2008 to 5 December 2008	5.00	5.00
6 January 2008 to 5 November 2008	5.75	6.00
6 August 2007 to 5 January 2008	6.50	6.75
6 September 2006 to 5 August 2007	5.75	6
6 September 2005 to 5 September 2006	5	5.25
6 September 2004 to 5 September 2005	5.75	6
6 December 2003 to 5 September 2004	5.25	5
6 August 2003 to 5 December 2003	4.25	4.25
6 November 2001 to 5 August 2003	5	5
6 May 2001 to 5 November 2001	5.75	6
6 February 2000 to 5 May 2001	6.5	6.75
6 March 1999 to 5 February 2000	5.75	5.75
6 January 1999 to 5 March 1999	6.5	6.5
6 August 1997 to 5 January 1999	7.25	7.5
6 February 1997 to 5 August 1997	6.25	6.25
6 February 1996 to 5 February 1997	6.25	
6 March 1995 to 5 February 1996	7	
6 October 1994 to 5 March 1995	6.25	
6 January 1994 to 5 October 1994	5.5	
6 March 1993 to 5 January 1994	6.25	
6 December 1992 to 5 March 1993	7	
6 November 1992 to 5 December 1992	7.75	

Period of application	Rate % pre-Pay and File	Rate % post-Pay and File
6 October 1991 to 5 November 1992	9.25	
6 July 1991 to 5 October 1991	10	
6 May 1991 to 5 July 1991	10.75	
6 March 1991 to 5 May 1991	11.5	

[¶7-650] Interest on tax repayments

(ICTA 1988, s. 826; SI 1998/3175, reg. 8)

(Tax Reporter: ¶811-350)

Repayment interest on corporation tax runs from later of:

(1)   due and payable date (nine months after end of accounting period); and

(2)   date of actual payment; except for

(a)   overpayments of instalments of corporation tax, when interest runs from the first instalment date on which the excess amount would have been due and payable or, if later, the date on which that excess arises; and

(b)   for companies outside the instalments regime, if tax was paid earlier than the normal due date, then interest on repayments in advance of agreement of liability runs from the first instalment date on which the excess amount would have been due and payable had the instalments regime applied or, the date on which the amount repayable was originally paid, whichever is later.

Interest on repayments of income tax deducted at source from income will run from the day after the end of the accounting period in which the income was received for accounting periods under self assessment.

Finance Act 2009 contained provisions to harmonise interest regimes across all HMRC taxes and duties except corporation tax (CT) and petroleum revenue tax (PRT). Legislation to apply the harmonised interest regime to CT and PRT is expected to be included in a Finance Bill to be introduced later in 2010.

[¶7-700] Rates of interest on tax repayments

Rates of interest on overpaid corporation tax

With effect for **interest** periods commencing on 6 February 1997, the rates of interest for the purposes of overpaid corporation tax are different from those for other taxes. The rate of interest on overpaid corporation tax will depend on the accounting period for which the tax is due and, under self assessment, the nature of the tax repayable:

Self assessment

For accounting periods within the self assessment regime (CTSA) i.e. APs on or after 1 July 1999, the rates of interest on repayments of overpaid corporation tax are distinct from those for pre-CTSA periods, because the interest is taxable (see below).

In addition, there are separate provisions for:

● overpaid instalments of corporation tax; and

● payments of corporation tax made after the normal due date.

Pay and File and earlier periods

For accounting periods within Pay and File (APs ending after 30 September 1993) and accounting periods before Pay and File, interest on overpaid corporation tax, repayments of income tax and payments of tax credits in respect of franked investment income received is given at the appropriate rate shown in the relevant table below.

CTSA (APs ending on or after 1 July 1999)

1. Overpaid CT (other than overpaid instalments and early payments of CT not due by instalments)

Period of application	Rate %
From 29 September 2009	0.5
27 January 2009 to 28 September 2009	0
6 January 2009 to 26 January 2009	1
6 December 2008 to 5 January 2009	2
6 November 2008 to 5 December 2008	3
6 January 2008 to 5 November 2008	4
6 August 2007 to 5 January 2008	5
6 September 2006 to 5 August 2007	4
6 September 2005 to 5 September 2006	3
6 September 2004 to 5 September 2005	4
6 December 2003 to 5 September 2004	3
6 August 2003 to 5 December 2003	2
6 November 2001 to 5 August 2003	3
6 May 2001 to 5 November 2001	4
6 February 2000 to 5 May 2001	5

Period of application	Rate %
6 March 1999 to 5 February 2000	4
6 January 1999 to 5 March 1999	5

2. Overpaid instalments and early payments of CT not due by instalments

Period of application	Rate %
From 21 September 2009	0.50
16 March 2009 to 20 September 2009	0.25
16 February 2009 to 15 March 2009	0.75
19 January 2009 to 15 February 2009	1.25
15 December 2008 to 18 January 2009	1.75
17 November 2008 to 14 December 2008	2.75
20 October 2008 to 16 November 2008	4.25
21 April 2008 to 19 October 2008	4.75
18 February 2008 to 20 April 2008	5.00
17 December 2007 to 17 February 2008	5.25
16 July 2007 to 16 December 2007	5.50
21 May 2007 to 15 July 2007	5.25
22 January 2007 to 20 May 2007	5.00
20 November 2006 to 21 January 2007	4.75
14 August 2006 to 19 November 2006	4.50
15 August 2005 to 13 August 2006	4.25
16 August 2004 to 14 August 2005	4.50
21 June 2004 to 15 August 2004	4.25
17 May 2004 to 20 June 2004	4.00
16 February 2004 to 16 May 2004	3.75
17 November 2003 to 15 February 2004	3.5
21 July 2003 to 16 November 2003	3.25
17 February 2003 to 20 July 2003	3.50

Period of application	Rate %
19 November 2001 to 16 February 2003	3.75
15 October 2001 to 18 November 2001	4.25
1 October 2001 to 14 October 2001	4.50
13 August 2001 to 30 September 2001	4.75
21 May 2001 to 12 August 2001	5.00
16 April 2001 to 20 May 2001	5.25
19 February 2001 to 15 April 2001	5.5
21 February 2000 to 18 February 2001	5.75
24 January 2000 to 20 February 2000	5.5
15 November 1999 to 23 January 2000	5.25
20 September 1999 to 14 November 1999	5.00
21 June 1999 to 19 September 1999	4.75
19 April 1999 to 20 June 1999	5.00
15 February 1999 to 18 April 1999	5.25
18 January 1999 to 14 February 1999	5.75
Before 18 January 1999	6.00

Pay and File

Period of application	Rate %
From 29 September 2009	0.50
27 January 2009 to 28 September 2009	0
6 January 2009 to 26 January 2009	0.50
6 December 2008 to 5 January 2009	1.25
6 November 2008 to 5 December 2008	2.00
6 January 2008 to 5 November 2008	2.75
6 August 2007 to 5 January 2008	3.50
6 September 2006 to 5 August 2007	2.75
6 September 2005 to 5 September 2006	2

Period of application	Rate %
6 September 2004 to 5 September 2005	2.75
6 December 2003 to 5 September 2004	2
6 August 2003 to 5 December 2003	1.25
6 November 2001 to 5 August 2003	2
6 May 2001 to 5 November 2001	2.75
6 February 2000 to 5 May 2001	3.5
6 March 1999 to 5 February 2000	2.75
6 January 1999 to 5 March 1999	3.25
6 August 1997 to 5 January 1999	4
6 February 1996 to 5 August 1997	3.25
6 March 1995 to 5 February 1996	4
6 October 1994 to 5 March 1995	3.25
6 January 1994 to 5 October 1994	2.5
1 October 1993 to 5 January 1994	3.25

Pre-Pay and File

Period of application	Rate %
From 29 September 2009	0.50
24 March 2009 to 28 September 2009	2.00
27 January 2009 to 23 March 2009	2.75
6 January 2009 to 26 January 2009	3.50
6 December 2008 to 5 January 2009	4.25
6 November 2008 to 5 December 2008	5.00
6 January 2008 to 5 November 2008	5.75
6 August 2007 to 5 January 2008	6.5
6 September 2006 to 5 August 2007	5.75
6 September 2005 to 5 September 2006	5
6 September 2004 to 5 September 2005	5.75

Period of application	Rate %
6 December 2003 to 5 September 2004	5
6 August 2003 to 5 December 2003	4.25
6 November 2001 to 5 August 2003	5
6 May 2001 to 5 November 2001	5.75
6 February 2000 to 5 May 2001	6.5
6 March 1999 to 5 February 2000	5.75
6 January 1999 to 5 March 1999	6.5
6 August 1997 to 5 January 1999	7.25
6 February 1996 to 5 August 1997	6.25
6 March 1995 to 5 February 1996	7
6 October 1994 to 5 March 1995	6.25
6 January 1994 to 5 October 1994	5.5
6 March 1993 to 5 January 1994	6.25
6 December 1992 to 5 March 1993	7
6 November 1992 to 5 December 1992	7.75
6 October 1991 to 5 November 1992	9.25
6 July 1991 to 5 October 1991	10
6 May 1991 to 5 July 1991	10.75
6 March 1991 to 5 May 1991	11.5

[¶7-900]   Time limits for elections and claims

(Tax Reporter: ¶812-150)

In the absence of any provision to the contrary (some of which are considered below), the normal rule is that a claim must be made within four years of the end of the accounting period to which it relates (six years prior to 1 April 2010) (FA 1998, Sch. 18, para. 55).

In certain cases HMRC *may* permit an extension of the strict time limit in relation to certain elections and claims.

Provision	Time limit	References
Stock transferred to a connected party on cessation of trade to be valued at higher cost or sale price	2 years from end of accounting period in which trade ceased	CTA 2009, s. 167(4)

Provision	Time limit	References
Carry-forward of trading losses	Relief is given automatically	CTA 2010, s. 45
Set-off of trading losses against profits of the same, or an earlier, accounting period[1]	2 years from end of accounting period in which loss incurred	CTA 2010, s. 37(7)
Group relief	Claims to group relief must be made (or withdrawn) by the later of: (1) 12 months after the claimant company's filing date for the return for the accounting period covered by the claim; (2) 30 days after a closure notice is issued on the completion of an enquiry [2]; (3) 30 days after HMRC issue a notice of amendment to a return following the completion of an enquiry (issued where the company fails to amend the return itself); or (4) 30 days after the determination of any appeal against an HMRC amendment (as in (3) above).	FA 1998, Sch. 18, para. 74
Set-off of loss on disposal of shares in unquoted trading company against income of investment company	2 years from end of accounting period	CTA 2010, s. 70(4)
Surrender of company tax refund within group	Before refund made to surrendering company	CTA 2010, s. 963(3)
Election to reallocate a chargeable gain or an allowable loss within a group [3]	2 years from end of accounting period during which the gain or loss accrues	TCGA 1992, s. 171A
Relief for a non-trading deficit on loan relationships (including any non-trading exchange losses)	2 years from end of period in which deficit arises, or, in the case of a claim to carry forward the deficit, 2 years from end of the accounting period following the deficit period, or within such further period as the Board may allow	CTA 2009, s. 458(2) and 460(1)

[1] The carry-back period is extended to three years for accounting periods ending in the period 23/11/08 to 24/11/2010 (FA 2009, s. 23, Sch. 6).

[2] 'Enquiry' in the above does not include a restricted enquiry into an amendment to a return (restricted because the time limit for making an enquiry into the return itself has expired), where the amendment consists of a group relief claim or withdrawal of claim.
These time limits have priority over any other general time limits for amending returns and are subject to HMRC permitting an extension to the time limits.

[3] Following the enactment of the *Finance Act* 2009, it is now possible for chargeable gains and allowable losses to be transferred within a group. For gains and losses made before 21 July 2009, this result could only be achieved by electing for the notional transfer of an asset before its disposal to a third party (TCGA 1992, s. 171A prior to the changes made by FA 2009, s. 31, Sch. 12). The election had to be made jointly on or before the second anniversary of the end of the actual vendor group company's accounting period in which it made the disposal.

CAPITAL ALLOWANCES

[¶8-000] Plant and machinery: overview of allowances

(CAA 2001)

(Tax Reporter: ¶235-000ff.)

Plant and machinery allowances are normally given by way of:

- annual investment allowances: see ¶8-100;
- first-year allowances: see ¶8-200; or
- writing-down allowances: see ¶8-300.

In specified circumstances, balancing allowances may be due or balancing charges may be made.

[¶8-100] Plant and machinery: annual investment allowances

(CAA 2001, s. 51A)

(Tax Reporter: ¶236-400ff.)

	Maximum (£)
From April 2012	25,000
April 2010 to April 2012	100,000
April 2008 to April 2010	50,000
Before April 2008	–

This figure is adjusted pro rata for chargeable periods shorter or longer than one year.

An apportionment is made for periods spanning any date on which the maximum allowance is changed.

Groups and certain other related parties share a single amount.

[¶8-200] Plant and machinery: first-year allowances – overview

Most first-year allowances are permanently available, and give immediate relief for the whole of the qualifying expenditure: see ¶8-210.

Other allowances are given on a temporary basis only, and at a lower level of relief: see below.

General exclusions

See ¶8-220 re general exclusions from first-year allowances (but see also ¶237-075 re leasing restriction for fixtures owned by landlords).

Temporary first-year allowances

(FA 2009, s. 24)

(Tax Reporter: ¶237-075)

Temporary first-year allowances at 40 per cent were given for general expenditure on plant or machinery incurred by businesses of any size in the year ended 31 March or 5 April 2010 (for corporation tax and income tax respectively).

Older first-year allowances

(CAA 2001, s. 52)

(Tax Reporter: ¶237-000ff.)

Until April 2008, entitlement to some first-year allowances depended on the size of the business.

Medium-sized enterprises (defined at ¶8-230) were entitled to a 40 per cent FYA on most plant and machinery.

Small enterprises (also defined at ¶8-230) were similarly entitled to first-year allowances on most plant and machinery. The first-year allowance rate of 40 per cent was increased to 50 per cent for the years 2004–05, 2006–07 (but not 2005–06) and 2007–08 (and for financial years 2004, 2006 and 2007 (but not 2005)).

[¶8-210]   Plant and machinery: 100 per cent first-year allowances

(CAA 2001, s. 52)

(Tax Reporter: ¶237-000ff.)

Subject to the general exclusions listed at ¶8-220, full 100 per cent allowances are available for the following types of expenditure incurred by a business of any size. If full FYAs are not claimed, WDA is normally available at 20 per cent on a reducing balance basis.

Nature of expenditure	Authority (CAA 2001)	Notes
Energy-saving plant or machinery	s. 45A–45C	Loss-making companies may claim tax rebate
Cars with very low CO_2 emissions	s. 45D	Threshold tightened from April 2008
Plant or machinery for certain refuelling stations	s. 45E	

Nature of expenditure	Authority (CAA 2001)	Notes
Plant or machinery (other than a long life asset) for use by a company wholly in a ring fence trade	s. 45F	
Environmentally beneficial plant or machinery	s. 45H–45J	Loss-making companies may claim tax rebate

It was announced in the Budget of March 2010, and confirmed in the emergency Budget of 22 June 2010, that a new 100 per cent first-year allowance will be introduced for expenditure incurred in a five year period from April 2010 on zero-emission goods vehicles. The stated intention is to legislate for this measure 'in a Finance Bill to be introduced as soon as possible after the summer recess'.

[¶8-220] Plant and machinery: first-year allowances – general exclusions

(CAA 2001, s. 46(2))

(Tax Reporter: ¶237-150)

No first-year allowances are available for:

- expenditure incurred in the final chargeable period;
- cars (other than those with very low CO_2 emissions);
- certain ships and railway assets;
- items excluded from the long-life asset treatment only by virtue of the transitional provisions;
- plant or machinery for leasing;
- in certain anti-avoidance cases where the obtaining of a FYA is linked to a change in the nature or conduct of a trade;
- where an asset was initially acquired for purposes other than those of the qualifying activity;
- where an asset was acquired by way of a gift;
- where plant or machinery that was provided for long funding leasing starts to be used for other purposes.

Capital Allowances

[¶8-230]   Plant and machinery: definition of small and medium-sized enterprises

(Former CAA 2001, s. 47)

(Tax Reporter: ¶237-200)

This concept was relevant for capital allowances purposes up to 31 March or 5 April 2008 (respectively for corporation tax and income tax purposes).

A company or business was a *small enterprise* if:

* it qualified (or was treated as qualifying) as small under the 'relevant companies legislation', for the financial year of the company in which the expenditure was incurred; and

* it was not a member of a medium or large group (*Companies Act* 1985, s. 249) at the time the expenditure was incurred.

A company or business was a *small or medium-sized enterprise* if:

* it qualified (or was treated as qualifying) as small or medium-sized under the 'relevant companies legislation', for the financial year of the company in which the expenditure was incurred; and

* it was not a member of a large group at the time the expenditure was incurred.

Type of company	Requirements	
Small company	Turnover	Not more than £5.6m
	Balance sheet total	Not more than £2.8m
	Number of employees	Not more than 50
Medium-sized company	Turnover	Not more than £22.8m
	Balance sheet total	Not more than £11.4m
	Number of employees	Not more than 250
Small group	Aggregate turnover	Not more than £5.6m net (or £6.72m gross)
	Aggregate balance sheet total	Not more than £2.8m net (or £3.36m gross)
	Aggregate number of employees	Not more than 50

Type of company	Requirements	
Medium-sized group	Aggregate turnover	Not more than £22.8m net (or £27.36m gross)
	Aggregate balance sheet total	Not more than £11.4m net (or £13.68m gross)
	Aggregate number of employees	Not more than 250

[¶8-300]   Plant and machinery: writing-down allowances

(CAA 2001, s. 56)

(Tax Reporter: ¶238-050ff.)

	Standard rate (%)	Special rate (%)
From April 2012	18	8
April 2008 to April 2012	20	10
Before April 2008	25	See notes

Notes

Before April 2008, long-life assets attracted allowances at six per cent.

Different rules apply for cars: see ¶8-500.

[¶8-400]   Plant and machinery: integral features

(CAA 2001, s. 33A)

(Tax Reporter: ¶243-400ff.)

The following assets are designated as integral features:

- electrical systems (including lighting systems);

- cold water systems;

- space or water heating systems, powered systems of ventilation, air cooling or air purification, and any floor or ceiling comprised in such systems;

- lifts, escalators and moving walkways; and

- external solar shading.

Expenditure on thermal insulation and long-life assets, and (from April 2009) higher emission cars (see ¶8-500), is also allocated to the 'special rate' pool.

[¶8-410]   Plant and machinery: expenditure unaffected by statutory restrictions re buildings

(CAA 2001, s. 23)

(Tax Reporter: ¶245-550)

The restrictions in CAA 2001, s. 21 and 22 (buildings, structures and other assets) do not apply to expenditure in List C at CAA 2001, s. 23. List C, as amended, is as follows:

(1)   Machinery (including devices for providing motive power) not within any other item in this list.

(2)   Gas and sewerage systems provided mainly

(a)   to meet the particular requirements of the qualifying activity;

(b)   to serve particular plant or machinery used for the purposes of the qualifying activity.

(3)   [omitted by Finance Act 2008].

(4)   Manufacturing or processing equipment; storage equipment (including cold rooms); display equipment; and counters, checkouts and similar equipment.

(5)   Cookers, washing machines, dishwashers, refrigerators and similar equipment; washbasins, sinks, baths, showers, sanitary ware and similar equipment; and furniture and furnishings.

(6)   Hoists.

(7)   Sound insulation provided mainly to meet the particular requirements of the qualifying activity.

(8)   Computer, telecommunication and surveillance systems (including their wiring or other links).

(9)   Refrigeration or cooling equipment.

(10) Fire alarm systems; sprinkler and other equipment for extinguishing or containing fires.

(11) Burglar alarm systems.

(12) Strong rooms in bank or building society premises; safes.

(13) Partition walls, where moveable and intended to be moved in the course of the qualifying activity.

(14) Decorative assets provided for the enjoyment of the public in hotel, restaurant or similar trades.

(15) Advertising hoardings; signs, displays and similar assets.

(16) Swimming-pools (including diving boards, slides and structures on which such boards or slides are mounted).

(17) Any glasshouse constructed so that the required environment (namely, air, heat, light, irrigation and temperature) for the growing of plants is provided automatically by means of devices forming an integral part of its structure.

(18) Cold stores.

(19) Caravans provided mainly for holiday lettings.

(20) Buildings provided for testing aircraft engines run within the buildings.

(21) Moveable buildings intended to be moved in the course of the qualifying activity.

(22) The alteration of land for the purpose only of installing plant or machinery.

(23) The provision of dry docks.

(24) The provision of any jetty or similar structure provided mainly to carry plant or machinery.

(25) The provision of pipelines or underground ducts or tunnels with a primary purpose of carrying utility conduits.

(26) The provision of towers to support floodlights.

(27) The provision of
 (a) any reservoir incorporated into a water treatment works; or
 (b) any service reservoir of treated water for supply within any housing estate or other particular locality.

(28) The provision of
 (a) silos provided for temporary storage; or
 (b) storage tanks.

(29) The provision of slurry pits or silage clamps.

(30) The provision of fish tanks or fish ponds.

(31) The provision of rails, sleepers and ballast for a railway or tramway.

(32) The provision of structures and other assets for providing the setting for any ride at an amusement park or exhibition.

(33) The provision of fixed zoo cages.

Items 1–16 of the above list do not, however, include any asset with the principal purpose of insulating or enclosing the interior of a building or of providing an interior wall, floor or ceiling that is intended to remain permanently in place.

[¶8-500] Plant and machinery: allowances for cars

(CAA 2001, s. 74ff.)

From April 2009

(Tax Reporter: ¶238-500ff.)

Expenditure on cars bought from April 2009 goes into the main 20 per cent pool if CO_2 emissions do not exceed 160g/km.

Expenditure on cars bought from April 2009 with higher emissions goes into 10 per cent 'special rate' pool.

Cars with private use go to single asset pool but still attract allowances at 20 per cent or 10 per cent as above, but then adjusted for private use percentage.

Cars with emissions that do not exceed 110g/km continue to attract first-year allowances at 100 per cent.

Cars bought before 1 or 6 April 2009 continue to attract allowances as before (see below).

Leased cars, where lease begins from 1 or 6 April 2009, suffer 15 per cent disallowance of relevant payments if CO_2 emissions exceed 160g/km; otherwise no disallowance.

Before April 2009

(Tax Reporter: ¶238-900ff.)

Bought cars attract allowances at standard 20 per cent (previously 25 per cent) rate, but cars costing more than £12,000 have annual WDA restricted to £3,000. No restriction on balancing allowances.

Cars with emissions that do not exceed 110g/km (previously 120g/km) attract first-year allowances at 100 per cent.

Permanent disallowance of a proportion of the hire cost of cars where the retail price when new exceeds £12,000.

[¶8-600] Industrial buildings, hotels and sports pavilions; agricultural buildings and structures

(CAA 2001, s. 271ff.)

(Tax Reporter: ¶246-750ff.)

These allowances are being phased out. To achieve this, the following percentages are applied to the writing-down allowances that would otherwise be available for industrial buildings, hotels and sports pavilions and agricultural buildings and structures.

Financial year beginning	Tax year	Percentage
1 April 2011 and later	2011–12 and later	0 per cent (ie no further allowances given)
1 April 2010	2010–11	25 per cent
1 April 2009	2009–10	50 per cent
1 April 2008	2008–09	75 per cent
1 April 2007 and earlier	2007–08 and earlier	100 per cent

Where a chargeable period straddles the financial or tax year, the WDA is to be apportioned on a strict time basis.

The restriction applies both to the standard four per cent WDA and to the higher WDA available to some used buildings.

No initial allowances are available.

[¶8-650]   Enterprise zones: industrial buildings, hotels, commercial buildings or structures

(CAA 2001, s. 271ff.)

(Tax Reporter: ¶250-950ff.)

Initial allowances (at 100 per cent) or writing-down allowances (at 25 per cent) are available for certain buildings in enterprise zones (industrial buildings; hotels and commercial buildings or structures).

Enterprise zones can be valid for up to a maximum of 20 years in total. Those that still fall within that 20-year period are as follows:

Statutory instrument	Area	Start date
1993/23	Lanarkshire (Hamilton)	1 February 1993
1993/24	Lanarkshire (Motherwell)	1 February 1993
1993/25	Lanarkshire (Monklands)	1 February 1993
1995/2624	Dearne Valley (Barnsley, Doncaster, Rotherham)	3 November 1995
1995/2625	Holmewood (North East Derbyshire)	3 November 1995
1995/2738	Bassetlaw	16 November 1995
1995/2758	Ashfield	21 November 1995
1995/2812	East Durham (No. 1 to No. 6)	29 November 1995
1996/106	Tyne Riverside (North Tyneside)	19 February 1996
1996/1981	Tyne Riverside (Silverlink North Scheme)	26 August 1996
1996/1981	Tyne Riverside (Silverlink Business Park Scheme)	26 August 1996
1996/1981	Tyne Riverside (Middle Engine Lane Scheme)	26 August 1996
1996/1981	Tyne Riverside (New York Industrial Park Scheme)	26 August 1996
1996/1981	Tyne Riverside (Balliol Business Park West Scheme)	26 August 1996
1996/2435	Tyne Riverside (Baltic Enterprise Park Scheme)	21 October 1996
1996/2435	Tyne Riverside (Viking Industrial Park – Wagonway West Scheme)	21 October 1996
1996/2435	Tyne Riverside (Viking Industrial Park – Blackett Street Scheme)	21 October 1996
1996/2435	Tyne Riverside (Viking Industrial Park – Western Road Scheme)	21 October 1996

[¶8-800]   Other allowances

Allowance	Date expenditure incurred (from)	Initial allowance (%)	WDA (%)	CAA 2001	BTR
Business premises renovation	11 April 2007	100	25	s. 360A	252-500
Flat conversion	11 May 2001	100	25	s. 393A	254-000
Mineral extraction	1 April 1986	–	25	s. 394	255-500
Research and development	5 November 1962	100	–	s. 437	256-000
Know-how	1 April 1986	–	25	s. 452	257-000
Patents	1 April 1986	–	25	s. 464	257-500
Dredging	1 April 1986	–	4	s. 484	258-000
Assured tenancy	1 April 1986 (to 31 March 1992)	–	4	s. 490	258-500

Capital Allowances

[¶8-950]   Time limits for elections and claims

(TMA 1970, s. 43(1))

In the absence of any provision to the contrary, under self-assessment for the purposes of income tax, the normal rule is that claims are to be made within four years from the end of the tax year to which they relate. Before 1 April 2010, the time limit was generally five years from 31 January following the end of the tax year.

Provision	Time limit	Statutory reference
General claim to capital allowances under self assessment	Claims to capital allowances must be made (or amended or withdrawn) by the later of:	FA 1998, Sch. 18, para. 82
	(1) 12 months after the claimant company's filing date for the return for the accounting period covered by the claim;	
	(2) 30 days after a closure notice is issued on the completion of an enquiry;	
	(3) 30 days after HMRC issue a notice of amendment to a return following the completion of an enquiry (issued where the company fails to amend the return itself); or	
	(4) 30 days after the determination of any appeal against an HMRC amendment (as in (3) above).	
	'Enquiry' in the above does not include a restricted enquiry into an amendment to a return (restricted because the time limit for making an enquiry into the return itself has expired), where the amendment consists of a group relief claim or withdrawal of a claim. These time limits have priority over any other general time limits for amending returns and are subject to HMRC permitting an extension to the time limits.	
Certain plant and machinery treated as 'short life' assets (income tax elections)	12 months from 31 January next following the tax year in which ends the chargeable period in which the qualifying expenditure was incurred	CAA 2001, s. 85
Certain plant and machinery treated as 'short life' assets (corporation tax elections)	2 years from end of the chargeable period in which the qualifying expenditure was incurred	CAA 2001, s. 85

Provision	Time limit	Statutory reference
Set-off of capital allowances on special leasing	2 years from end of accounting period	CAA 2001, s. 260(3), (6)
Transfer between connected parties of certain assets, eligible for capital allowances, at tax-written down value	2 years from date of sale	CAA 2001, s. 570(5)

Capital Allowances

NATIONAL INSURANCE CONTRIBUTIONS

[¶9-000]   NIC rates: general

There are six classes of National Insurance contributions payable according to the individual circumstances of the payer.

Class 1 contributions

Class 1 contributions are earnings-related and payable by employer and employee on earnings above the earnings threshold. The primary threshold (PT) for employees is currently set at the same level as the secondary threshold (ST) for employers. From April 2003, employees pay at the main rate up to the upper earnings limit (UEL) and the 1 per cent additional rate above the limit. Rates are set to rise by one percentage point in April 2011, but starting thresholds will also rise to provide some protection from the rate rise for the lower paid.

Where the employee is a member of the employer's contracted-out pension scheme, a contracted-out rebate reduces the contributions due from both on any earnings between the lower earnings limit (LEL) and, until 5 April 2009, the UEL and, from 6 April 2009, the upper accruals point (UAP). Earnings between the LEL and the PT/ST attract the rebate despite there being no contributions due at that level.

The reduced rate applies to married women or widows with a valid certificate of election and affects only primary contributions.

Men over 65 and women over state pension age (60-65 since 6 April 2010) pay no primary contributions, though employers still pay the secondary contribution, at the not contracted-out rate, regardless of the previous category of contribution liability. Children under 16 and their employers pay no contributions.

[¶9-045]   Class 1 NIC: 2010–11

Class 1 contributions

Class 1 primary (employee) contributions 2010–11	
Lower earnings limit (LEL)[1]	£97 weekly £421 monthly £5,044 yearly
Primary threshold (PT)	£110 weekly £476 monthly £5,715 yearly
Upper earnings limit (UEL)	£844 weekly £3,656 monthly £43,875 yearly

National Insurance Contributions

Upper accrual point (UAP)	£770 weekly £3,337 monthly £40,040 yearly
Rate on earnings up to PT[1]	0%
Not contracted-out rate	11% on £110.01 to £844 weekly 1% on excess over £844
Contracted-out rate	9.4% on £110.01 to £770 weekly 11% on £770.01 to £844 weekly 1% on excess over £844
Reduced rate	4.85% on £110.01 to £844 weekly 1% on excess over £844 (no rebate even if contracted-out)

Notes

[1] Earnings from the LEL, up to and including the primary threshold (PT), count towards the employee's basic state pension, even though no contributions are paid on those earnings. Similarly, earnings between the LEL and the PT count towards the employee's entitlement to certain benefits including the second state pension (S2P). Employees in contracted-out employment earn no S2P rights and receive a rebate of contributions of 1.6 per cent. This applies from the LEL to the UAP, so earnings from LEL to PT attract a 'negative' contribution of 1.6 per cent and the rate for earnings from PT to UAP becomes 9.4 per cent. Earnings from UAP to UEL are subject to the main not contracted-out rate.
Monthly and annual LEL, UEL and UAP figures are calculated as per SI 2001/1004, reg. 11.

[2] It was announced in the June 2010 Budget that the not contracted-out rate on earnings between the PT and the UEL will be 12 per cent for 2011-12 and the rate on earnings above the UEL will be 2 per cent. The UEL will continue to be aligned with the income tax higher rate threshold. An increase in the PT already planned for 2011-12 and announced in the PBR 2009 is to go ahead. The reduced rate for married women will be 5.85 per cent for 2011-12.

Class 1 secondary (employer) contributions 2010–11	
Secondary earnings threshold (ST)	£110 weekly £476 monthly £5,715 yearly
Not contracted-out rate	12.8% on earnings above the ST
Contracted-out rate[1]	9.1% for salary-related (COSR) and 11.4% for money-purchase (COMP) schemes on earnings from ST to UAP (plus 3.7% and 1.4% rebates for earnings from LEL to ST), then 12.8% above UAP.

Notes

[1] Although employer contributions do not *per se* give any benefit entitlements, earnings between the LEL and ST are those classed as relevant for S2P. Employers with contracted-out occupational pension schemes receive a rebate of contributions for scheme members of 3.7 per cent (COSR) or 1.4 per cent (COMP). This applies from the LEL to the UAP, so earnings from LEL to ST attract a 'negative' contribution and the rate for earnings from ST to UAP is reduced as shown

[2] It was announced in the June 2010 Budget that the not contracted-out rate on earnings above the ST will be 13.8 per cent for 2011-12. However, the ST for 2011-12 will be increased by an extra £21 a week above indexation. It was also announced that a scheme will be introduced under which new businesses setting up in targeted areas of the UK during a three-year qualifying period will not have to pay the first £5,000 of Class 1 employer NICs due in the

first 12 months of employment. This will apply for each of the first 10 employees hired in the first year of business. The scheme is intended to start no later than September 2010.

[¶9-050]   Class 1 NIC: 2009–10

Class 1 contributions

Class 1 primary (employee) contributions 2009–10	
Lower earnings limit (LEL)[1]	£95 weekly £412 monthly £4,940 yearly
Primary threshold (PT)	£110 weekly £476 monthly £5,715 yearly
Upper earnings limit (UEL)	£844 weekly £3,656 monthly £43,875 yearly
Upper accrual point (UAP)	£770 weekly £3,337 monthly £40,040 yearly
Rate on earnings up to PT[1]	0%
Not contracted-out rate	11% on £110.01 to £844 weekly 1% on excess over £844
Contracted-out rate	9.4% on £110.01 to £770 weekly 11% on £770.01 to £844 weekly 1% on excess over £844
Reduced rate	4.85% on £110.01 to £844 weekly 1% on excess over £844 (no rebate even if contracted-out)

Notes

[1]   Earnings from the LEL, up to and including the primary threshold (PT), count towards the employee's basic state pension, even though no contributions are paid on those earnings. Similarly, earnings between the LEL and the PT count towards the employee's entitlement to certain benefits including the second state pension (S2P). Employees in contracted-out employment earn no S2P rights and receive a rebate of contributions of 1.6 per cent. This applies from the LEL to the UAP, so earnings from LEL to PT attract a 'negative' contribution of 1.6 per cent and the rate for earnings from PT to UAP becomes 9.4 per cent. Earnings from UAP to UEL are subject to the main not contracted-out rate.

Monthly and annual LEL, UEL and UAP figures are calculated as per SI 2001/1004, reg. 11.

National Insurance Contributions

Class 1 secondary (employer) contributions 2009–10	
Secondary earnings threshold (ST)	£110 weekly £476 monthly £5,715 yearly
Not contracted-out rate	12.8% on earnings above the ST
Contracted-out rate[1]	9.1% for salary-related (COSR) and 11.4% for money-purchase (COMP) schemes on earnings from ST to UAP (plus 3.7% and 1.4% rebates for earnings from LEL to ST), then 12.8% above UAP.

Notes
[1] Although employer contributions do not *per se* give any benefit entitlements, earnings between the LEL and ST are those classed as relevant for S2P. Employers with contracted-out occupational pension schemes receive a rebate of contributions for scheme members of 3.7 per cent (COSR) or 1.4 per cent (COMP). This applies from the LEL to the UAP, so earnings from LEL to ST attract a 'negative' contribution and the rate for earnings from ST to UAP is reduced as shown

[¶9-100]   Class 1 NIC: 2008–09

Class 1 contributions

Class 1 primary (employee) contributions 2008–09	
Lower earnings limit (LEL)[1]	£90 weekly £390 monthly £4,680 yearly
Primary threshold (PT)	£105 weekly £453 monthly £5,435 yearly
Upper earnings limit (UEL)	£770 weekly £3,337 monthly £40,040 yearly
Rate on earnings up to PT[1]	0%
Not contracted-out rate	11% on £105.01 to £770 weekly 1% on excess over £770
Contracted-out rate	9.4% on £105.01 to £770 weekly 1% on excess over £770
Reduced rate	4.85% on £105.01 to £770 weekly 1% on excess over £770 (no rebate even if contracted-out)

Notes

[1]   Earnings from the LEL, up to and including the primary threshold (PT), count towards the employee's basic state pension, even though no contributions are paid on those earnings. Similarly, earnings between the LEL and the primary threshold count towards the employee's entitlement to certain benefits including the second state pension (S2P). Employees in contracted-out employment earn no S2P rights and receive a rebate of contributions of 1.6 per cent. This applies from the LEL to the UEL, so earnings from LEL to PT attract a 'negative' contribution of 1.6 per cent and the rate for earnings from PT to UEL becomes 9.4 per cent.

Monthly LEL and UEL figures are calculated per SI 2001/1004, reg. 11 (as amended by SI 2008/133). The equivalent annual figures are calculated as 52 times the weekly figure (NIM 12021).

Class 1 secondary (employer) contributions 2008–09	
Secondary earnings threshold (ST)	£105 weekly £453 monthly £5,435 yearly
Not contracted-out rate	12.8% on earnings above the ST
Contracted-out rate[1]	9.1% for salary-related (COSR) and 11.4% for money-purchase (COMP) schemes (plus 3.7% and 1.4% rebates for earnings from LEL to ST), then 12.8% above UEL.

Notes

[1]   As for employees, earnings between the LEL and the ST will count towards the employee's entitlement to S2P. Employers with contracted-out occupational pension schemes receive a rebate of contributions for scheme members of 3.7 per cent (COSR) or 1.4 per cent (COMP). This applies from the LEL to the UEL, so earnings from LEL to ST attract a 'negative' contribution and the rate for earnings from ST to UEL is reduced as shown.

[¶9-150]   Class 1 NIC: 2007–08

Class 1 contributions

Class 1 primary (employee) contributions 2007–08	
Lower earnings limit (LEL)[1]	£87 weekly £377 monthly £4,524 yearly
Primary threshold (PT)	£100 weekly £435 monthly £5,225 yearly
Upper earnings limit (UEL)	£670 weekly £2,904 monthly £34,840 yearly
Rate on earnings up to PT[1]	0%
Not contracted-out rate	11% on £100.01 to £670 weekly 1% on excess over £670

National Insurance Contributions

Class 1 primary (employee) contributions 2007–08	
Contracted-out rate[1]	9.4% on £100.01 to £670 weekly 1% on excess over £670 (1.6% also rebated for earnings from LEL £87 to PT £100)
Reduced rate	4.85% on £100.01 to £670 weekly 1% on excess over £670 (no rebate even if contracted-out)

Notes

[1] Earnings from the LEL, up to and including the PT will count towards the employee's basic state pension, even though no contributions will have been paid on those earnings. Similarly, earnings between the LEL and the PT will count towards the employee's entitlement to certain benefits including the additional pension, the second state pension (S2P). Employees in contracted-out employment receive a rebate of contributions of 1.6%. This applies from the LEL to the UEL, so earnings from LEL to PT attract a 'negative' contribution of 1.6% and the rate for earnings from PT to UEL becomes 9.4%.

Class 1 secondary (employer) contributions 2007–08	
Secondary earnings threshold (ST)	£100 weekly £435 monthly £5,225 yearly
Not contracted-out rate	12.8% on earnings above threshold
Contracted-out rate[1]	9.1% for salary-related (COSR) and 11.4% for money-purchase (COMP) schemes (plus 3.7% and 1.4% rebates for earnings from LEL to secondary threshold), then 12.8% above UEL.
Reduced rate	12.8% on earnings above the threshold, rebated as above if the woman is in contracted-out employment

Notes

[1] As for employees, earnings between the LEL and the ST will count towards the employee's entitlement to S2P. Employers with contracted-out occupational pension schemes receive a rebate of contributions for scheme members of 3.7% (COSR) or 1.4% (COMP). This applies from the LEL to the UEL, so earnings from LEL to ST attract a 'negative' contribution and the rate for earnings from ST to UEL is reduced as shown.

[¶9-200]   Class 1 NIC: 2006–07

Class 1 contributions

Class 1 primary (employee) contributions 2006–07	
Lower earnings limit (LEL)[1]	£84 weekly £364 monthly £4,368 yearly
Primary threshold (PT)	£97 weekly £420 monthly £5,035 yearly
Upper earnings limit (UEL)	£645 weekly £2,795 monthly £33,540 yearly
Rate on earnings up to PT[1]	0%
Not contracted-out rate	11% on £97.01 to £645 weekly 1% on excess over £645
Contracted-out rate[1]	9.4% on £97.01 to £645 weekly 1% on excess over £645 (1.6% also rebated for earnings from LEL £84 to PT £97)
Reduced rate	4.85% on £97.01 to £645 weekly 1% on excess over £645 (no rebate even if contracted-out)

Notes
[1]   As 2007–08 above.

Class 1 secondary (employer) contributions 2006–07	
Secondary earnings threshold (ST)	£97 weekly £420 monthly £5,035 yearly
Not contracted-out rate	12.8% on earnings above the ST
Contracted-out rate[1]	9.3% for salary-related (COSR) and 11.8% for money-purchase (COMP) schemes on earnings from secondary threshold to the UEL, then 12.8% on earnings above the UEL (plus 3.5% (COSR) and 1% (COMP) rebates for earnings from LEL to ST)

National Insurance Contributions

Class 1 secondary (employer) contributions 2006–07	
Reduced rate	12.8% on earnings above the ST, rebated as above if the woman is in contracted-out employment

Notes

(1) As for employees, earnings between the LEL and the PT will count towards the employee's entitlement to SERPS and S2P. Employers with contracted-out occupational pension schemes receive a rebate of contributions for scheme members of 3.5% (COSR) or 1% (COMP). This applies from the LEL to the UEL, so earnings from LEL to PT attract a 'negative' contribution and the rate for earnings from PT to UEL is reduced as shown.

[¶9-350]   Class 1A contributions

Since 6 April 2000, employers (but not employees) have paid NICs on an annual basis on benefits in kind provided to employees earning at the rate of £8,500 p.a. or more or to directors (SSCBA 1992, s. 10). Contributions for the year are due by 19 July following the end of the tax year to which they relate (22 July for electronic payment). Rates applying are always the full Class 1 secondary (employer) rate for each year, with no rebate for contracted-out employees. They have been as follows:

2005-06 to 2010-11 – 12.8%

For rates of interest on late paid Class 1A contributions, see ¶9-650

[¶9-400]   Return deadlines for Class 1 and 1A contributions

Forms	Date	Penalty provision
End of year returns P14, P35, P38 and P38A	19 May following year of assessment	TMA 1970, s. 98A (to change to FA 2009, Sch. 55 once enacted)
P11D(b)	6 July following year of assessment	SI 2001/1004, reg. 81(2)

Note

In cases of PAYE and NIC default there are provisions to prevent double charging. Class 1A contributions are recorded annually in arrears. Penalties will only be imposed if there is a delay in the submission of the relevant year's PAYE return or P11Ds and P11D(b).

[¶9-450]   Class 1B contributions

Class 1B contributions are payable by employers on the amount of earnings in a PAYE settlement agreement (PSA) that are chargeable to Class 1 or Class 1A NICs, together with the total amount of income tax payable under the agreement (SSCBA 1992, s. 10A). Class 1B contributions are charged at the same rate as Class 1A contributions (see above) and are payable by 19 October after the end of the tax year to which the PSA applies (22 October for electronic payment).

[¶9-500] Class 2 contributions

Class 2 contributions are paid at a flat rate by a self-employed person unless he has applied for and been granted exception because his earnings are below the small earnings exception (SEE) limit for Class 2 contributions. If a person is excepted, he may still pay the contributions voluntarily to keep up his right to the benefits they provide.

Rates and SEE limit

| | Weekly contribution rate | | | |
Tax year	Rate £	Share fishermen £	Volunteer development workers £	Small earnings exception limit £
2010–11	2.40	3.05	4.85	5,075
2009–10	2.40	3.05	4.75	5,075
2008–09	2.30	2.95	4.50	4,825
2007–08	2.20	2.85	4.35	4,635
2006–07	2.10	2.75	4.20	4,465

[¶9-550] Class 3 contributions

Class 3 contributions are paid voluntarily by persons not liable for contributions, or who have been excepted from Class 2 contributions, or whose contribution record is insufficient to qualify for benefits. They are paid at a flat rate.

Rate and earnings factor

Tax year	Weekly contribution rate £	Earnings factor for each contribution in col. 2 £
2010–11	12.05	97.00
2009–10	12.05	95.00
2008–09	8.10	90.00
2007–08	7.80	87.00
2006–07	7.55	84.00

National Insurance Contributions

[¶9-600] Class 4 contributions

Self-employed people whose profits or gains are over a certain amount have to pay Class 4 contributions as well as Class 2 contributions. These contributions are earnings-related and paid at a main rate on trading profits (earnings) between the lower and upper annual limits (which are the same as the Class 1 earnings threshold and upper earnings limit), with an additional 1 per cent on profits above the upper limit since 6 April 2003.

Tax year	Rate on profits between upper and lower limits %	Annual lower profits limit £	Annual upper profits limit £	Rate on profits in excess of upper limit %	Maximum contribution £
2010–11	8	5,715	43,875	1	unlimited
2009–10	8	5,715	43,875	1	unlimited
2008–09	8	5,435	40,040	1	unlimited
2007–08	8	5,225	34,840	1	unlimited
2006–07	8	5,035	33,540	1	unlimited

Notes
(1) The maximum Class 4 contribution is now based on 8 per cent of profits above the lower annual limit up to the upper annual limit, plus 1 per cent of any excess, and 53 weeks of Class 2 contributions. Until April 2003, the value was fixed, as the Class 4 liability was capped, but the introduction of the 1 per cent contribution on trading profits above the annual limit means that the annual maximum has become variable, since the 1 per cent is without limit.
(2) It was announced in the June 2010 Budget that Class 4 contributions for 2011-12 will be 9 per cent of profits above the lower annual limit up to the upper annual limit, plus 2 per cent of any excess. The upper annual limit will continue to be aligned with the income tax higher rate threshold.

[¶9-650] Rates of interest on overdue National Insurance contributions

The tables at ¶1-500 give the rates of interest applicable under FA 1989, s. 178 or FA 2009 and prescribed rates of interest on late-paid National Insurance contributions (SSCBA 1992, Sch. 1, para 6(2)).

[¶9-670] Rates of interest on National Insurance contributions repayments

Interest on NIC repayments qualifying for repayment interest is given in the tables at ¶1-550.

TAX CREDITS

[¶10-000]   Working tax credits

Maximum rates 2006–07 to 2010–11

Element	2010–11 £	2009–10 £	2008–09 £	2007–08 £	2006–07 £
Basic element	1,920	1,890	1,800	1,730	1,665
Disability element	2,570	2,530	2,405	2,310	2,225
Severe disability element	1,095	1,075	1,020	980	945
30-hour element	790	775	735	705	680
Second adult element	1,890	1,860	1,770	1,700	1,640
Lone parent element	1,890	1,860	1,770	1,700	1,640
50-plus element:					
(a) working at least 16 hours but less than 30 hours per week	1,320	1,300	1,235	1,185	1,140
(b) working at least 30 hours per week	1,965	1,935	1,840	1,770	1,705
Childcare element: percentage of eligible costs covered	80%	80%	80%	80%	80%
• maximum eligible cost for one child	175	175	175	175	175
• maximum eligible cost for two or more children	300	300	300	300	300

Notes

[1] It was announced in the Emergency Budget 2010 that the Government will use the consumer prices index (CPI) for the price indexation of tax credits from April 2011.

[¶10-100]   Child tax credits

Maximum rates 2006–07 to 2010–11

Element	Circumstance	Maximum annual rate 2010–11 £	Maximum annual rate 2009–10 £	Maximum annual rate 2008–09 £	Maximum annual rate 2007–08 £	Maximum annual rate 2006–07 £
Family	Normal case	545	545	545	545	545
	Where there is a child under the age of one	1,090	1,090	1,090	1,090	1,090
Individual	Each child or young person	2,300	2,235	2,085	1,845	1,765
	Each disabled child or young person	5,015	4,905	4,625	4,285	4,115
	Each severely disabled child or young person	6,110	5,980	5,645	5,265	5,060

Notes
[1] It was announced in the Emergency Budget 2010 that the Government will use the consumer prices index (CPI) for the price indexation of tax credits from April 2011. The child element of the child tax credit will increase by £150 above CPI in April 2011 and by £60 above CPI in April 2012.
[2] In the Emergency Budget 2010 it was announced that the 'baby element' of the child tax credit (i.e. where there is a child under the age of one) will be abolished from April 2011.

Income thresholds and withdrawal rates 2006–07 to 2010–11

	2010–11	2009–10	2008–09	2007–08	2006–07
First income threshold	£6,420	£6,420	£6,420	£5,220	£5,220
First withdrawal rate	39%	39%	39%	37%	37%
Second income threshold	£50,000	£50,000	£50,000	£50,000	£50,000
Second withdrawal rate	6.67%	6.67%	6.67%	6.67%	6.67%
First threshold for those entitled to child tax credit only	£16,190	£16,040	£15.575	£14,495	£14,155
Income disregard	£25,000	£25,000	£25,000	£25,000	£25,000

Notes
[1] The Emergency Budget 2010 announced changes to the income thresholds and withdrawal rates for 2011-12 so that they will become:

* first withdrawal rate 41 per cent;
* second income threshold £40,000;
* second withdrawal rate 41 per cent; and
* income disregard £10,000.

STATE BENEFITS AND STATUTORY PAYMENTS

[¶10-500]   Taxable state benefits

(ITEPA 2003, s. 577, 580, 660)

(BTR: ¶490-000ff.)

The following benefits are liable to income tax.

Rates were most recently updated by the *Social Security Benefits Up-rating Order* 2010 (SI 2010/793) and may be found via the DWP website at *http://www.dwp.gov.uk/ directgov/*.

The site of the Social Security Agency of Northern Ireland also contains relevant information, and is better presented: http://www.dsdni.gov.uk/benefit_rates.

Another useful site is the 'toolkit' area of http://www.rightsnet.org.uk/, which lists the current benefit and tax credit rates.

Benefit	Weekly rate from				
	April 2010 £	April 2009 £	April 2008 £	April 2007 £	April 2006 £
Bereavement allowance	97.65	95.25	90.70	87.30	84.25
Carer's allowance	53.90	53.10	50.55	48.65	46.95
Dependent adults					
with retirement pension[1]	57.05	57.05	54.35	52.30	50.50
with carer's allowance[1]	31.70	31.70	30.20	29.05	28.05
with severe disablement allowance	31.90	31.90	30.40	29.25	28.05
Employment & Support Allowance					
Age 25+ contributions-based ESA	65.45	64.30	n/a	n/a	n/a
Industrial death benefit: Widow's pension					
Permanent rate –					
higher	97.65	95.25	90.70	87.30	84.25
lower	29.30	28.58	27.21	26.19	25.28

State Benefits and Stat. Payments

Benefit	Weekly rate from				
	April 2010 £	April 2009 £	April 2008 £	April 2007 £	April 2006 £
Incapacity benefit (long term)					
Rate	91.40	89.80	84.50	81.35	78.50
Increase for age:					
higher rate	15.00	15.65	17.75	17.10	16.50
lower rate	5.80	6.55	8.90	8.55	8.25
Jobseeker's allowance See ¶10-600.					
Incapacity benefit (short term)					
Higher rate:					
under pensionable age[2]	81.60	80.15	75.40	72.55	70.05
over pensionable age[2]	91.40	89.80	84.50	81.35	78.50
Non-contributory retirement pension					
Standard rate	58.50	57.05	54.35	52.30	50.50
Age addition (at age 80)	0.25	0.25	0.25	0.25	0.25
Retirement pension					
Standard rate	97.65	95.25	90.70	87.30	84.25
Age addition (at age 80)	0.25	0.25	0.25	0.25	0.25
SSP, SMP, SPP and SAP See ¶10-650ff.					
Widow's pension[3]					
Pension (standard rate)	97.65	95.25	90.70	87.30	84.25
Widowed parent's allowance	97.65	95.25	90.70	87.30	84.25

Notes

[1] No new claims for adult dependency increases payable with the state retirement pension or the carer's allowance may be made on or after 6 April 2010. Adult dependency increases already in payment immediately before 6 April 2010 will be phased out between 2010 and 2020.

[2] Pensionable age is 60 for women, 65 for men. From 6 April 2020, the state pension age for women will be 65, the same as for men. From 2010, women's state pension age is gradually increasing by one month every two months to bring it up to age 65 by 2020.

[3] Bereavement allowance replaced widow's pension from 9 April 2001 for all new claims by widows and widowers.

[4] It was announced in the June 2010 Budget that the Government will use the consumer prices index (CPI) for the price indexation of benefits from April 2011.

[¶10-550]   Non-taxable state benefits

(ITEPA 2003, s. 677(1): see also EIM 76100)

(BTR: ¶490-000ff.)

The following UK social security benefits are wholly exempt from tax, except where indicated otherwise.

- Attendance allowance
- Back to work bonus (see EIM 76223)
- Bereavement payment (see EIM 76171)
- Child benefit
- Child's special allowance
- Child tax credit
- Constant attendance allowance: see 'Industrial injuries benefit'
- Council tax benefit
- Disability living allowance
- Employment & support allowance — income-related (ESA(IR)) (see EIM 76186)
- Exceptionally severe disablement allowance: see 'Industrial injuries benefit'
- Guardian's allowance
- Housing benefit
- Incapacity benefit (for first 28 weeks only – see EIM 76180)
- Income support (certain payments – see EIM 76190)
- Industrial injuries benefit ('a general term covering industrial injuries pension, reduced earnings allowance, retirement allowance, constant attendance allowance and exceptionally severe disablement allowance': EIM 76100)
- Invalidity benefit (replaced by Incapacity benefit from April 1995 but still payable where invalidity commenced before April 1995)
- In-work credit, In-work emergency discretion fund payment, In-work emergency fund payment
- Maternity allowance (see EIM 76361)
- Pensioner's Christmas bonus
- Pension credit
- Reduced earnings allowance: see 'Industrial injuries benefit'
- Retirement allowance: see 'Industrial injuries benefit'
- Return to work credit and self-employment credit
- Severe disablement allowance
- Statutory redundancy payments (ITEPA 2003, s. 309)
- Social fund payments – budgeting loan, cold weather payment, community care grant, crisis loan, funeral payment, maternity payment, winter fuel payments
- Vaccine damage
- War widow's pension (see EIM 76103)
- Winter fuel payment (or 'cold weather payment')
- Working tax credit

See EIM 74302 for the tax treatment of various special payments to those who have served in the armed forces and see EIM 74700 for allowances payable to civilians in respect of war injuries.

See EIM 76009 for the treatment of certain foreign social security payments that are exempt from tax.

State Benefits and Stat. Payments

Benefit rates

	Weekly rate from				
Benefit	April 2010 £	April 2009 £	April 2008 £	April 2007 £	April 2006 £
Attendance allowance					
Higher rate (day and night)	71.40	70.35	67.00	64.50	62.25
Lower rate (day or night)	47.80	47.10	44.85	43.15	41.65
Child benefit(2)					
For the eldest qualifying child	20.30	20.00	18.80	18.10	17.45
For each other child	13.40	13.20	12.55	12.10	11.70
Constant attendance allowance					
Exceptional rate	116.80	115.00	109.60	105.40	101.80
Intermediate rate	87.60	86.25	82.20	79.05	76.35
Normal maximum rate	58.40	57.50	54.80	52.70	50.90
Part-time rate	29.20	28.75	27.40	26.35	25.45
Exceptionally severe disablement allowance	58.40	57.50	54.80	52.70	50.90
Employment & support allowance – income-related based (ESA(IR)) Involves over 30 potential components					
Maternity and paternity allowances	See ¶10-700ff.				
Disability living allowance (care component)					
Higher rate	71.40	70.35	67.00	64.50	62.25
Middle rate	47.80	47.10	44.85	43.15	41.65
Lower rate	18.95	18.65	17.75	17.10	16.50
Disability living allowance (mobility component)					
Higher rate	49.85	49.10	46.75	45.00	43.45
Lower rate	18.95	18.65	17.75	17.10	16.50

	Weekly rate from				
Benefit	April 2010 £	April 2009 £	April 2008 £	April 2007 £	April 2006 £
Incapacity benefit (short term)[3] Lower rate:					
under pensionable age[4]	68.95	67.75	63.75	61.35	59.20
over pensionable age[4]	87.75	86.20	81.10	78.05	75.35

Notes

[1] Child special allowance and child dependency increases with retirement pension, widow's benefit, short-term incapacity benefit at the higher rate and long-term incapacity benefit, invalid care allowance, severe disablement allowance, higher rate individual death benefit, unemployability supplement and short-term incapacity benefit if beneficiary over pension age.

[2] It was announced in the June 2010 Budget that both rates of child benefit will be frozen for three years from 2011-12. Child benefit increases for 2009 were paid from January rather than April 2009.

[3] Incapacity benefit and contributory employment & support allowance (ESA(C)) are taxable, under the *Income Tax (Earnings and Pensions) Act* 2003, Part 10, Chapter 3, except for short-term benefit payable at the lower rate. It is not taxable, however, if the recipient started receiving invalidity benefit or sickness benefit before 6 April 1995 and has continued receiving long-term incapacity benefit since then.

[4] Pensionable age is 60 for women, 65 for men. From 6 April 2020, the state pension age for women will be 65, the same as for men. From 2010, women's state pension age is gradually increasing by one month every two months to bring it up to age 65 by 2020.

[5] It was announced in the June 2010 Budget that the Government will use the consumer prices index (CPI) for the price indexation of benefits from April 2011 (but see footnote (2) above regarding the freezing of child benefit rates).

[¶10-600]   Income support and jobseeker's allowance

(BTR: ¶490-250)

	Weekly rate from				
Benefit: Income support	April 2010 £	April 2009 £	April 2008 £	April 2007 £	April 2006 £
Single					
Under 18 usual rate	51.85	50.95	47.95	35.65	34.60
Under 18 – higher rate payable in specific circumstances	51.85	50.95	47.95	46.85	45.50
18 to 24	51.85	50.95	47.95	46.85	45.50
25 or over	65.45	64.30	60.50	59.15	57.45
Lone parent					
Under 18 – usual rate	51.85	50.95	47.95	35.65	34.60
Under 18 – higher rate payable	51.85	50.95	47.95	46.85	45.50
18 or over	65.45	64.30	60.50	59.15	57.45

Benefit: Income support	Weekly rate from				
	April 2010 £	April 2009 £	April 2008 £	April 2007 £	April 2006 £
Couple					
Both under 18	51.85	50.95	47.95	35.65	34.60
Both under 18, one disabled	51.85	50.95	47.95	46.85	45.50
Both under 18, with resp. for a child	78.30	76.90	72.35	70.70	68.65
One under 18, one 18–24	51.85	50.95	47.95	46.85	45.50
One under 18, one 25+	65.45	64.30	60.50	59.15	57.45
Both 18 or over	102.75	100.95	94.95	92.80	90.10
Dependent children	57.57	56.11	52.59	47.45	45.58

Benefit: Jobseeker's allowance	Weekly rate from				
	April 2010 £	April 2009 £	April 2008 £	April 2007 £	April 2006 £
Contributions based JSA – personal rates					
Under 18	51.85	50.95	47.95	35.65	34.60
18 to 24	51.85	50.95	47.95	46.85	45.50
25 or over	65.45	64.30	60.50	59.15	57.45
Income based JSA – personal allowances					
Under 18	51.85	50.95	47.95	35.65	34.60
18 to 24	51.85	50..95	47.95	46.85	45.50
25 or over	65.45	64.30	60.50	59.15	57.45
Lone parent					
Under 18	51.85	50.95	47.95	35.65	34.60
Under 18 – higher rate payable in specific circumstances	51.85	50.95	47.95	46.85	45.50
18 or over	65.45	64.30	60.50	59.15	57.45
Couple					
Both under 18	51.85	50.95	47.95	35.65	34.60
Both under 18, one disabled	51.85	50.95	47.95	46.85	45.50
Both under 18, with resp. for a child	78.30	76.90	72.35	70.70	68.65
One under 18, one 18–24	51.85	50.95	47.95	46.85	45.50
One under 18, one 25+	65.45	64.30	60.50	59.15	57.45
Both 18 or over	102.75	100.95	94.95	92.80	90.10
Dependent children	57.57	56.11	52.59	47.45	45.58

Premium: Income support and Jobseeker's allowance	Weekly rate from				
	April 2010 £	April 2009 £	April 2008 £	April 2007 £	April 2006 £
Family/lone parent	17.40	17.30	16.75	16.43	16.25
Pensioner					
Single	67.15	65.70	63.55	59.90	56.60
Couple	99.65	97.50	94.40	88.90	83.95
Pensioner (higher)					
Single	67.15	65.70	63.55	59.90	56.60
Couple	99.65	97.50	94.40	88.90	83.95
Disability					
Single	28.00	27.50	25.85	25.25	24.50
Couple	39.85	39.15	36.85	36.00	34.95
Enhanced disability premium					
single rate	13.65	13.40	12.60	12.30	11.95
Disabled child rate	21.00	20.65	19.60	18.76	18.13
Couple rate	19.65	19.30	18.15	17.75	17.25
Severe disability					
Single	53.65	52.85	50.35	48.45	46.75
couple (lower rate)	53.65	52.85	50.35	48.45	46.75
couple (higher rate)	107.30	105.70	100.70	96.90	93.50
Disabled child	52.08	51.24	48.72	46.69	45.08
Carer	30.05	29.50	27.75	27.15	26.35
Bereavement	n/a	n/a	n/a	26.80	26.80

Notes
[1] It was announced in the June 2010 Budget that the Government will use the consumer prices index (CPI) for the price indexation of benefits from April 2011.

State Benefits and Stat. Payments

[¶10-650] Statutory sick pay (SSP)

Employers are liable to pay SSP in any period of incapacity for work to a maximum of 28 weeks at the SSP rate in force. Statutory sick pay is treated as wages and is subject to PAYE income tax and to National Insurance contributions. Statutory sick pay is not payable for certain periods in which statutory maternity pay is being paid.

The amount of SSP payable to an employee depends on the earnings band into which he or she falls. The earnings bands and the associated SSP payments are as follows:

Year to	Average gross weekly earnings £	Weekly SSP rate[1] £
5 April 2011	97.00 or more	79.15
5 April 2010	95.00 or more	79.15
5 April 2009	90.00 or more	75.40
5 April 2008	87.00 or more	72.55
5 April 2007	84.00 or more	70.05

Note

[1] The daily rate of SSP is ascertained by dividing the weekly rate by the number of qualifying days in the week (beginning on Sunday), then multiplying by the number of qualifying days of incapacity in the week, rounded up to the nearest penny.

[2] It was announced in the June 2010 Budget that the Government will use the consumer prices index (CPI) for the price indexation of benefits from April 2011.

Maximum entitlement

An employee reaches his maximum entitlement to SSP in one spell of incapacity when he has been paid 28 times the appropriate rate, i.e. £79.15 × 28 = £2,216.20.

[¶10-700] Statutory maternity pay (SMP)

Women expecting a baby who satisfy the qualifying conditions are entitled to a maximum of 39 weeks' SMP (26 weeks up to April 2007). These include having 'average weekly earnings' of:

* £87 if their baby was due on or before 19 July 2008;
* £90 if their baby was due between 20 July 2008 and 18 July 2009;
* £95 if their baby is due between 19 July 2009 and 17 July 2010; and
* £97 if their baby is due between 18 July 2010 and 16 July 2011.

In other words, 'average weekly earnings' must reach or exceed the then-current NIC LEL in the eight weeks leading up to the fifteenth week before the expected week of childbirth (or placement of an adopted child).

Period	First 6 weeks	Remaining weeks
From 6 April 2010	90% average weekly earnings	Lower of 90% of weekly earnings and £124.88
From 6 April 2009	90% average weekly earnings	Lower of 90% of weekly earnings and £123.06
From 6 April 2008	90% average weekly earnings	Lower of 90% of weekly earnings and £117.18
From 6 April 2007	90% average weekly earnings	Lower of 90% of weekly earnings and £112.75
From 6 April 2006	90% average weekly earnings	Lower of 90% of weekly earnings and £108.85

Note
[1] It was announced in the Emergency Budget 2010 that the Government will use the consumer prices index (CPI) for the price indexation of benefits from April 2011.

[¶10-750]   Statutory paternity pay (SPP)

SPP was introduced from 6 April 2003 and is payable for a maximum of two weeks. For babies born from 4 April 2011, a mother may return to work early and pass her entitlement to leave and lower rate benefit to the father, for up to 26 weeks. This may affect families whose babies are born prematurely from November 2010 onwards. The weekly rate of SPP is as follows:

Period	Weekly rate of SPP
From 6 April 2010	Lower of 90% of average weekly earnings and £124.88
From 6 April 2009	Lower of 90% of average weekly earnings and £123.06
From 6 April 2008	Lower of 90% of average weekly earnings and £117.18
From 6 April 2007	Lower of 90% of average weekly earnings and £112.75
From 6 April 2006	Lower of 90% of average weekly earnings and £108.85

Notes
[1] It was announced in the Emergency Budget 2010 that the Government will use the consumer prices index (CPI) for the price indexation of benefits from April 2011.

Additional statutory paternity pay has been introduced for fathers of children due on or after 3 April 2011 if they take statutory leave during the mother's maternity pay period after she has returned to work. This will be paid at the same rate as SPP.

State Benefits and Stat. Payments

[¶10-800]   Statutory adoption pay (SAP)

SAP was introduced, like SPP, in April 2003.

Employees who are adopting a child and are notified that they have been matched with a child or received official notification that they are eligible to adopt a child from abroad who satisfy the qualifying conditions are entitled to a maximum of 39 weeks' SAP. These include having average weekly earnings of:

- £87 if they are notified that they have been matched with a child or received official notification that they are eligible to adopt a child from abroad on or before 5 April 2008;

- £90 if they are notified that they have been matched with a child or received official notification that they are eligible to adopt a child from abroad on or after 6 April 2008.

- £95 if they are notified that they have been matched with a child or received official notification that they are eligible to adopt a child from abroad on or after 6 April 2009.

- £97 if they are notified that they have been matched with a child or received official notification that they are eligible to adopt a child from abroad on or after 6 April 2010.

The weekly rate is the lesser of £124.88 or 90 per cent of the employee's average weekly earnings. The adoptive parents are treated in effect as if they have had a baby and qualified for SMP. Rates since 2003 have been as shown in the SMP table above.

It was announced in the Emergency Budget 2010 that the Government will use the consumer prices index (CPI) for the price indexation of benefits from April 2011.

GENERAL

Retail prices index

[¶11-000]   Retail prices index: general

The Retail Prices Index (RPI), issued by the Department of Employment, is used to calculate the indexation allowance for the purposes of calculating capital gains on corporation tax. (Since April 1998, the indexation allowance has ceased to be available when calculating gains liable to capital gains tax.) Certain personal and other reliefs are also linked to the RPI, subject to Parliament determining otherwise.

With effect from February 1987 the reference date to which the price level in each subsequent month is related was changed from 'January 1974 = 100' to 'January 1987 = 100'.

Movements in the RPI in the months after January 1987 are calculated with reference to January 1987 = 100. (With a base of January 1974 = 100, January 1987's RPI was 394.5). A new formula has been provided by the Department of Employment for calculating movements in the index over periods which span January 1987:

'The index for the later month (January 1987 = 100) is multiplied by the index for January 1987 (January 1974 = 100) and divided by the index for the earlier month (January 1974 = 100). 100 is subtracted to give the percentage change between the two months.'

CCH has prepared the following table in accordance with this formula:

	1982	1983	1984	1985	1986	1987	1988	1989	1990	1991
Jan.		82.61	86.84	91.20	96.25	100.0	103.3	111.0	119.5	130.2
Feb.		82.97	87.20	91.94	96.60	100.4	103.7	111.8	120.2	130.9
March	79.44	83.12	87.48	92.80	96.73	100.6	104.1	112.3	121.4	131.4
April	81.04	84.28	88.64	94.78	97.67	101.8	105.8	114.3	125.1	133.1
May	81.62	84.64	88.97	95.21	97.85	101.9	106.2	115.0	126.2	133.5
June	81.85	84.84	89.20	95.41	97.79	101.9	106.6	115.4	126.7	134.1
July	81.88	85.30	89.10	95.23	97.52	101.8	106.7	115.5	126.8	133.8
Aug.	81.90	85.68	89.94	95.49	97.82	102.1	107.9	115.8	128.1	134.1
Sept.	81.85	86.06	90.11	95.44	98.30	102.4	108.4	116.6	129.3	134.6
Oct.	82.26	86.36	90.67	95.59	98.45	102.9	109.5	117.5	130.3	135.1
Nov.	82.66	86.67	90.95	95.92	99.29	103.4	110.0	118.5	130.0	135.6
Dec.	82.51	86.89	90.87	96.05	99.62	103.3	110.3	118.8	129.9	135.7

General

	1992	1993	1994	1995	1996	1997	1998	1999	2000	2001
Jan.	135.6	137.9	141.3	146.0	150.2	154.4	159.5	163.4	166.6	171.1
Feb.	136.3	138.8	142.1	146.9	150.9	155.0	160.3	163.7	167.5	172.0
March	136.7	139.3	142.5	147.5	151.5	155.4	160.8	164.1	168.4	172.2
April	138.8	140.6	144.2	149.0	152.6	156.3	162.6	165.2	170.1	173.1
May	139.3	141.1	144.7	149.6	152.9	156.9	163.5	165.6	170.7	174.2
June	139.3	141.0	144.7	149.8	153.0	157.5	163.4	165.6	171.1	174.4
July	138.8	140.7	144.0	149.1	152.4	157.5	163.0	165.1	170.5	173.3
Aug.	138.9	141.3	144.7	149.9	153.1	158.5	163.7	165.5	170.5	174.0
Sept.	139.4	141.9	145.0	150.6	153.8	159.3	164.4	166.2	171.7	174.6
Oct.	139.9	141.8	145.2	149.8	153.8	159.5	164.5	166.5	171.6	174.3
Nov.	139.7	141.6	145.3	149.8	153.9	159.6	164.4	166.7	172.1	173.6
Dec.	139.2	141.9	146.0	150.7	154.4	160.0	164.4	167.3	172.2	173.4

	2002	2003	2004	2005	2006	2007	2008	2009	2010	2011
Jan.	173.3	178.4	183.1	188.9	193.4	201.6	209.8	210.1	217.9	
Feb.	173.8	179.3	183.8	189.6	194.2	203.1	211.4	211.4	219.2	
March	174.5	179.9	184.6	190.5	195.0	204.4	212.1	211.3	220.7	
April	175.7	181.2	185.7	191.6	196.5	205.4	214.0	211.5	222.8	
May	176.2	181.5	186.5	192.0	197.7	206.2	215.1	212.8	223.6	
June	176.2	181.3	186.8	192.2	198.5	207.3	216.8	213.4		
July	175.9	181.3	186.8	192.2	198.5	206.1	216.5	213.4		
Aug.	176.4	181.6	187.4	192.6	199.2	207.3	217.2	214.4		
Sept.	177.6	182.5	188.1	193.1	200.1	208.0	218.4	215.3		
Oct.	177.9	182.6	188.6	193.3	200.4	208.9	217.7	216.0		
Nov.	178.2	182.7	189.0	193.6	201.1	209.7	216.0	216.6		
Dec.	178.5	183.5	189.9	194.1	202.7	210.9	212.9	218.0		

The RPI figures for the month of December 1974 to December 1981 are given below for the purpose of calculating partnership retirement annuities.

	1974	1975	1976	1977	1978	1979	1980	1981
December	116.9	146.0	168.0	188.4	204.2	239.4	275.6	308.8

[¶11-020] Indexation allowance up to 5 April 1998
(TCGA 1992, s. 53 and 54)

Indexation allowance in respect of changes shown by the retail prices indices for months after April 1998 shall be allowed only for the purposes of corporation tax. For disposals made by individuals, trustees and personal representatives after April 1998 and before 6 April 2008, indexation allowance up to 5 April 1998 and taper relief (see above) could be obtained.

The table below sets out the figure that is determined by the formula of $(RD - RI)/RI$ where RD is the Retail Prices Index for April 1998 and RI is the Retail Prices Index for the later of March 1982 and the date that the item of relevant allowable expenditure was incurred. The indexation allowance is the aggregate of the indexed rise in each item of relevant allowable expenditure. In relation to each item of expenditure, the indexed rise is a sum produced by multiplying the amount of that item of expenditure by the appropriate figure in the table below.

	Jan.	Feb.	Mar.	Apr.	May	Jun.	Jul.	Aug.	Sep.	Oct.	Nov.	Dec.
1982	–	–	1.047	1.006	0.992	0.987	0.986	0.985	0.987	0.977	0.967	0.971
1983	0.968	0.960	0.956	0.929	0.921	0.917	0.906	0.898	0.889	0.883	0.876	0.871
1984	0.872	0.865	0.859	0.834	0.828	0.823	0.825	0.808	0.804	0.793	0.788	0.789
1985	0.783	0.769	0.752	0.716	0.708	0.704	0.707	0.703	0.704	0.701	0.695	0.693
1986	0.689	0.683	0.681	0.665	0.662	0.663	0.667	0.662	0.654	0.652	0.638	0.632
1987	0.626	0.620	0.616	0.597	0.596	0.596	0.597	0.593	0.588	0.580	0.573	0.574
1988	0.574	0.568	0.562	0.537	0.531	0.525	0.524	0.507	0.500	0.485	0.478	0.474
1989	0.465	0.454	0.448	0.423	0.414	0.409	0.408	0.404	0.395	0.384	0.372	0.369
1990	0.361	0.353	0.339	0.300	0.288	0.283	0.282	0.269	0.258	0.248	0.251	0.252
1991	0.249	0.242	0.237	0.222	0.218	0.213	0.215	0.213	0.208	0.204	0.199	0.198
1992	0.199	0.193	0.189	0.171	0.167	0.167	0.171	0.171	0.166	0.162	0.164	0.168
1993	0.179	0.171	0.167	0.156	0.152	0.153	0.156	0.151	0.146	0.147	0.148	0.146
1994	0.151	0.144	0.141	0.128	0.124	0.124	0.129	0.124	0.121	0.120	0.119	0.114
1995	0.114	0.107	0.102	0.091	0.087	0.085	0.091	0.085	0.080	0.085	0.085	0.079
1996	0.083	0.078	0.073	0.066	0.063	0.063	0.067	0.062	0.057	0.057	0.057	0.053
1997	0.053	0.049	0.046	0.040	0.036	0.032	0.032	0.026	0.021	0.019	0.019	0.016
1998	0.019	0.014	0.011	–	–	–	–	–	–	–	–	–

General

[¶11-480]   RPI: March 2010 to May 2010

Tables follow showing the indexed rise to be used for disposals between March 2010 and May 2010. The amount of indexation allowances is restricted where the indexation allowance gives rise to a loss.

RD Month (Mar. 2010–May. 2010) January 1987 = 100

	2010 Mar.	Apr.	May
RI Month			
1982 *Mar.*	1.778	1.805	1.815
April	1.723	1.749	1.759
May	1.704	1.730	1.739
June	1.696	1.722	1.732
July	1.696	1.721	1.731
Aug.	1.695	1.720	1.730
Sept.	1.696	1.722	1.732
Oct.	1.683	1.709	1.718
Nov.	1.670	1.695	1.705
Dec.	1.675	1.700	1.710
1983 *Jan.*	1.672	1.697	1.707
Feb.	1.660	1.685	1.695
Mar.	1.655	1.681	1.690
April	1.619	1.643	1.653
May	1.608	1.632	1.642
June	1.601	1.626	1.636
July	1.587	1.612	1.621
Aug.	1.576	1.600	1.610
Sept.	1.565	1.589	1.598
Oct.	1.556	1.580	1.589
Nov.	1.547	1.571	1.580
Dec.	1.540	1.564	1.573
1984 *Jan.*	1.541	1.566	1.575
Feb.	1.531	1.555	1.564
Mar.	1.523	1.547	1.556
April	1.490	1.513	1.522
May	1.481	1.504	1.513
June	1.474	1.498	1.507
July	1.477	1.501	1.510
Aug.	1.454	1.477	1.486
Sept.	1.449	1.472	1.481
Oct.	1.434	1.457	1.466
Nov.	1.427	1.450	1.458
Dec.	1.429	1.452	1.461
1985 *Jan.*	1.420	1.443	1.452
Feb.	1.401	1.423	1.432
Mar.	1.378	1.401	1.409
April	1.329	1.351	1.359
May	1.318	1.340	1.349
June	1.313	1.335	1.344
July	1.317	1.339	1.348
Aug.	1.311	1.333	1.342
Sept.	1.313	1.335	1.343
Oct.	1.309	1.331	1.339
Nov.	1.301	1.323	1.331
Dec.	1.298	1.320	1.328
1986 *Jan.*	1.293	1.315	1.323

RD Month (Mar. 2010–May. 2010) January 1987 = 100

	2010		
	Mar.	Apr.	May
RI Month			
Feb.	1.285	1.306	1.315
Mar.	1.282	1.303	1.312
April	1.260	1.281	1.289
May	1.256	1.277	1.285
June	1.257	1.278	1.286
July	1.263	1.285	1.293
Aug.	1.256	1.278	1.286
Sept.	1.245	1.266	1.275
Oct.	1.242	1.263	1.271
Nov.	1.223	1.244	1.252
Dec.	1.215	1.237	1.245
1987 Jan.	1.207	1.228	1.236
Feb.	1.198	1.219	1.227
Mar.	1.194	1.215	1.223
April	1.168	1.189	1.196
May	1.166	1.186	1.194
June	1.166	1.186	1.194
July	1.168	1.189	1.196
Aug.	1.162	1.182	1.190
Sept.	1.155	1.176	1.184
Oct.	1.145	1.165	1.173
Nov.	1.134	1.155	1.162
Dec.	1.136	1.157	1.165
1988 Jan.	1.136	1.157	1.165
Feb.	1.128	1.149	1.156
Mar.	1.120	1.140	1.148
April	1.086	1.106	1.113
May	1.078	1.098	1.105
June	1.070	1.090	1.098
July	1.068	1.088	1.096
Aug.	1.045	1.065	1.072
Sept.	1.036	1.055	1.063
Oct.	1.016	1.035	1.042
Nov.	1.006	1.025	1.033
Dec.	1.001	1.020	1.027
1989 Jan.	0.988	1.007	1.014
Feb.	0.974	0.993	1.000
Mar.	0.965	0.984	0.991
April	0.931	0.949	0.956
May	0.919	0.937	0.944
June	0.912	0.931	0.938
July	0.911	0.929	0.936
Aug.	0.906	0.924	0.931
Sept.	0.893	0.911	0.918
Oct.	0.878	0.896	0.903
Nov.	0.862	0.880	0.887
Dec.	0.858	0.875	0.882
1990 Jan.	0.847	0.864	0.871
Feb.	0.836	0.854	0.860
Mar.	0.818	0.835	0.842
April	0.764	0.781	0.787
May	0.749	0.765	0.772

General

RD Month (Mar. 2010–May. 2010) January 1987 = 100

| | 2010 | | |
	Mar.	Apr.	May
RI Month			
June	0.742	0.758	0.765
July	0.741	0.757	0.763
Aug.	0.723	0.739	0.746
Sept.	0.707	0.723	0.729
Oct.	0.694	0.710	0.716
Nov.	0.698	0.714	0.720
Dec.	0.699	0.715	0.721
1991 Jan.	0.695	0.711	0.717
Feb.	0.686	0.702	0.708
Mar.	0.680	0.696	0.702
April	0.658	0.674	0.680
May	0.653	0.669	0.675
June	0.646	0.661	0.667
July	0.649	0.665	0.671
Aug.	0.646	0.661	0.667
Sept.	0.640	0.655	0.661
Oct.	0.634	0.649	0.655
Nov.	0.628	0.643	0.649
Dec.	0.626	0.642	0.648
1992 Jan.	0.628	0.643	0.649
Feb.	0.619	0.635	0.640
Mar.	0.614	0.630	0.636
April	0.590	0.605	0.611
May	0.584	0.599	0.605
June	0.584	0.599	0.605
July	0.590	0.605	0.611
Aug.	0.589	0.604	0.610
Sept.	0.583	0.598	0.604
Oct.	0.578	0.593	0.598
Nov.	0.580	0.595	0.601
Dec.	0.585	0.601	0.606
1993 Jan.	0.600	0.616	0.621
Feb.	0.590	0.605	0.611
Mar.	0.584	0.599	0.605
April	0.570	0.585	0.590
May	0.564	0.579	0.585
June	0.565	0.580	0.586
July	0.569	0.584	0.589
Aug.	0.562	0.577	0.582
Sept.	0.555	0.570	0.576
Oct.	0.556	0.571	0.577
Nov.	0.559	0.573	0.579
Dec.	0.555	0.570	0.576
1994 Jan.	0.562	0.577	0.582
Feb.	0.553	0.568	0,574
Mar.	0.549	0.564	0.569
April	0.531	0.545	0.551
May	0.525	0.540	0.545
June	0.525	0.540	0.545
July	0.533	0.547	0.553
Aug.	0.525	0.540	0.545
Sept.	0.522	0.537	0.542
Oct.	0.520	0.534	0.540
Nov.	0.519	0.533	0.539
Dec.	0.512	0.526	0.532

RD Month (Mar. 2010–May. 2010) January 1987 = 100

| | 2010 | | |
	Mar.	Apr.	May
RI Month			
1995 Jan.	0.512	0.526	0.532
Feb.	0.502	0.517	0.522
Mar.	0.496	0.511	0.516
April	0.481	0.495	0.501
May	0.475	0.489	0.495
June	0.473	0.487	0.493
July	0.480	0.494	0.500
Aug.	0.472	0.486	0.492
Sept.	0.465	0.479	0.485
Oct.	0.473	0.487	0.493
Nov.	0.473	0.487	0.493
Dec.	0.464	0.478	0.484
1996 Jan.	0.469	0.483	0.489
Feb.	0.463	0.476	0.482
Mar.	0.457	0.471	0.476
April	0.446	0.460	0.465
May	0.443	0.457	0.462
June	0.442	0.456	0.461
July	0.448	0.462	0.467
Aug.	0.442	0.455	0.460
Sept.	0.435	0.449	0.454
Oct.	0.435	0.449	0.454
Nov.	0.434	0.448	0.453
Dec.	0.329	0.443	0.448
1997 Jan.	0.429	0.443	0.448
Feb.	0.424	0.437	0.443
Mar.	0.420	0.434	0.439
April	0.412	0.425	0.431
May	0.407	0.420	0.425
June	0.401	0.415	0.420
July	0.401	0.415	0.420
Aug.	0.392	0.406	0.411
Sept.	0.385	0.399	0.404
Oct.	0.384	0.397	0.402
Nov.	0.383	0.396	0.401
Dec.	0.379	0.393	0.398
1998 Jan.	0.384	0.397	0.402
Feb.	0.377	0.390	0.395
Mar.	0.373	0.386	0.391
April	0.357	0.370	0.375
May	0.350	0.363	0.368
June	0.351	0.364	0.368
July	0.354	0.367	0.372
Aug.	0.348	0.361	0.366
Sept.	0.342	0.355	0.360
Oct.	0.342	0.354	0.359
Nov.	0.342	0.355	0.360
Dec.	0.342	0.355	0.360
1999 Jan.	0.351	0.364	0.368
Feb.	0.348	0.361	0.366
Mar.	0.345	0.358	0.363
April	0.336	0.349	0.354
May	0.333	0.345	0.350

RD Month (Mar. 2010–May. 2010) January 1987 = 100

	2010 Mar.	Apr.	May
RI Month			
June	0.333	0.345	0.350
July	0.337	0,349	0.354
Aug.	0.334	0.346	0.351
Sept.	0.328	0.341	0.345
Oct.	0.326	0.338	0.343
Nov.	0.324	0.337	0.341
Dec.	0.319	0.332	0.337
2000 Jan.	0.325	0.337	0.342
Feb.	0.318	0.330	0.335
Mar.	0.311	0.323	0.328
April	0.297	0.310	0.315
May	0.293	0.305	0.310
June	0.290	0.302	0.307
July	0.294	0.307	0.311
Aug.	0.294	0.307	0.311
Sept.	0.285	0.298	0.302
Oct.	0.286	0.298	0.303
Nov.	0.282	0.295	0.299
Dec.	0.282	0.294	0.298
2001 Jan.	0.290	0.302	0.307
Feb.	0.283	0.295	0.300
Mar.	0.282	0.294	0.298
April	0.275	0.287	0.292
May	0.267	0.279	0.284
June	0.265	0.278	0.282
July	0.274	0.286	0.290
Aug.	0.268	0.280	0.285
Sept.	0.264	0.276	0.281
Oct.	0.266	0.278	0.283
Nov.	0.271	0.283	0.288
Dec.	0.273	0.285	0.290
2002 Jan.	0.274	0.286	0.290
Feb.	0.270	0.282	0.287
Mar.	0.265	0.277	0.281
April	0.256	0.268	0.273
May	0.253	0.264	0.269
June	0.253	0.264	0.269
July	0.255	0.267	0.271
Aug.	0.251	0.263	0.268
Sept.	0.243	0.255	0.259
Oct.	0.241	0.252	0.257
Nov.	0.238	0.250	0.255
Dec.	0.236	0.248	0.253
2003 Jan.	0.237	0.249	0.253
Feb.	0.231	0.243	0.247
Mar.	0.227	0.238	0.243
April	0.218	0.230	0.234
May	0.216	0.228	0.232
June	0.217	0.229	0.233
July	0.217	0.229	0.233
Aug.	0.215	0.227	0.231
Sep.	0.209	0.221	0.225

RD Month (Mar. 2010–May. 2010) January 1987 = 100

	2010		
	Mar.	*Apr.*	*May*
RI Month			
Oct.	0.209	0.220	0.225
Nov.	0.208	0.219	0.224
Dec.	0.203	0.214	0.219
2004 *Jan.*	0.205	0.217	0.221
Feb.	0.201	0.212	0.217
Mar.	0.196	0.207	0.211
April	0.188	0.200	0.204
May	0.183	0.195	0.199
June	0.181	0.193	0.197
July	0.181	0.193	0.197
Aug.	0.178	0.189	0.193
Sep.	0.173	0.184	0.189
Oct.	0.170	0.181	0.186
Nov.	0.168	0.179	0.183
Dec.	0.162	0.173	0.177
2005 *Jan.*	0.168	0.179	0.184
Feb.	0.164	0.175	0.179
Mar.	0.159	0.170	0.174
Apr.	0.152	0.163	0.167
May	0.149	0.160	0.165
June	0.148	0.159	0.163
July	0.148	0.159	0.163
Aug.	0.146	0.157	0.161
Sep.	0.143	0.154	0.158
Oct.	0.142	0.153	0.157
Nov.	0.140	0.151	0.155
Dec.	0.137	0.148	0.152
2006 *Jan.*	0.141	0.152	0.156
Feb.	0.136	0.147	0.151
Mar.	0.132	0.143	0.147
April	0.123	0.134	0.138
May	0.116	0.127	0.131
June	0.112	0.122	0.126
July	0.112	0.122	0.126
Aug.	0.108	0.118	0.122
Sept.	0.103	0.113	0.117
Oct.	0.101	0.112	0.116
Nov.	0.097	0.108	0.112
Dec.	0.089	0.099	0.103
2007 *Jan.*	0.095	0.105	0.109
Feb.	0.087	0.097	0.101
Mar.	0.080	0.090	0.094
April	0.074	0.085	0.089
May	0.070	0.081	0.084
June	0.065	0.075	0.079
July	0.071	0.081	0.085
Aug.	0.065	0.075	0.079
Sept.	0.061	0.071	0.075
Oct.	0.056	0.067	0.070
Nov.	0.052	0.062	0.066
Dec.	0.046	0.056	0.060
2008 *Jan.*	0.052	0.062	0.066

General

RD Month (Mar. 2010–May. 2010) January 1987 = 100

	2010		
	Mar.	*Apr.*	*May*
RI Month			
Feb.	0.044	0.054	0.058
Mar.	0.041	0.050	0.054
April	0.031	0.041	0.045
May	0.026	0.036	0.040
June	0.018	0.028	0.031
July	0.019	0.029	0.033
August	0.016	0.026	0.029
Sept.	0.011	0.020	0.024
Oct.	0.014	0.023	0.027
Nov.	0.022	0.031	0.035
Dec.	0.037	0.047	0.050
2009 *Jan.*	0.050	0.060	0.064
Feb.	0.044	0.054	0.058
Mar.	0.044	0.054	0.058
April	0.043	0.053	0.057
May	0.037	0.047	0.051
June	0.034	0.044	0.048
July	0.034	0.044	0.048
August	0.029	0.039	0.043
Sept.	0.025	0.035	0.039
Oct.	0.022	0.031	0.035
Nov.	0.019	0.029	0.032
Dec.	0.012	0.022	0.026
2010 *Jan.*	0.013	0.022	0.026
Feb.	0.007	0.016	0.020
Mar.	Nil	0.010	0.013
Apr.	–	Nil	0.004
May	–	–	Nil

Foreign exchange rates

[¶12-000] Foreign exchange rates: general

HMRC publish annually currency exchange rates for the purposes of converting foreign currencies into sterling.

The currency exchange rates for the US dollar, German deutschmark, Japanese yen and euro are reproduced below.

Average exchange rates for year to 31 December

Average for year to 31 December	US $	DM	Yen	Euro
1984	1.3300	3.7900	316.00	
1985	1.2800	3.7800	305.00	
1986	1.4700	3.1600	246.00	
1987	1.6300	2.9400	236.41	
1988	1.7810	3.1240	226.92	
1989	1.6387	3.0786	225.64	
1990	1.7854	2.8749	257.45	
1991	1.8710	2.8375	233.75	
1992	1.7655	2.7528	223.76	
1993	1.5023	2.4828	166.9335	
1994	1.5318	2.4826	156.4429	
1995	1.5783	2.2603	148.283	
1996	1.5619	2.3506	169.593	
1997	1.638	2.8391	198.189	
1998	1.6573	2.9147	216.6834	
1999	1.6181	2.9702	183.969	
2000	1.5163	3.2114	163.378	
2001	1.4401	3.1461	174.8889	
2002	1.5023	N/A	187.8315	1.5906
2003	1.6348	N/A	189.3354	1.4457
2004	1.8318	N/A	198.065	1.474
2005	1.8195	N/A	200.2141	1.4626
2006	1.8424	N/A	214.3005	1.4666
2007	2.0020	N/A	235.6273	1.4604
2008	1.8511	N/A	192.26	1.2586
2009	1.5633	N/A	146.366	1.1235

Average exchange rates for year to 31 March

Average for year to 31 March	US $	DM	Yen	Euro
1985	1.2500	3.7300	305.00	
1986	1.3700	3.7100	285.00	
1987	1.4900	3.0300	238.00	
1988	1.7000	2.9800	234.76	

General

Average for year

to 31 March	US $	DM	Yen	Euro
1989	1.7970	3.2460	229.33	
1990	1.6305	2.9144	235.64	
1991	1.7390	2.9090	258.31	
1992	1.7355	2.8550	231.00	
1993	1.6924	2.6526	211.59	
1994	1.5066	2.5203	162.2872	
1995	1.5553	2.4256	154.3941	
1996	1.5656	2.2375	150.75	
1997	1.5866	2.4642	178.8762	
1998	1.642	2.912	201.5651	
1999	1.6542	2.878	211.499	
2000	1.6114	3.0548	179.386	
2001	1.4793	3.1886	163.482	
2002	1.432	3.1677	179.0169	
2003	1.5466	N/A	188.3036	1.5573
2004	1.6348	N/A	190.9326	1.4400
2005	1.8445	N/A	198.171	1.467
2006	1.79738	N/A	201.2374	1.4664
2007	1.8932	N/A	221.4527	1.475
2008	2.0080	N/A	229.3116	1.4178
2009	1.7138	N/A	173.793	1.2042
2010	1.5962	N/A	148.193	1.1298

[¶12-660]   Foreign exchange rates 2009–10

		Average rates for the year to 31 December 2009 and the year to 31 March 2010			
		Average for the year to 31 December 2009		Average for the year to 31 March 2010	
Country	Unit of currency	Currency units per £1	Sterling value of currency unit £	Currency units per £1	Sterling value of currency unit £
Algeria	Algerian Dinar	113.373	0.0088204	115.670	0.0086453
Argentina	Peso	5.8426	0.17116	6.0580	0.16507
Australia	Australian Dollar	1.9923	0.50193	1.8829	0.5311
Bahrain	Dinar	0.5896	1.69607	0.6005	1.66528
Bangladesh	Taka	108.191	0.0092429	110.103	0.0090824
Barbados	Barbados Dollar	3.1280	0.31969	3.1853	0.31394
Bolivia	Boliviano	10.9794	0.09108	11.1804	0.089442
Botswana	Pula	11.0911	0.090163	10.8900	0.091827
Brazil	Real	3.1109	0.32145	2.9799	0.33558
Brunei	Brunei Dollar	2.2743	0.4397	2.2677	0.44098
Bulgaria	Lev	2.1974	0.45508	2.2063	0.45325

2009–10 Average foreign exchange rates (cont'd)

		Average rates for the year to 31 December 2009 and the year to 31 March 2010			
		Average for the year to 31 December 2009		Average for the year to 31 March 2010	
Country	Unit of currency	Currency units per £1	Sterling value of currency unit £	Currency units per £1	Sterling value of currency unit £
Burma	Kyat	10.0277	0.099724	10.2089	0.097954
Burundi	Burundi Franc	1929.10	0.00051838	1959.83	0.00051025
Canada	Canadian Dollar	1.7801	0.56177	1.7398	0.57478
Cayman Islands	C.I. Dollar	1.2851	0.77815	1.3067	0.76529
Chile	Chilean Peso	870.827	0.0011483	854.751	0.0011699
China	Yuan	10.7044	0.09342	10.8798	0.091913
Colombia	Colombia Peso	3358.97	0.00029771	3183.33	0.00031414
Congo (Dem Rep)	Congolese Franc	1263.11	0.0007917	1354.89	0.00073807
Costa Rica	Colon	898.802	0.0011126	906.539	0.0011031
Cuba	Cuban Peso	1.5673	0.63804	1.5935	0.62755
Czech Republic	Koruna	29.8025	0.033554	29.3613	0.034058
Denmark	Danish Krone	8.3581	0.11964	8.4083	0.11893
Egypt	Egyptian £	8.6820	0.11518	8.8012	0.11362
El Salvador	Colon	13.7107	0.072936	13.9391	0.071741
Ethiopia	Ethiopian Birr	18.7056	0.05346	19.7973	0.050512
European Union	Euro	1.1235	0.89008	1.1298	0.88511
Fiji Islands	Fiji Dollar	3.0833	0.32433	3.1723	0.31523
French Cty/Africa	CFA Franc	736.978	0.0013569	739.927	0.0013515
French Pacific Islands	CFP Franc	133.979	0.0074639	134.515	0.0074341
Gambia	Dalasi	41.6103	0.024033	42.4940	0.023533
Ghana	Cedi	2.2426	0.44591	2.3068	0.4335
Grenada/Wind. Isles	East Carib Dollar	4.2229	0.2368	4.3023	0.23243
Guyana	Guyana Dollar	316.241	0.0031621	322.95	0.0030965
Honduras	Lempira	29.6097	0.033773	30.1084	0.033213
Hong Kong	HK Dollar	12.1317	0.082429	12.3810	0.080769
Hungary	Forint	316.187	0.0031627	308.141	0.0032453
Iceland	Icelandic Krona	193.524	0.0051673	200.920	0.0049771
India	Indian Rupee	75.6294	0.013222	75.5588	0.013235
Indonesia	Rupiah	16175.8	0.000061821	15601.1	0.000064098
Iran	Rial	15443.8	0.000064751	15770.0	0.000063412
Iraq	New Iraqi Dinar	1802.03	0.00055493	1838.48	0.00054393
Israel	Shekel	6.1341	0.16302	6.1280	0.16319
Jamaica	Jamaican Dollar	137.646	0.007265	141.387	0.0070728
Japan	Yen	146.366	0.0068322	148.193	0.006748
Jordan	Jordanian Dinar	1.1077	0.90277	1.1278	0.88668
Kenya	Kenyan Shilling	120.848	0.0082749	121.942	0.0082006
Korea (South)	Won	1993.87	0.00050154	1924.48	0.00051962
Kuwait	Kuwaiti Dinar	0.4508	2.21828	0.4582	2.18245
Laos	New Kip	13295.8	0.000075212	13502.7	0.000074059
Latvia	Lats	0.7936	1.26008	0.7975	1.25392

2009–10 Average foreign exchange rates (cont'd)

| Country | Unit of currency | Average rates for the year to 31 December 2009 and the year to 31 March 2010 | | | |
| | | Average for the year to 31 December 2009 | | Average for the year to 31 March 2010 | |
		Currency units per £1	Sterling value of currency unit £	Currency units per £1	Sterling value of currency unit £
Lebanon	Lebanese Pound	2348.60	0.00042579	2391.71	0.00041811
Libya	Libyan Dinar	1.9538	0.51182	1.9751	0.5063
Lithuania	Litas	3.8793	0.25778	3.8949	0.25675
Malawi	Kwacha	221.896	0.0045066	229.365	0.0043599
Malaysia	Ringgit	5.5051	0.18165	5.5113	0.18145
Mauritius	Mauritius Rupee	49.8915	0.020043	49.6959	0.020122
Mexico	Mexican Peso	21.0920	0.047411	20.8849	0.047881
Morocco	Dirham	12.6491	0.079057	12.7327	0.078538
Nepal	Nepalese Rupee	121.294	0.0082444	120.696	0.0082853
N'nd Antilles	Antilles Guilder	2.8053	0.35647	2.8523	0.35059
New Zealand	NZ Dollar	2.4870	0.40209	2.3637	0.42307
Nicaragua	Gold Cordoba	31.9532	0.031296	32.8596	0.030433
Nigeria	Naira	234.162	0.0042706	239.591	0.0041738
Norway	Nor Krone	9.8078	0.10196	9.6327	0.10381
Oman	Rial Omani	0.6022	1.66058	0.6132	1.63079
Pakistan	Pakistan Rupee	127.926	0.007817	132.082	0.0075711
Papua New Guinea	Kina	4.2283	0.2365	4.2584	0.23483
Paraguay	Guarani	7783.09	0.00012848	7779.04	0.00012855
Peru	New Sol	4.6983	0.21284	4.6586	0.21466
Philippines	Peso	74.5322	0.013417	75.1918	0.013299
Poland	Zloty	4.8775	0.20502	4.7177	0.21197
Qatar	Riyal	5.6946	0.1756	5.7982	0.17247
Romania	New Leu	4.7645	0.20989	4.7312	0.21136
Russia	Rouble	49.7386	0.020105	48.6544	0.020553
Rwanda	Franc	891.257	0.001122	908.223	0.0011011
Saudi Arabia	Riyal	5.8657	0.17048	5.9728	0.16743
Seychelles	Rupee	21.1657	0.047246	19.6567	0.050873
Sierra Leone	Leone	5314.64	0.00018816	5723.55	0.00017472
Singapore	Singapore Dollar	2.2711	0.44032	2.2719	0.44016
Solomon Islands	SI Dollar	12.4682	0.080204	12.7244	0.078589
Somali Republic	Shilling	2161.21	0.0004627	2236.85	0.00044706
South Africa	Rand	13.0021	0.076911	12.4676	0.080208
Sri Lanka	Rupee	180.184	0.0055499	183.205	0.0054584
Sudan	Sudanese Pound	3.6544	0.27364	3.7308	0.26804
Surinam	Dollar	4.3020	0.23245	4.3741	0.22862
Swaziland	Lilangeni	12.9656	0.077127	12.3156	0.081198
Sweden	Krona	11.9491	0.083688	11.7215	0.085313
Switzerland	Franc	1.6968	0.58935	1.6961	0.58959
Syria	Pound	72.0249	0.013884	73.1795	0.013665
Taiwan	Dollar	51.6003	0.01938	51.7867	0.01931

2009–10 Average foreign exchange rates (cont'd)

| | | Average rates for the year to 31 December 2009 and the year to 31 March 2010 | | | |
| | | Average for the year to 31 December 2009 | | Average for the year to 31 March 2010 | |
Country	Unit of currency	Currency units per £1	Sterling value of currency unit £	Currency units per £1	Sterling value of currency unit £
Tanzania	Shilling	2071.20	0.00048281	2118.02	0.00047214
Thailand	Baht	53.6478	0.01864	53.7107	0.018618
Tonga Islands	Pa'anga	3.1526	0.3172	3.1071	0.32184
Trinidad & Tobago	Dollar	9.8537	0.10148	10.0652	0.099352
Tunisia	Dinar	2.1093	0.47409	2.1345	0.46849
Turkey	New Lira	2.4264	0.41213	2.4160	0.41391
Uganda	New Shilling	3177.46	0.00031472	3237.06	0.00030892
United Arab Emirates	Dirham	5.7445	0.17408	5.8497	0.17095
Uruguay	Peso Uruguay	35.2328	0.028383	34.3153	0.029142
USA	US Dollar	1.5633	0.63967	1.5962	0.62649
Venezuela	Bolivar Fuerte	3.3620	0.29744	1/4/09 to 10/1/10: 0.28987 11/1/10 to 31/3/10: 0.14969*	1/4/09 to 10/1/10: 3.4498 11/1/10 to 31/3/10: 6.6804*
Vietnam	Dong	28019.6	0.000035689	28974.5	0.000034513
Yemen	Rial	318.436	0.0031403	329.603	0.0030340
Zambia	Kwacha	7870.74	0.00012705	7741.14	0.00012918

*Rate shown for Venezuela from 11/1/10 is 'petro-dollar' rate, preferential rate is fixed at 2.6 to the US dollar

Table of spot rates on 31 December 2009 and 31 March 2010

| | | 31 December 2009 | | 31 March 2010 | |
Country	Unit of Currency	Currency units per £1	Sterling value of currency unit £	Currency units per £1	Sterling value of currency unit £
Australia	Australian Dollar	1.7956	0.55692	1.6527	0.60507
Canada	Canadian Dollar	1.6930	0.59067	1.5390	0.64977
Denmark	Danish Krone	8.3750	0.1194	8.3459	0.11982
European Union	Euro	1.1255	0.88849	1.1211	0.89198
Hong Kong	HK Dollar	12.5217	0.079861	11.7783	0.084902
Japan	Yen	150.335	0.0066518	141.739	0.0070552
Norway	Nor Krone	9.3287	0.1072	9.0038	0.11106
South Africa	Rand	11.8914	0.084094	11.1401	0.089766
Sweden	Krona	11.5302	0.086729	10.9171	0.091599
Switzerland	Franc	1.6693	0.59905	1.5967	0.62629
USA	US Dollar	1.6149	0.61923	1.5169	0.65924

General

[¶13-000]   Clearances and approvals provided for in the Taxes Acts

Full details of this service can be found at *www.hmrc.gov.uk/cap/index.htm*.

[¶13-200]   Clearance service for businesses

Guidance is for the use of the business customers can be found at *www.hmrc.gov.uk/cap/links-dec07.htm*. Non-business customers should continue to refer to the existing guidance at Code of Practice 10 or VAT Notice 700-6.

Business owners who would like tomake clearance applications in relation to inheritance tax business property relief (IHT-BPR) should see the separate guidance Inheritance Tax clearance service for business (see *www.hmrc.gov.uk/cap/clearanceiht.htm*).

[¶14-000]   Double tax treaties

The following table lists all the territories with which the UK has concluded agreements to avoid international double taxation and also facilitate the exchange of information to prevent tax evasion.

Algeria (A)
Andorra (EC)
Anguilla (TIE)
Antigua and Barbuda (C/TIE)
Argentina (C)
Aruba (TIE)
Australia (C)
Austria (C/SS)
Azerbaijan (C)
Bahamas (TIE)
Bahrain (C)
Bangladesh (C)
Barbados (C/SS)
Belarus (C)[1]
Belgium (C/SS)
Belize (C/TIE)
Bermuda (TIE/SS)
Bolivia (C)
Bosnia-Herzegovina (C/SS)[2]
Botswana (C)
Brazil (SA)
British Virgin Islands (TIE)
Brunei (C)
Bulgaria (C)
Burma (Myanmar) (C)
Cameroon (A)
Canada (C/SS)
Cayman Islands (TIE)
Chile (C)[3]
China (C/A)
Croatia (C/SS)[2]
Cyprus (C/SS)
Czech Republic (C)
Denmark (C/SS)
Dominica (TIE)
Egypt (C)
Estonia (C/SS)[1]
Ethiopia (A)
Falkland Islands (C)
Faroe Islands (C)
Fiji (C)
Finland (C/SS)
France (includes Guadeloupe,
   Guyane, Martinique and
   Réunion (C/EIG/SS)
Gambia (C)
Georgia (C)
Germany (C/SS)
Ghana (C)
Gibraltar (TIE/SS)

Greece (C/SS)
Grenada (C/TIE)
Guernsey (includes Alderney,
   Herm and Lithou) (C/SS/TIE)
Guyana (C)
Hong Kong SAR (SA)
Hungary (C/SS)
Iceland (C/SS)
India (C/EIG)[3]
Indonesia (C)
Iran (A)
Ireland (C/EIG/SS)
Isle of Man (C/SS/TIE)
Israel (C/SS)
Italy (C/EIG/SS)
Ivory Coast (Cote d'Ivoire) (C)
Jamaica (C/SS)
Japan (C/SS)
Jersey (C/SS/TIE)
Jordan (C)
Kazakstan (C)
Kenya (C)
Kiribati and Tuvalu (C)
Korea (C)
Kuwait (C)
Latvia (C)
Lebanon (SA)
Lesotho (C)
Libya (C)
Liechtenstein (EC/SS/TIE)
Lithuania (C/SS)
Luxembourg (C/SS)
Macedonia (C/SS)
Malawi (C)
Malaysia (C)
Malta (C/SS)
Mauritius (C/SS)
Mexico (C)
Moldova (C)
Monaco (EC)
Mongolia (C)
Montenegro (C/SS)[2]
Montserrat (C/TIE)
Morocco (C)
Namibia (C)
Netherlands (C/EIG/SS)
Netherlands Antilles (TIE)
New Zealand (C/SS)

Nigeria (C)
Norway (C/SS)
Oman (C)
Pakistan (C/EIG)[3]
Papua New Guinea (C)
Philippines (C/SS)
Poland (C/SS)
Portugal (C/SS)
Qatar (C)
Romania (C)
Russia (C)
St. Christopher (St. Kitts) & Nevis
   (C/TIE)
St. Lucia (TIE)
St. Vincent and the Grenadines (TIE)
San Marino (EC/TIE)
Saudi Arabia (C/A)
Serbia (C/SS)[2]
Sierra Leone (C)
Singapore (C)
Slovak Republic (C/SS)
Slovenia (C/SS)[2]
Solomon Islands (C)
South Africa (C/EIG)
South Korea (C/SS)
Spain (C/SS)
Sri Lanka (C)
Sudan (C)
Swaziland (C)
Sweden (C/EIG/SS)
Switzerland (C/EC/EIG/SS/EC)
Taiwan (C)
Tajikistan (C)[1]
Thailand (C)
Trinidad and Tobago (C)
Tunisia (C)
Turkey (C/SS)
Turkmenistan (C)[1]
Turks & Caicos Islands (TIE)
Uganda (C)
Ukraine (C)
USA (C/EIG/SS)
Uzbekistan (C)
Venezuela (C)
Vietnam (C)
Zaire (SA)
Zambia (C)
Zimbabwe (C)

General

These agreements may be of various types which are indicated below by the following letters:

- (C) – comprehensive agreements covering a wide range of areas of possible double taxation of income and capital gains;

- (SA) – agreements limited to shipping and air transport profits;

- (A) – agreements limited to air transport profits only;

- (EIG) – agreements relating to tax on estates, inheritances and gifts;

- (TIE) – tax information exchange agreements relating to the taxation of savings income received by individuals; and

- (EC) – tax information exchange agreements concluded by the EC on behalf of its member states with third countries.

Notes

(1) The Convention of 31 July 1985 with the former USSR is regarded as continuing in force (see SP 04/01).

(2) The Convention of 5 November 1981 with the former Yugoslavia is regarded as continuing in force (see SP 03/07).

(3) The estate, inheritance and gifts agreements with India and Pakistan have not been formally terminated despite the fact that estate duties in those countries were abolished on 15 March 1985 and 29 July 1979 respectively.

[¶15-000]   Recognised stock exchanges

(ITA 2007, s. 1005)

With effect from 19 July 2007, a 'recognised stock exchange' is defined for the purposes of the Income Tax Acts as being one which is designated as such by an Order of the Commissioners for HMRC and which falls within one of two categories:

- 'recognised investment exchanges' designated by the Financial Services Authority; and

- markets outside the UK (see below).

From 19 July 2007, UK recognised stock exchanges, as designated by HMRC, are:

- the London Stock Exchange; and

- the PLUS-listed market segment of the PLUS exchange.

Under the previous legislation 'the Stock Exchange' (strictly known as 'the London Stock Exchange') was the only UK 'recognised stock exchange'.

Recognised stock exchanges outside the UK

Below is a list of stock exchanges designated as 'recognised stock exchanges' by Order of the Commissioners for HMRC, together with the date of recognition.

The Athens Stock Exchange	14 Jun 1993
The Australian Stock Exchange and any of its subsidiaries(1)	22 Sep 1988
The Bahamas International Securities Exchange	19 April 2010
The Bermuda Stock Exchange	4 Dec 2007

The Bond Exchange of South Africa	16 April 2008
The Cayman Islands Stock Exchange	4 Mar 2004
The Colombo Stock Exchange	21 Feb 1972
The Copenhagen Stock Exchange	22 Oct 1970
The Cyprus Stock Exchange	22 June 2009
The Helsinki Stock Exchange	22 Oct 1970
The Iceland Stock Exchange	31 Mar 2006
The Johannesburg Stock Exchange	22 Oct 1970
The Korea Stock Exchange	10 Oct 1994
The Kuala Lumpur Stock Exchange	10 Oct 1994
The London Stock Exchange	19 July 2007
The Malta Stock Exchange	29 Dec 2005
The Mexico Stock Exchange	10 Oct 1994
The NASDAQ OMX Tallin	5 May 2010
The New Zealand Stock Exchange	22 Sep 1988
The Plus-listed Market	19 July 2007
The Rio De Janeiro Stock Exchange	17 Aug 1995
The Sao Paulo Stock Exchange	11 Dec 1995
The Singapore Stock Exchange	30 Jun 1977
The Stockholm Stock Exchange	16 Jul 1985
The Stock Exchange of Thailand	10 Oct 1994
The Swiss Stock Exchange[2]	12 May 1997
The Warsaw Stock Exchange[3]	25 February 2010

Notes
[1] Replaces an Order dated 22 October 1970 recognising any Australian stock exchange which was a prescribed member exchange of the Australian Associated Stock Exchanges.
[2] Formed on the merger of the Zurich, Basle and Geneva exchanges, that were all previously recognised by an Order dated 30 June 1970.
[3] The markets accepted as 'listed' are The Main Market, The Parallel Market and the EU Regulated Market . Other markets operated by the Warsaw Stock Exchange, the Catalyst Multi-lateral Trading Facility and the New Connect Market are not recognised.

General

In addition, a recognised stock exchange is any stock exchange in the following countries which is a stock exchange within the meaning of the law of the particular country relating to stock exchanges (or as specified below).

Austria	22 Oct 1970
Belgium	22 Oct 1970
Canada, any stock exchange prescribed for the purpose of the Canadian Income Tax Act	22 Oct 1970
France	22 Oct 1970
Germany	5 Aug 1971
Guernsey	10 Dec 2002
Hong Kong, any stock exchange which is recognised under s. 2A(1) of the Hong Kong Companies Ordinance	26 Feb 1971
Ireland, Republic of[1]	22 Oct 1970
Italy	3 May 1972
Japan	22 Oct 1970
Luxembourg	21 Feb 1972
Netherlands[2]	22 Oct 1970
Norway	22 Oct 1970
Portugal	21 Feb 1972
Spain	5 Aug 1971
USA, any exchange registered with the Securities and Exchange Commission of the United States as a national securities exchange	22 Oct 1970
USA, the NASDAQ Stock Market as maintained through the facilities of the National Association of Securities Dealers, Inc. and its subsidiaries	10 Mar 1992

Note
[1] On 23 March 1973, the stock exchanges in the Republic of Ireland became part of 'the Stock Exchange'. In December 1995, the Irish Stock Exchange demerged from 'the Stock Exchange'.
[2] Includes the European Options Exchange

Alternative finance investment bonds

(ITA 2007, s. 564G)

'Alternative finance investment bonds' (Sharia compliant financial instruments commonly known as 'sukuk') must be listed on a recognised stock exchange. An alternative finance investment bond listed on an exchange recognised under ITA 2007, s. 1005 will meet this requirement. In addition, certain other exchanges are designated as recognised stock exchanges *solely* for the purposes of ITA 2007, s. 564G. These are listed below, together with the dates of recognition.

Abu Dhabi Securities Market	1 April 2007
Bahrain Stock Exchange	1 April 2007
Dubai Financial Market	1 April 2007
Dubai International Financial Exchange	1 April 2007
Labuan International Financial Exchange	1 April 2007
Saudi Stock Exchange (Tadawul)	1 April 2007
Surabaya Stock Exchange	1 April 2007

General

[¶15-050]   Recognised futures exchanges
(TCGA 1992, s. 288(6))

The following futures exchanges have been designated by the Board of Her Majesty's Revenue and Customs as 'recognised futures exchanges'[1]:

Notes
[1] When the Board recognises a futures exchange this is announced in the *London Gazette*.

Date	Exchange
From 6 August 1985	International Petroleum Exchange of London London Metal Exchange London Wool Terminal Market
From 12 December 1985	London Gold Market London Silver Market
From 19 December 1986	Chicago Mercantile Exchange Philadelphia Board of Trade New York Mercantile Exchange
From 24 April 1987	Chicago Board of Trade
From 29 July 1987	Montreal Exchange Mid-America Commodity Exchange
From 15 December 1987	Hong Kong Futures Exchange New York Coffee Sugar and Cocoa Exchange
From 25 August 1988	Commodity Exchange, Inc (COMEX) Citrus Associates of the New York Cotton Exchange Inc New York Cotton Exchange
From 31 October 1988	Sydney Futures Exchange Ltd
From 18 March 1992	OM Stockholm London Commodity Exchange[2] OMLX (formerly OM London)
From 22 March 1992	London International Financial Futures and Options Exchange (LIFFE)[3]

Notes
[2] The following futures exchanges, which are recognised from 6 August 1985, are now part of the London Commodity Exchange (also known as London FOX): Baltic International Freight Futures Exchange; London Cocoa Terminal Market; London Coffee Terminal Market; London Futures and Options Exchange; London Grain Futures Market; London Meat Futures Market; London Potato Futures Market; London Rubber Market; London Soya Bean Meal Futures Market; London Sugar Terminal Market. The name of the London International Financial Futures Exchange changed to London Commodity Exchange from 1 July 1993.
[3] The London International Financial Futures Exchange and the London Traded Options Market merged on 22 March 1992, forming the London International Financial Futures and Options Exchange (LIFFE).

[¶15-150]   Recognised investment exchanges

(ITEPA 2003, s. 702)

(BTR; ¶494-300)

A 'recognised investment exchange' (RIE) is an investment exchange in relation to which a recognition order made by the Financial Services Authority is in force (*Financial Services and Markets Act* 2000, s. 285ff.).

Where the Financial Services Authority does issue a recognition order for a 'recognised investment exchange' this has consequences for the rules relating to the operation of PAYE on the provision of 'readily convertible asset' for employees. If an employer provides an employee with an asset that can be sold, or otherwise realised, on a recognised investment exchange (RIE); the London Bullion Market; the New York Stock Exchange; or any market specified in PAYE Regulations, that asset is a 'readily convertible asset' and the employer is obliged to operate PAYE (ITEPA 2003, s. 696, s. 702. Similarly any asset, such as a gold bar, capable of sale or realisation on the London Bullion Market is a 'readily convertible asset'. As at December 2009, the FSA has currently issued recognition orders for the following RIEs (with the effective date shown in parentheses):

EDX London Ltd (1 July 2003)

ICE Futures (22 November 2001)

LIFFE Administration and Management (22 November 2001)

London Stock Exchange plc (22 November 2001)

PLUS Markets plc (19 July 2007)

The London Metal Exchange Limited (22 November 2001)

Cantor Financial Futures Exchange [CFEE] (22 November 2001)

Chicago Board of Trade [CBOT] (22 November 2001)

EUREX [Zurich] (23 November 2001)

ICE Futures US Inc. (17 May 2007)

National Association of Securities Dealers Automated Quotations [NASDAQ] (23 November 2001)

New York Mercantile Exchange Inc. [NYMEX Inc.] (23 November 2001)

Sydney Futures Exchange Limited (30 January 2002)

The Chicago Mercantile Exchange [CME] (23 November 2001)

SIX Swiss Exchange AG [ROIE] (23 November 2001)

General

HMRC Information

[¶15-500]   HMRC forms

For a complete list see *http://search2.hmrc.gov.uk/kbroker/hmrc/forms/start.jsp.*

[¶15-550]   HMRC leaflets and booklets

For a complete list see *www.hmrc.gov.uk/leaflets/index.htm.*

[¶15-600]   HMRC manuals

For a complete list see *www.hmrc.gov.uk/thelibrary/manuals-a-z.htm.*

[¶15-650]   HMRC websites

HMRC home page

http://www.hmrc.gov.uk

The HMRC website contains full details of contact addresses and numbers, including in particular the following:

*   All local Tax Offices, National Insurance Contribution Offices, and Valuation Offices: *http://www.hmrc.gov.uk/local/index.htm*
*   Specialist offices: *http://www.hmrc.gov.uk/menus/officesmenu.htm*
*   HMRC enquiry centres: *http://www.hmrc.gov.uk/enq/index.htm*

Other useful parts of the HMRC website are:

HMRC self assessment pages

http://www.hmrc.gov.uk/sa/index.htm

HMRC benefits in kind

http://www.hmrc.gov.uk/stats/taxable_benefits/menu.htm

HMRC employers information

http://www.hmrc.gov.uk/employers/index.htm

HMRC tax credits

http://www.hmrc.gov.uk/taxcredits

[¶15-800]   Other useful websites

Adjudicator

http://www.adjudicatorsoffice.gov.uk/

CCTA Government Information Service

http://www.direct.gov.uk

CIOT

http://www.tax.org.uk

ICAEW Tax Faculty

*http://www.icaew.com/index.cfm/route/159000/icaew_ga/en/Faculties/Tax/
Tax_Faculty_home/Tax_faculty*

Office of Public Sector Information – Statutory Instruments

http://www.opsi.gov.uk/stat.htm

For statutory instruments made by the National Assembly for Wales –

http://www.opsi.gov.uk/legislation/wales/w-stat.htm

For statutory instruments made by the Scottish Parliament –

http://www.opsi.gov.uk/legislation/scotland/s-stat.htm

Parliament

http://www.parliament.uk/

Parliamentary Ombudsman

http://www.ombudsman.org.uk/

Treasury Home Page

http://www.hm-treasury.gov.uk/

Tribunals service

http://www.tribunals.gov.uk/tax/

Valuation Office Agency

http://www.voa.gov.uk/

General

[¶15-950] Finance Acts

Year	Budget		Royal Assent	
1976	6 April	1976	29 July	1976
1977	29 March	1977	29 July	1977
1978	11 April	1978	31 July	1978
1979	3 April	1979	4 April	1979
1979 (No. 2)	12 June	1979	26 July	1979
1980	26 March	1980	1 August	1980
1981	10 March	1981	27 July	1981
1982	9 March	1982	30 July	1982
1983	15 March	1983	13 May	1983
1983 (No. 2)	15 March	1983	26 July	1983
1984	13 March	1984	26 July	1984
1985	19 March	1985	25 July	1985
1986	18 March	1986	25 July	1986
1987	17 March	1987	15 May	1987
1987 (No. 2)	17 March	1987	23 July	1987
1988	15 March	1988	29 July	1988
1989	14 March	1989	27 July	1989
1990	20 March	1990	26 July	1990
1991	19 March	1991	26 July	1991
1992	10 March	1992	16 March	1992
1992 (No. 2)	10 March	1992	16 July	1992
1993	16 March	1993	27 July	1993
1994	30 November	1993	3 May	1994
1995	29 November	1994	1 May	1995
1996	28 November	1995	29 April	1996
1997	26 November	1996	19 March	1997
1997 (No. 2)	2 July	1997	31 July	1997
1998	17 March	1998	31 July	1998
1999	9 March	1999	27 July	1999
2000	21 March	2000	28 July	2000
2001	7 March	2001	11 May	2001
2002	17 April	2002	24 July	2002
2003	9 April	2003	10 July	2003
2004	17 March	2004	22 July	2004
2005	16 March	2005	7 April	2005
2005 (No. 2)	16 March	2005	20 July	2005
2006	22 March	2006	19 July	2006
2007	21 March	2007	19 July	2007
2008	12 March	2008	21 July	2008
2009	22 April	2009	21 July	2009
2010	24 March	2010	8 April	2010
2010 (No. 2)	22 June	2010		
2010 (No. 3)	22 June	2010		

STAMP TAXES

Stamp duty land tax

[¶16-000] Stamp duty land tax rates

Applies to contracts entered into (or varied) after 10 July 2003 and completed after 30 November 2003 and to leases granted after that date.

FA 2003, s. 77A removes the requirement to notify HMRC of a transaction involving residential and non-residential property where chargeable consideration is less than £40,000 for transactions on or after 12 March 2008.

An exemption from stamp duty land tax is available to buyers of new zero-carbon homes in the period from 1 October 2007 to 30 September 2012 (FA 2003, s. 58A). The *Finance Act* 2008 extended this relief to zero-carbon flats.

All land in UK

Rates from 1 January 2010

Rate (%)	Residential	Non-residential
Zero	£125,000	£150,000
1	Over £125,000–£250,000[1]	Over £150,000–£250,000
3	Over £250,000–£500,000	Over £250,000–£500,000
4	Over £500,000	Over £500,000

Rates from 3 September 2008 to 31 December 2009

Rate (%)	Residential	Non-residential
Zero	£175,000	£150,000
1	Over £175,000–£250,000	Over £150,000–£250,000
3	Over £250,000–£500,000	Over £250,000–£500,000
4	Over £500,000	Over £500,000

[1] First time buyers can claim relief from SDLT on transactions up to £250,000 between 25 March 2010 and 25 March 2012 (FA 2003, s. 57AA and Sch. 9, para. 15).
[2] From 3 September 2008 until 21 April 2009, the £175,000 threshold only applied to freehold or assigned leases with 21 years or more remaining.
[3] The £175,000 threshold does not apply to the residential element of a mixed use property.
[4] A rate of 5% will apply to transactions over £1,000,000 on or after 6 April 2011 (FA 2010, s. 7).

Rates from 23 March 2006 to 2 September 2008

Rate (%)	Residential	Non-residential
Zero	£125,000	£150,000
1	Over £125,000–£250,000	Over £150,000–£250,000
3	Over £250,000–£500,000	Over £250,000–£500,000
4	Over £500,000	Over £500,000

Rates from 17 March 2005 to 22 March 2006

Rate (%)	Residential	Non-residential
Zero	£120,000	£150,000
1	Over £120,000–£250,000	Over £150,000–£250,000
3	Over £250,000–£500,000	Over £250,000–£500,000
4	Over £500,000	Over £500,000

Rates from 1 December 2003 to 16 March 2005

Rate (%)	Residential	Non-residential
Zero	£60,000	£150,000
1	Over £60,000–£250,000	Over £150,000–£250,000
3	Over £250,000–£500,000	Over £250,000–£500,000
4	Over £500,000	Over £500,000

Land in disadvantaged areas

Note

For transactions between 3 September 2008 and 2 September 2009, the standard rules shown above are more advantageous, and should therefore be used for purchases up to £175,000.

Rates from 17 March 2005

Rate (%)	Residential	Non-residential[1]
Zero	£150,000	£150,000
1	Over £150,000–£250,000	Over £150,000–£250,000
3	Over £250,001–£500,000	Over £250,001–£500,000
4	Over £500,000	Over £500,000

[1] The exemption for non-residential transactions in land situated in a disadvantaged area was abolished for transactions with an effective date after 16 March 2005. Certain contracts entered into before then where the transaction takes place after abolition may continue to benefit from exemption.

Rates from 1 December 2003 to 16 March 2005

Rate (%)	Residential	Non-residential
Zero	£150,000	All
1	Over £150,000–£250,000	
3	Over £250,001–£500,000	
4	Over £500,000	

Note
FA 2003, s. 125 confirms that property that is not land, shares or interests in partnerships is not subject to stamp duty from 1 December 2003.

Lease rentals

Duty on new leases from 1 January 2010

Rate (%)	Net present value of rent	
	Residential	Non-residential
Zero	£0–£125,000	£0–£150,000
1	Over £125,000	Over £150,000

Notes
(1) Duty on premium is the same as for transfers of land (except special rules apply for premium where rent exceeds £1,000 annually).

Duty on new leases 3 September 2008 – 31 December 2009

Rate (%)	Net present value of rent	
	Residential	Non-residential
Zero	£0–£175,000	£0–£150,000
1	Over £175,000	Over £150,000

Notes
(1) Duty on premium is the same as for transfers of land (except special rules apply for premium where rent exceeds £1,000 annually).
(2) Until 22 April 2009 if the net present value exceeded £175,000, the charge was on the excess over £125,000.

Duty on new leases 23 March 2006 – 2 September 2008

Rate (%)	Net present value of rent	
	Residential	Non-residential
Zero	£0–£125,000	£0–£150,000
1	Over £125,000	Over £150,000

Notes

(1) Duty on premium is the same as for transfers of land (except special rules apply for premium where rent exceeds £1,000 annually (£600 annually before 12 March 2008)

Duty on new leases 17 March 2005–22 March 2006

	Net present value of rent	
Rate (%)	**Residential**	**Non-residential**
Zero	£0–£120,000	£0–£150,000
1	Over £120,000	Over £150,000

Notes

(1) Duty on premium is the same as for transfers of land (except special rules apply for premium where rent exceeds £600 annually).

Duty on new leases 1 December 2003–16 March 2005

	Net present value of rent	
Rate (%)	**Residential**	**Non-residential**
Zero	£0–£60,000	£0–£150,000
1	Over £60,000	Over £150,000

Notes

(1) Duty on premium is the same as for transfers of land (except special rules apply for premium where rent exceeds £600 annually).

[¶16-200]   Stamp duty land tax penalties

Failure to deliver a land transaction return by the filing date (FA 2003, Sch. 10, para. 3 and 4)	£100 if return delivered within 3 months of filing date, otherwise £200. If not delivered within 12 months, maximum penalty of amount of tax chargeable
Failure to comply with a notice to deliver return within specified period (FA 2003, Sch. 10, para. 5)	Maximum of £60 for each day on which the failure continues after notification
Failure to keep or preserve records under FA 2003, Sch. 10, para. 9 or Sch. 11, para. 4 (FA 2003, Sch. 10, para. 11, Sch. 11, para. 6)	Maximum of £3,000 unless other documentary evidence provided
Failure to comply with notice to produce documents under FA 2003, Sch. 10, para. 14 (FA 2003, Sch. 10, para. 16)	Initial penalty of £50 with further maximum penalty of £30 (if determined by HMRC) or £150 (if determined by courts) for each day the failure continues
Failure to disclose certain SDLT proposals or arrangements (SI 2005/1868;SI 2005/1869)	Initial penalty of £5,000 with maximum penalty of £600 for each day failure continues

Stamp Taxes

[¶16-250]   Stamp duty land tax interest

The rates are as follows:

	Rate %	
Period of application	Underpayments	Repayments
From 29 September 2009	3.00	0.50
24 March 2009 to 28 September 2009	2.50	0.00
27 January 2009 to 23 March 2009	3.50	0.00
6 January 2009 to 26 January 2009	4.50	0.75
6 December 2008 to 5 January 2009	5.50	1.50
6 November 2008 to 5 December 2008	6.50	2.25
6 January 2008 to 5 November 2008	7.50	3.00
6 August 2007 to 5 January 2008	8.50	4.00
6 September 2006 to 5 August 2007	7.50	3.00
26 September 2005 to 5 September 2006	6.50	2.25

FA 2009, s. 101–104 and Sch. 53 and 54 contain provisions to harmonise interest regimes across all HMRC taxes and duties.

Stamp duty

[¶17-000]   Stamp duty rates

Conveyance or transfer on sale of shares and securities

(FA 1999, Sch. 13, para. 3)

Instrument	Rate of tax after 26 October 1986 %
Stock transfer	$1/_2$[1][2]
Conversion of shares into depositary receipts	$1 1/_2$[3]
Take overs and mergers	$1/_2$[1][2]
Purchase by company of own shares	[1][2]
Letters of allotment	$1/_2$

Notes

[1] Because duty at $1/_2$% is equivalent to £5 per £1,000 of consideration and duty is rounded up to the next multiple of £5 (FA 1999, s. 112(1)(b)), duty is effectively £5 per £1,000 (or part of £1,000) of consideration.

[2] Loan capital is generally exempt from transfer on sale duty subject to specific exclusions (designed to prevent exemption applying to quasi-equity securities) (FA 1986, s. 79).

[3] FA 1986, s. 67(3).

[4] FA 2008, s. 98 exempts transfers that would attract duty not exceeding £5. This applies to instruments executed after 13 March 2008.

Fixed duties

(FA 1999, s. 112(2))

In relation to instruments executed on or after 1 October 1999, the amount of fixed stamp duty is £5.

[¶17-200] Stamp duty penalties

Type of document	Penalties applicable if document presented for stamping more than
Document executed in UK	30 days after execution
Document executed abroad relating to UK land and buildings	30 days after execution
Other document executed abroad	30 days after document first received in UK[1]

Note

[1] Free standing penalty (see table further below) may apply if written information confirming date of receipt in UK is incorrect.

The maximum penalties are:

- £300 or the amount of duty, whichever is less; on documents submitted up to one year late; and

- £300 or the amount of duty, whichever is greater; on documents submitted more than one year late.

Mitigated penalties due on late stamping

The Stamp Office publishes tables (booklet SO10) of mitigated penalty levels that will be applied in straightforward cases.

Cases involving ad valorem duties

Months late	Up to £300	£300– £700	£705– £1,350	£1,355– £2,500	£2,505– £5,000	Over £5,000
Under 3	Nil	£20	£40	£60	£80	£100
Under 6	£20*	£40	£60	£80	£100	£150
Under 9	£40*	£60	£80	£100	£150	£200
Under 12	£60*	£80	£100	£150	£200	£300
Under 15	15% of the duty or £100 if greater					
Under 18	25% of the duty or £150 if greater					See
Under 21	35% of the duty or £200 if greater					below
Under 24	45% of the duty or £250 if greater					

Note

* Or the amount of the duty if that is less.

Cases over one year late involving duty over £5,000 and any case over two years late are considered individually.

Cases involving fixed duties

	Maximum penalty per document	Penalty after mitigation
Up to 12 months late	Nil	Nil
Over 1 year late	£10	According to circumstances
Over 2 years late	£25	According to circumstances

In all cases above the penalties will not apply if the person responsible for stamping can show a 'reasonable excuse' for the failure to submit the document(s) within the time limit. Interest is due on any unpaid penalty.

Free standing penalties (maximum amount)

- fraud in relation to stamp duty; (£3,000)

- failure to set out true facts, relating to stamp duty liability, in a document; (£3,000)

- failure to stamp document within 30 days of issue of a Notice of Decision on Adjudication; (£300)

- failure to allow inspection of documents; (£300)

- registering or enrolling a chargeable document that is not duly stamped; (£300)

- circulating a blank transfer; (£300)

- issuing an unstamped foreign security. (£300)

[¶17-250]   Stamp duty interest

In respect of instruments executed on or after 1 October 1999, interest is chargeable on stamp duty that is not paid within 30 days of execution of a stampable document, wherever execution takes place (SA 1891, s. 15A). Interest is payable on repayments of overpaid duty, calculated from the later of 30 days from the date of execution of the instrument, or lodgement with the Stamp Office of the duty repayable (FA 1999, s. 110). Interest is rounded down (if necessary) to the nearest multiple of £5. No interest is payable if that amount is under £25. The applicable interest rate is as prescribed under FA 1989, s. 178.

For interest periods from 1 October 1999 onwards, the rate of interest charged on underpaid or late paid stamp duty and SDRT exceeds that on repayments:

	Rate %	
Period of application	Underpayments	Repayments
From 29 September 2009	3.00	0.50
24 March 2009 to 28 September 2009	2.50	0.00
27 January 2009 to 23 March 2009	3.50	0.00
6 January 2009 to 26 January 2009	4.50	0.75
6 December 2008 to 5 January 2009	5.50	1.50
6 November 2008 to 5 December 2008	6.50	2.25
6 January 2008 to 5 November 2008	7.50	3.00
6 August 2007 to 5 January 2008	8.50	4.00
6 September 2006 to 5 August 2007	7.50	3.00
6 September 2005 to 5 September 2006	6.50	2.25
6 September 2004 to 5 September 2005	7.50	3.00[1]
6 December 2003 to 5 September 2004	6.50	2.25[1]
6 August 2003 to 5 December 2003	5.50	1.50[1]
6 November 2001 to 5 August 2003	6.50	2.25[1]
6 May 2001 to 5 November 2001	7.50	3.00[1]
5 February 2000 to 5 May 2001	8.50	4.00
1 October 1999 to 5 February 2000	7.50	3.00

Note
[1] Rates revised by HMRC (press release 5 September 2005).

FA 2009, s. 101–104 and Sch. 53 and 54 contain provisions to harmonise interest regimes across all HMRC taxes and duties.

Stamp Taxes

Stamp duty reserve tax

[¶18-000] Stamp duty reserve tax rates
(FA 1986, s. 87)

Principal charge

Subject matter of charge	Rate of tax %
Agreements to transfer chargeable securities[1] for money or money's worth	0.5
Renounceable letters of allotment	0.5
Shares converted into depositary receipts	1.5
but transfer of shares or securities on which stamp duty payable	1
Shares put into clearance system	1.5
but transfer of shares or securities on which stamp duty payable	1

Note

[1] Chargeable securities = stocks, shares, loan capital, units under unit trust scheme (FA 1986, s. 99(3)).

[¶18-050] Stamp duty reserve tax interest
(TMA 1970, s. 86, FA 1986, s. 92 and FA 1989, s. 178 via SI 1986/1711, reg. 11 and 13)

SDRT carries interest as follows:

- interest is charged on SDRT paid late;
- repayments of SDRT carry interest from the date that SDRT was paid; and
- similarly, SDRT is repaid with interest if an instrument is duly stamped within six years of the date of the agreement.

The same rates apply as for stamp duty – see above.

VALUE ADDED TAX

[¶19-000] Rates

(VATA 1994, s. 2)

(VAT Reporter: ¶18-014)

Period of application	Standard rate %	Higher rate %
From 4/1/11	20	N/A
1/1/10–3/1/11	17.5	N/A
1/12/08–31/12/09	15	N/A
1/4/91–30/11/08	$17^1/_2$	N/A
18/6/79–31/3/91	15	N/A
12/4/76–17/6/79	8	$12^1/_2$

Notes

[1] Supplies of fuel and power for domestic, residential and charity non-business use and certain other supplies are charged at five per cent (VATA 1994, Sch. 7A).

[2] Imports of certain works of art, antiques and collectors' items are charged at an effective rate of five per cent from 27 July 1999 (VATA 1994, s. 21(4)–(6)).

[3] The zero rate has applied from 1 April 1973 to date.

[¶19-020] Fractions

(VATA 1994, s. 2)

(VAT Reporter: ¶18-018)

Fractions are used to determine the amount of VAT at a given rate contained in a tax-inclusive figure.

Example

VAT rate 20%

VAT fraction is $20/120 = {}^1/_6$

Retail price (excluding VAT) £1; VAT at 20% = 20p.

Retail price (including VAT) £1.20; multiply by ${}^1/_6$ = 20p.

VAT rate

%	*VAT fraction*
2$\frac{1}{2}$	1/41
5	1/21
8	2/27
10	1/11
12$\frac{1}{2}$	1/9
15	3/23
17$\frac{1}{2}$	7/47
20	1/6
25	1/5

[¶19-040] Flat-rate scheme

(VATA 1994, s. 26B; *Value Added Tax Regulations* 1995 (SI 1995/2518), reg. 55A-55V; Notice 733; HMRC 'Flat rate scheme' manual)

(VAT Reporter: ¶55-350)

Generally, the percentage that applies to the flat-rate scheme (FRS) for small firms is cut by one per cent for the first year of VAT registration.

Flat-rate percentages applying after 3 January 2011

Category of business	Appropriate percentage
Accountancy or book-keeping	14.5
Advertising	11
Agricultural services	11
Any other activity not listed elsewhere	12
Architect, civil and structural engineer or surveyor	14.5
Boarding or care of animals	12
Business services that are not listed elsewhere	12
Catering services including restaurants and takeaways	12.5
Computer and IT consultancy or data processing	14.5
Computer repair services	10.5
Dealing in waste or scrap	10.5
Entertainment or journalism	12.5
Estate agency or property management services	12
Farming or agriculture that is not listed elsewhere	6.5
Film, radio, television or video production	13
Financial services	13.5
Forestry or fishing	10.5
General building or construction services *	9.5
Hairdressing or other beauty treatment services	13

Category of business	Appropriate percentage
Hiring or renting goods	9.5
Hotel or accommodation	10.5
Investigation or security	12
Labour-only building or construction services *	14.5
Laundry or dry-cleaning services	12
Lawyer or legal services	14.5
Library, archive, museum or other cultural activity	9.5
Management consultancy	14
Manufacturing fabricated metal products	10.5
Manufacturing food	9
Manufacturing that is not listed elsewhere	9.5
Manufacturing yarn, textiles or clothing	9
Membership organisation	8
Mining or quarrying	10
Packaging	9
Photography	11
Post offices	5
Printing	8.5
Publishing	11
Pubs	6.5
Real estate activity not listed elsewhere	14
Repairing personal or household goods	10
Repairing vehicles	8.5
Retailing food, confectionary, tobacco, newspapers or children's clothing	4
Retailing pharmaceuticals, medical goods, cosmetics or toiletries	8
Retailing that is not listed elsewhere	7.5
Retailing vehicles or fuel	6.5
Secretarial services	13
Social work	11
Sport or recreation	8.5
Transport or storage, including couriers, freight, removals and taxis	10
Travel agency	10.5
Veterinary medicine	11
Wholesaling agricultural products	8
Wholesaling food	7.5
Wholesaling that is not listed elsewhere	8.5

Value Added Tax

Note

* 'Labour-only building or construction services' means building or construction services where the value of materials supplied is less than 10 per cent of relevant turnover from such services; any other building or construction services are 'general building or construction services'.

Flat-rate percentages applying after 31 December 2009 and before 4 January 2011

Category of business	Appropriate percentage
Accountancy or book-keeping	13
Advertising	10
Agricultural services	10
Any other activity not listed elsewhere	10.5
Architect, civil and structural engineer or surveyor	13
Boarding or care of animals	10.5
Business services that are not listed elsewhere	10.5
Catering services including restaurants and takeaways	11
Computer and IT consultancy or data processing	13
Computer repair services	9.5
Dealing in waste or scrap	9.5
Entertainment or journalism	11
Estate agency or property management services	10.5
Farming or agriculture that is not listed elsewhere	6
Film, radio, television or video production	11.5
Financial services	12
Forestry or fishing	9.5
General building or construction services *	8.5
Hairdressing or other beauty treatment services	11.5
Hiring or renting goods	8.5
Hotel or accommodation	9.5
Investigation or security	10.5
Labour-only building or construction services *	13
Laundry or dry-cleaning services	10.5
Lawyer or legal services	13
Library, archive, museum or other cultural activity	8.5

Category of business	Appropriate percentage
Management consultancy	12.5
Manufacturing fabricated metal products	9.5
Manufacturing food	8
Manufacturing that is not listed elsewhere	8.5
Manufacturing yarn, textiles or clothing	8
Membership organisation	7
Mining or quarrying	9
Packaging	8
Photography	10
Post offices	4.5
Printing	7.5
Publishing	10
Pubs	6
Real estate activity not listed elsewhere	12.5
Repairing personal or household goods	9
Repairing vehicles	7.5
Retailing food, confectionary, tobacco, newspapers or children's clothing	3.5
Retailing pharmaceuticals, medical goods, cosmetics or toiletries	7
Retailing that is not listed elsewhere	6.5
Retailing vehicles or fuel	6
Secretarial services	11.5
Social work	10
Sport or recreation	7.5
Transport or storage, including couriers, freight, removals and taxis	9
Travel agency	9.5
Veterinary medicine	10
Wholesaling agricultural products	7
Wholesaling food	6.5
Wholesaling that is not listed elsewhere	7.5

Value Added Tax

Note

* 'Labour-only building or construction services' means building or construction services where the value of materials supplied is less than 10 per cent of relevant turnover from such services; any other building or construction services are 'general building or construction services'.

Flat-rate percentages applying after 30 November 2008 and before 1 January 2010

Category of business	Appropriate percentage
Accountancy or book-keeping	11.5
Advertising	8.5
Agricultural services	7
Any other activity not listed elsewhere	9
Architect, civil and structural engineer or surveyor	11
Boarding or care of animals	9.5
Business services that are not listed elsewhere	9.5
Catering services including restaurants and takeaways	10.5
Computer and IT consultancy or data processing	11.5
Computer repair services	10
Dealing in waste or scrap	8.5
Entertainment or journalism	9.5
Estate agency or property management services	9.5
Farming or agriculture that is not listed elsewhere	5.5
Film, radio, television or video production	9.5
Financial services	10.5
Forestry or fishing	8
General building or constructions services *	7.5
Hairdressing or other beauty treatment services	10.5
Hiring or renting goods	7.5
Hotel or accommodation	8.5
Investigation or security	9
Labour-only building or construction services *	11.5
Laundry or dry-cleaning services	9.5
Lawyer or legal services	12
Library, archive, museum or other cultural activity	7.5

Category of business	Appropriate percentage
Management consultancy	11
Manufacturing that is not listed elsewhere	7.5
Manufacturing fabricated metal products	8.5
Manufacturing food	7
Manufacturing yam, textiles or clothing	7.5
Membership organisation	5.5
Mining or quarrying	8
Packaging	7.5
Photography	8.5
Post offices	2
Printing	6.5
Publishing	8.5
Pubs	5.5
Real estate activity not listed elsewhere	11
Repairing personal or household goods	7.5
Repairing vehicles	6.5
Retailing food, confectionary, tobacco, newspapers or children's clothing	2
Retailing pharmaceuticals, medical goods, cosmetics or toiletries	6
Retailing that is not listed elsewhere	5.5
Retailing vehicles or fuel	5.5
Secretarial services	9.5
Social work	8
Sport or recreation	6
Transport or storage, including couriers, freight, removals and taxis	8
Travel agency	8
Veterinary medicine	8
Wholesaling agricultural products	5.5
Wholesaling food	5
Wholesaling that is not listed elsewhere	6

Value Added Tax

Note

* 'Labour-only building or construction services' means building or construction services where the value of materials supplied is less than 10 per cent of relevant turnover from such services; and other building or construction services are 'general building or construction services'.

Flat-rate percentages applying after 31 December 2003 and before 1 December 2008

Trade Sector (from 1 January 2004)	Flat Rate Percentage
Retailing food, confectionery, tobacco, newspapers or children's clothing	2
Membership organisation	5.5
Postal and courier services	
Pubs	
Wholesaling food	
Farming or agriculture that is not listed elsewhere	6
Retailing that is not listed elsewhere	
Wholesaling agricultural products	
Retailing pharmaceuticals, medical goods, cosmetics or toiletries	7
Retailing vehicles or fuel	
Sport or recreation	
Wholesaling that is not listed elsewhere	
Agricultural services	7.5
Library, archive, museum or other cultural activity	
Manufacturing food	
Printing	
Repairing vehicles	
General building or construction services *	8.5
Hiring or renting goods	
Manufacturing that is not listed elsewhere	
Manufacturing yarn, textiles or clothing	
Packaging	
Repairing personal or household goods	
Social work	

Trade Sector (from 1 January 2004)	Flat Rate Percentage
Forestry or fishing	9
Mining or quarrying	
Transport or storage, including couriers, freight, removals and taxis	
Travel agency	
Advertising	9.5
Dealing in waste or scrap	
Hotel or accommodation	
Photography	
Publishing	
Veterinary medicine	
Any other activity not listed elsewhere	10
Investigation or security	
Manufacturing fabricated metal products	
Boarding or care of animals	10.5
Film, radio, television or video production	
Business services that are not listed elsewhere	11
Computer repair services	
Entertainment or journalism	
Estate agency or property management services	
Laundry or dry-cleaning services	
Secretarial services	
Financial services	11.5
Catering services, including restaurants and takeaways	12
Hairdressing or other beauty treatment services	
Real estate activity not listed elsewhere	
Architect, civil and structural engineer or surveyor	12.5
Management consultancy	

Value Added Tax

Trade Sector (from 1 January 2004)	Flat Rate Percentage
Accountancy or book-keeping	13
Computer and IT consultancy or data processing	
Lawyer or legal services	
Labour-only building or construction services *	13.5

Note

* 'Labour-only building or construction services' means services where the value of materials supplied is under 10% of turnover of such services. Other building or construction services are 'General building or construction services'.

[¶19-060] Farmer's flat-rate scheme

(VATA 1994, s. 54; *Value Added Tax Regulations* 1995 (SI 1995/2518), reg. 202ff., *Value Added Tax (Flat-rate Scheme for Farmers) (Designated Activities) Order* 1992 (SI 1992/3220), *Value Added Tax (Flat-rate Scheme for Farmers) (Percentage Addition) Order* 1992 (SI 1992/3221); Notice 700/46; HMRC 'VAT – Agricultural flat rate scheme' manual)

(VAT Reporter: ¶53-500)

The rate which applies to the farmers' flat-rate scheme is four per cent.

[¶19-080] Registration limits

(1) Taxable supplies

(VATA 1994, Sch. 1; Notice 700/1)

(VAT Reporter: ¶43-025)

Past turnover limits

Period of application	Past turnover (£)		Future turnover (£)
	1 year £	Unless turnover for next year will not exceed £	30 days £
From 1/4/10	70,000	68,000	70,000
1/5/09–31/03/10	68,000	66,000	68,000
1/4/08–30/04/09	67,000	65,000	67,000
1/4/07–31/03/08	64,000	62,000	64,000
1/4/06–31/03/07	61,000	59,000	61,000
1/4/05–31/03/06	60,000	58,000	60,000
1/4/04–31/03/05	58,000	56,000	58,000

Future prospects rule: in addition, *future taxable* turnover must be considered. Registration is required if there are reasonable grounds for believing that the value of *taxable* supplies in a period of 30 days (before 21 March 1990 this period was one year) will exceed the given limit. This limit is the same as that for the 12 months above, but applies to 30 days from any time.

Notes

Taxable supplies at *both* the zero rate and positive rates are included in the above limits. *All* of a person's taxable supplies are considered, because it is 'persons' not 'businesses' who can or must register.

These limits are *exclusive* of VAT as VAT is not chargeable unless a person is registered or liable to be registered.

Quarter means *calendar* quarter to the end of March, June, September or December.

The limit which applies for a particular past period is that which is in force at the *end* of the period.

There are now two *alternative* tests of the liability to notify HMRC of a person's liability to register as a result of making taxable supplies:

(1)   past 12 months turnover limit; and

(2)   future 30 days turnover limit.

The following are *excluded* from the supplies for the purpose of applying the registration limits.

(1)   value of capital supplies (other than of land)

(2)   any taxable supplies which would not be taxable supplies apart from VATA 1994, s. 7(4), which concerns removal of goods to the UK.

Any supplies made at a previous time when the person was registered are *disregarded* if all necessary information was given to HMRC when the earlier registration was cancelled.

If a person took over a business as a 'going concern', he is *deemed* to have made the vendor's supplies for the purposes of registration.

(2) Supplies from other member states

(VATA 1994, Sch. 2; Notice 700/1)

(VAT Reporter: ¶43-030)

Period of application	Cumulative relevant supplies from 1 January in year to any day in same year £
From 1/1/93	70,000

(VATA 1994, Sch. 2; Notice 700/1).

Generally, the value of relevant supplies is of those made by persons in other member states to non-taxable persons in the UK.

If certain goods, which are subject to excise duty, are removed to the UK, the person who removes the goods is liable to register in the UK because all such goods must be taxed in the country of destination. There is no de minimis limit.

(3) Acquisitions from other member states

(VATA 1994, Sch. 3; Notice 700/1)

(VAT Reporter: ¶43-035)

Period of application	Cumulative relevant supplies from 1 January in year to any day in same year £
From 1/4/10	70,000
1/5/09–31/03/10	68,000
1/4/08–30/04/09	67,000

Value Added Tax

Period of application	Cumulative relevant supplies from 1 January in year to any day in same year £
1/4/07–31/03/08	64,000
1/4/06–31/03/07	61,000
1/4/05–31/03/06	60,000
1/4/04–31/03/05	58,000

Future prospects rule: a person is also liable to register at any time if there are reasonable grounds for believing that the value of his relevant acquisitions in the period of 30 days then beginning will exceed the given limit. This limit is the same as that for the period starting on 1 January above.

(4) Assets supplied in the UK by overseas persons

(VATA 1994, Sch. 3A; Notice 700/1)

(VAT Reporter: ¶43-045)

From 21 March 2000, any person without an establishment in the UK making or intending to make 'relevant supplies' must VAT register, regardless of the value of those supplies.

'Relevant supplies' are taxable supplies of goods, including capital assets, in the UK where the supplier has recovered UK VAT under:

(1)   Directive 2008/9 (for claims made before 1 January 2010: Directive 79/1072 (the eighth VAT directive)) for a person in a member state as regards VAT incurred in another member state; or

(2)   Directive 86/560 (the thirteenth VAT directive) for claimants established outside the member states.

This applies where:

•   the supplier (or his predecessor in business) was charged VAT on the purchase of the goods, or on anything incorporated in them, and has either claimed it back or intends to do so; or

•   the VAT being claimed back was VAT paid on the import of goods into the UK.

(5) Electronic services

(VATA 1994, Sch. 3B; Notice 700/1)

(VAT Reporter: ¶43-047)

A person can register under if he makes or intends to make qualifying supplies, i.e. electronically supplied services to a person who belongs in the UK or another member state and who receives such services otherwise than for business purposes. The person who registers must have neither a business establishment nor a fixed establishment in the UK or in another member state in relation to any supply. Generally the person must also be neither registered nor required to be registered for VAT in the UK or the Isle of Man or, under equivalent legislation, in another member state.

[¶19-100]   De-registration limits

(1) Taxable supplies

(VATA 1994, Sch. 1; Notice 700/1)

(VAT Reporter: ¶43-925)

De-registration at any time

A registered person ceases to be liable to be registered if at *any* time HMRC are satisfied that the value of his taxable supplies in the period of one year then beginning will not exceed a certain limit. The limits and periods of application are set out below:

Period of application	Future turnover £
From 1/4/10	68,000
1/5/09–31/3/10	66,000
1/4/08–30/4/09	65,000
1/4/07–31/3/08	62,000
1/4/06–31/3/07	59,000
1/4/05–31/3/06	58,000
1/4/04–31/3/05	56,000

Notes

The value of supplies of capital assets is *excluded* from the supplies for the purpose of applying the de-registration limits.

The de-registration limits *exclude* VAT.

Taxable supplies at both the *zero* rate and positive rates are included in the above limits.

Since 15 May 1987 the question of de-registration is determined by the above test only, i.e. only *future turnover* is relevant.

(2) Supplies from other member states

(VATA 1994, Sch. 2; Notice 700/1)

(VAT Reporter: ¶43-930)

Period of application	Past relevant supplies in last year to 31 December £	Future relevant supplies in immediately following year £
From 1/1/93	70,000	70,000

Generally, the value of supplies is of those made by persons in other member states to non-taxable persons in the UK.

(3) Acquisitions from other member states

(VATA 1994, Sch. 3; Notice 700/1)

(VAT Reporter: ¶43-940)

Value Added Tax

Period of application	Past relevant acquisitions in last year to 31 December £	Future relevant acquisitions in immediately following year £
From 1/4/10	70,000	70,000
1/5/09–31/3/10	68,000	68,000
1/4/08–30/4/09	67,000	67,000
1/4/07–31/3/08	64,000	64,000
1/4/06–31/3/07	61,000	61,000
1/4/05–31/3/06	60,000	60,000
1/4/04–31/3/05	58,000	58,000

(4) Assets supplied in the UK by overseas persons

(VATA 1994, Sch. 3A; Notice 700/1)

(VAT Reporter: ¶43-945)

If HMRC are satisfied that a person registered under VATA 1994, Sch. 3A has ceased to make relevant supplies, HMRC can de-register the person from the date on which he so ceased or from an agreed later date. However, HMRC must not de-register a person unless they are satisfied that he is not liable to be registered under another provision in VATA 1994.

(5) Electronic services

(VATA 1994, Sch. 3B; Notice 700/1)

(VAT Reporter: ¶43-946)

HMRC cancel a person's registration under VATA 1994, Sch. 3B if he notifies them, or they determine, that he ceased to make, or have the intention of to make, qualifying supplies.

[¶19-120]   Special accounting limits

Cash accounting: admission to the scheme

(*Value Added Tax Regulations* 1995 (SI 1995/2518), reg. 56-65; Notice 731; HMRC 'VAT – Cash accounting scheme' manual)

(VAT Reporter: ¶55-450)

Period of application	Annual turnover limit[1] £
From 1/4/07	1,350,000
1/4/04–31/3/07	660,000
1/4/01–31/3/04	600,000
1/4/93–31/3/01	350,000
1/10/90–31/3/93	300,000

Note

(1) Includes zero-rated supplies, but excludes any capital assets previously used in the business. Exempt supplies are also excluded.

(2) A person must stop using the cash accounting scheme at the end of the prescribed accounting period if the value of his taxable supplies in the one year ending at the end of the prescribed accounting period has exceeded (from 1 April 2007) £1,600,000 (*Value Added Tax Regulations* 1995 (SI 1995/2518), Pt. VIII; Notice 731).

(3) Outstanding VAT on supplies made and received while using the cash accounting scheme may be brought into account on a cash basis for a further six months after withdrawal from the scheme, but only where withdrawal was voluntary or because the turnover threshold was exceeded.

Annual accounting: admission to the scheme

(*Value Added Tax Regulations* 1995 (SI 1995/2518), reg. 49-55; Notice 732; HMRC 'VAT – Annual accounting scheme' manual)

(VAT Reporter: ¶55-300)

Period of application	Annual turnover limit(1) £
From 1/4/06	1,350,000
1/4/04–31/3/06	600,000
1/4/01–31/3/04	600,000
9/4/91–31/3/01	300,000

Note

(1) Positive and zero-rated supplies excluding any supplies of capital assets and any exempt supplies.

(2) A person must stop using the annual accounting scheme at the end of a prescribed accounting period if the value of his taxable supplies in the one year ending at the end of the prescribed accounting period has exceeded (from 1 April 2006) £1,600,000 (*Value Added Tax Regulations* 1995 (SI 1995/2518), Pt. VII; Notice 732).

(3) Persons with a taxable turnover of up to (from 10 April 2003) £150,000 may join the annual accounting scheme immediately, i.e. without having to be registered for at least 12 months.

Flat-rate scheme for small businesses: admission to the scheme

(*Value Added Tax Regulations* 1995 (SI 1995/2518), reg. 55A-55V; Notice 733; HMRC 'Flat rate scheme' manual)

(VAT Reporter: ¶55-350)

From 1 April 2009, the only test for eligibility to be admitted to the flat-rate scheme is the taxable turnover of the business, i.e. the £150,000 limit in the middle column in the table below.

Period of application	Annual taxable turnover limit(1) £	Annual total turnover limit(2) £
From 1/4/09	150,000	Test discontinued
10/4/03 – 31/3/09	150,000	187,500
25/4/02 – 9/4/03	100,000	125,000

Note

(1) Zero-rated and positive-rated supplies excluding VAT. Exempt supplies are excluded.

(2) Total of VAT-exclusive turnover and exempt and/or other non-taxable income.

(3) Net VAT liability is calculated by applying a flat-rate percentage to the VAT-inclusive turnover. The flat-rate percentage depends upon the trader sector (*Value Added Tax Regulations* 1995 (SI 1995/2518), Pt. VIIA; Notice

Value Added Tax

733). However from 1 January 2004, in the first year of VAT registration, the flat-rate percentage can be reduced by one per cent, i.e. if the normal rate is ten per cent, then nine per cent applies.

[4] From 4 January 2011, a person must leave the flat-rate scheme if either his VAT-inclusive annual flat-rate turnover exceeds £230,000 or his VAT-inclusive turnover in the next 30 days can reasonably be expected to exceed £230,000. (Before 4 January 2011, both exit thresholds were £225,000.)

If a user of the flat rate scheme exceeds the annual exit threshold as a result of a one-off transaction, but in the subsequent year he expects his VAT-inclusive annual flat-rate turnover to be under £191,500 (before 4 January 2011: £187,500), he may remain in the scheme with HMRC's agreement (*Value Added Tax Regulations* 1995 (SI 1995/2518), Pt. VIIA; Notice 733).

[¶19-140]   Zero-rated supplies

(VATA 1994, Sch. 8)

(VAT Reporter: ¶20-000)

A zero-rated supply is a taxable supply, but the tax rate is nil.

Group	
1.	Food (this includes most food for human and animal consumption - the exceptions are mainly food supplied in the course of catering, confectionary, pet foods and hot take-away food)
2.	Sewerage services and water (except distilled and bottled water) but not if supplied to industry
3.	Books, pamphlets, newspapers, journals, maps, music etc. (but not stationery and posters)
4.	Talking books for the blind and handicapped and wireless sets for the blind
5.	Construction of buildings etc
6.	Protected buildings
7.	International services
8.	Transport
9.	Caravans and houseboats
10.	Gold
11.	Bank notes
12.	Drugs, medicines, aids for the handicapped etc
13.	Imports, exports etc
14.	(repealed for supplies made after 30 June 1999) Tax-free shops
15.	Charities etc
16.	Clothing and footwear
17.	(for supplies made after 30 July 2009, but later repealed for supplies made after 31 October 2010 when the reverse charge applies) Emissions allowances

Notes

Except for exported goods and certain transactions in commodities, generally a supply is not zero-rated *unless* it is specified in the zero-rated schedule (VATA 1994, Sch. 8). A supply which can be classified as zero-rated overrides exemption. A supply which is not outside the scope of VAT is standard-rated *unless* it falls within one of the categories of exempt or zero-rated or reduced-rate supplies.

[¶19-160]   Exempt supplies
(VATA 1994, Sch. 9)

(VAT Reporter: ¶27-000)

No VAT is chargeable on an exempt supply, but input tax cannot be reclaimed except as computed under the provisions on partial exemption.

Group	
1.	Land
2.	Insurance
3.	Postal services (restricted after 30 January 2011 to supplies of public postal services and incidental goods made by the universal service provider)
4.	Betting, gaming and lotteries
5.	Finance
6.	Education
7.	Health and welfare
8.	Burial and cremation
9.	Subscriptions to trade unions, professional bodies and other public interest bodies
10.	Sport, sports competitions and physical education
11.	Works of art etc.
12.	Fund-raising events by charities and other qualifying bodies
13.	Cultural services etc.
14.	Supplies of goods where input tax cannot be recovered (from 1 March 2000)
15.	Investment gold (from 1 January 2000)

Notes
The descriptions of the zero-rated and exempt groups are for ease of reference only and do not affect the interpretation of the groups (VATA 1994, s. 96(10)). Some suppliers can unilaterally opt to tax certain land and buildings (VATA 1994, Sch. 10, para. 2–4).

[¶19-180]   Reduced-rate supplies
(VATA 1994, Sch. 7A)

(VAT Reporter: ¶32-000)

VAT is chargeable at five per cent on a reduced-rated supply

Group	
1.	Domestic fuel and power
2.	Installation of energy-saving materials
3.	Grant-funded installation of heating equipment or security goods or connection of gas supply.
4.	Women's sanitary products

Value Added Tax

Group	
5.	Children's car seats
6.	Residential conversions
7.	Residential renovations and alterations
8.	Contraceptive products (from 1 July 2006)
9.	Welfare advice or information (from 1 July 2006)
10.	Installation of mobility aids for the elderly (from 1 July 2007)
11.	Smoking cessation products (from 1 July 2007)

Notes

[1] The 'Listed Places of Worship Grants Scheme', which is administered by the Department for Culture, Media and Sport (DCMS), effectively leaves a listed place of worship bearing VAT at five per cent on repairs by funding the difference between VAT at five per cent and at the standard rate. This runs along with the scheme for UK charities which refunds the VAT charged on qualifying supplies made after 15 March 2005 in the construction, renovation and maintenance of certain memorials.

[¶19-200] Partial exemption

(*Value Added Tax Regulations* 1995 (SI 1995/2518), reg. 99-111; Notice 706; HMRC 'Partial exemption' manual)

(VAT Reporter: ¶19-400)

The law on partial exemption may restrict the amount of deductible input tax.

Where input tax cannot be attributed directly to taxable or exempt supplies (residual input tax), the standard method apportions the residual input tax according to the values of taxable and exempt supplies made in a period. In relation to input tax incurred after 17 April 2002, persons must adjust the input tax deductible under the standard method at the end of their tax year if that amount is substantially different from an attribution based on the use of purchases. 'Substantially' means:

● £50,000 or greater; or

● 50% or more of the value of the residual input tax, but not less than £25,000.

Where the residual input tax is less than £50,000 per year, the standard method can be used, unless the person is defined as a group undertaking under the Companies Acts and the residual input tax is greater than £25,000 per year.

Generally, the established de minimis limit for applying the partial exemption rules is as follows:

Period	Exempt input tax not exceeding
Tax years beginning after 30/11/94	● £625 per month on average; and ● 50% of total input tax for prescribed accounting period

In order to establish whether the de minimis limit has been breached, for partial exemption years starting after 31 March 2010, some taxable persons need only carry out simplified tests, rather than carry out detailed partial exemption calculations. The simplest test is whether total input tax incurred by a taxable person is less than £625 per month on average. If so, as long as 50% or less of the turnover is exempt, the de minimis test is passed. If that test is failed, the next simplified test is to strip out all input tax that is directly and solely attributable to taxable supplies. If the remainder is less than £625 per month on average then, as long as the value of exempt supplies does not exceed one-half of the value of all supplies, the de minimis test is passed.

For accounting periods commencing after 31 March 2005, rounding up the recovery rate under the standard method to the next whole number is only allowed for persons incurring no more than £400,000 residual input tax per month on average. Other persons round to two decimal places.

HMRC's approval of a partial exemption special method from 1 April 2007 is subject to a declaration by the taxable person that to the best of his knowledge and belief the proposed method is fair and reasonable.

[¶19-220] Capital goods scheme

(*Value Added Tax Regulations* 1995 (SI 1995/2518), reg. 112-116; Notice 706/2)

(VAT Reporter: ¶19-800)

The capital goods scheme affects the acquisition, etc. by a partially exempt person for use in a business of certain items as follows:

Item	Value	Adjustment period
Computers and computer equipment	£50,000 or more	5 years
Land and buildings[1]	£250,000 or more	10 years (5 years where interest had less than 10 years to run on acquisition)

Note
[1] From 3 July 1997, the capital goods scheme affects:
- civil engineering works; and
- the refurbishment or fitting out of a building by the owner.

Where the capital goods scheme applies, any initial deduction of input tax is made in the ordinary way, but must then be reviewed over the adjustment period by reference to the use of the asset concerned.

Revised rules apply to all capital goods scheme adjustments for intervals starting on or after 10 March 1999, to ensure that such adjustments compare the later use of the asset with the actual initial deduction of input VAT, after any other partial exemption adjustments.

[¶19-240] Particulars to be shown on a valid VAT invoice

(*Value Added Tax Regulations* 1995 (SI 1995/2518), reg.14; Notice 700, para. 16.1ff. (2002 edn))

(VAT Reporter: ¶55-800)

Value Added Tax

VAT invoices generally where supplied to a person who is also in the UK

1.	A sequential number based on one or more series which uniquely identifies the document
2.	The time of the supply
3.	The date of issue of the document
4.	The name, address and registration number of the supplier
5.	The name and address of the person to whom the goods or services are supplied
6.	A description sufficient to identify the goods or services supplied
7.	For each description, the quantity of the goods or the extent of the services, the rate of VAT and the amount payable, excluding VAT, expressed in any currency.
8.	The gross total amount payable, excluding VAT, expressed in any currency
9.	The rate of any cash discount offered
10.	The total amount of VAT chargeable, expressed in sterling
11.	The unit price
12.	From 1 October 2007, where a margin scheme applies (a) to second-hand goods, antiques, works of art, collectors' items or (b) to certain supplies made by a tour operator, a relevant reference to the appropriate provision in Directive 2006/112 or any indication that a margin scheme has been applied. For example, the invoice may include the legend 'This invoice is for a second-hand margin scheme supply' or 'This is a tour operators' margin scheme supply'.
13.	From 1 October 2007, where a VAT invoice relates in whole or part to a supply where the person supplied is liable to pay the tax, a relevant reference to the appropriate provision in Directive 2006/112 or any indication that the supply is one where the customer is liable to pay the tax . For example, the invoice may include the legend 'This supply is subject to the reverse charge'.

Generally, VAT officers adopt a 'light touch' for about one year after any change to the requirements for a valid VAT invoice in order to give reasonable time to change procedures and help minimise the cost of change.

Persons providing VAT invoices for leasing certain motor cars must state on the invoice whether the car is a qualifying vehicle. This enables the lessee to claim the correct proportion of the VAT charged by the lessor.

The requirements for invoices concerning supplies intra-EU member states are in the *Value Added Tax Regulations* 1995 (SI 1995/2518), reg. 14(2).

Also, a VAT invoice must be provided for an exempt supply made to a person in another member state for the purposes of that person's business.

Retailers' invoices

If the supplier sells directly to the public, he is only required to issue a VAT invoice if the customer requests it. Furthermore, if the supply is for £250 (before 1 January 2004, £100) or less, *including* VAT, a less-detailed VAT invoice can be issued setting out only the following:

1.	The name, address and registration number of the retailer
2.	The time of the supply
3.	A description sufficient to identify the goods or services supplied
4.	The total amount payable including VAT
5.	The rate of VAT in force at the time of the supply

See Notice 700 concerning the special rules for invoices concerning:

- petrol, derv, paraffin, and heating oil;
- credit cards;
- another form of modified VAT invoice for retailers;
- cash and carry wholesalers;
- computer invoicing; and
- calculation of VAT on invoices.

Continuous supplies of services

Certain additional particulars are required to be shown on a VAT invoice for a supply of continuous services, if the supplier chooses to use the advance invoicing facility (*Value Added Tax Regulations* 1995 (SI 1995/2518), reg. 90). Similar provisions apply for advance invoicing in respect of long leases (reg. 85) and in respect of supplies of water, gas, power, heat, refrigeration and ventilation (reg. 86).

[¶19-260] 'Blocked' input tax

(VATA 1994, s. 24)

(VAT Reporter: ¶19-004)

Any input tax charged on the following items is 'blocked', i.e. non-recoverable:

- motor cars, other than certain motor cars acquired by certain persons but after 31 July 1995 (1) any person can recover input tax on motor cars used exclusively for business and (2) only 50 per cent of VAT on car leasing charges is recoverable if lessee makes any private use of the car and if lessor recovered the VAT on buying the car;
- entertainment, except of employees;
- in the case of claims by builders, articles of a kind not ordinarily installed by builders as fixtures in new houses;
- goods supplied under the second-hand scheme;
- goods imported for private purposes;
- non-business element of supplies to be used only partly for business purposes. This may contravene European law where the supplies are of goods: strictly the input tax is deductible, but output tax is due on non-business use. VAT on supplies not intended for business use does not rank as input tax, so cannot be recovered; and
- goods and services acquired by a tour operator for re-supply as a designated travel service.

Value Added Tax

In addition, 'exempt input tax' is not recoverable. From 10 March 1999, the partial exemption simplification rule that allowed some businesses to claim back all their input tax, providing that their exempt input tax is only incurred in relation to certain exempt supplies, has been abolished.

[¶19-280]   Input tax and mileage allowances

(Value Added Tax (Input Tax) (Reimbursement by Employers of Employees' Business Use of Road Fuel) Regulations 2005 (SI 2005/3290))

(VAT Reporter: ¶19-071)

An employer can reclaim the VAT incurred by employees on fuel costs that are reimbursed by the employer on the basis of cost or via a mileage allowance. VAT can only be reclaimed by an employer on fuel which is used in the course of the business to make taxable supplies. However, the key practical change is that employers must obtain and retain a valid VAT invoice to support the reclaim. Generally, a retailer's invoice (also known as a 'less-detailed invoice') should suffice, because the amount of fuel that is purchased by an employee in a single supply is likely to be within the VAT-inclusive limit of £250 for a retailer's invoice.

Generally, the invoiced amount does not match the input tax claim for the fuel in any one claim period and invoices may concern more than one period. For example, if fuel is purchased towards the end of a period, it may not be fully used until a subsequent period. An invoice may cover more than one claim and this needs to be taken into account when checking the evidence to support claims. Another possible reason why the invoiced amount does not match the claim is that often some of the fuel is used by the employee for private journeys. Generally, the VAT can be reclaimed if the invoice(s) are for sufficient fuel to cover the claimed mileage, and cover the relevant period. Strictly, a claim cannot be supported by an invoice that is dated after the dates covered by the claim.

HMRC publish 'advisory fuel rates' to determine the business fuel cost, but rates set by recognised motoring agencies, such as the RAC and the AA, are usually acceptable. HMRC first published the rates in 2002 (*www.hmrc.gov.uk/cars/fuel_company_cars.htm*).

For journeys after 31 May 2010 and until further notice, rate per mile

Engine size	Petrol	Diesel	LPG
1400cc or less	12p	11p	8p
1401cc to 2000cc	15p	11p	10p
Over 2000cc	21p	16p	14p

For journeys after 30 November 2009, but before 1 June 2010, rate per mile

Engine size	Petrol	Diesel	LPG
1400cc or less	11p	11p	7p
1401cc to 2000cc	14p	11p	8p
Over 2000cc	20p	14p	12p

For journeys after 30 June 2009, but before 1 December 2009, rate per mile

Engine size	Petrol	Diesel	LPG
1400cc or less	10p	10p	7p
1401cc to 2000cc	12p	10p	8p
Over 2000cc	18p	13p	12p

For journeys after 31 December 2008, but before 1 July 2009, rate per mile

Engine size	Fuel cost per mile (petrol)	Fuel cost per mile (diesel)	Fuel cost per mile (liquid petroleum gas)
1400cc or less	10p	11p	7p
1401cc to 2000cc	12p	11p	9p
Over 2000cc	17p	14p	12p

For journeys after 30 June 2008, but before 1 January 2009, the rate per mile is as follows:

Engine size	Fuel cost per mile (petrol)	Fuel cost per mile (diesel)	Fuel cost per mile (liquid petroleum gas)
1400cc or less	12p	13p	7p
1401cc to 2000cc	15p	13p	9p
Over 2000cc	21p	17p	13p

For journeys after 31 December 2007 but before 1 July 2008, the rate per mile is as follows:

Engine size	Fuel cost per mile (petrol)	Fuel cost per mile (diesel)	Fuel cost per mile (liquid petroleum gas)
1400cc or less	11p	11p	7p
1401cc to 2000cc	13p	11p	8p
Over 2000cc	19p	14p	11p

[¶19-300]   VAT on private fuel (scale charges)

(VATA 1994, s. 57; Notice 700/64)

(VAT Reporter: ¶18-320ff.)

From 4 JANUARY 2011 (20 per cent VAT rate)

Fuel scale charges for 12-month period

CO_2 band	VAT fuel scale charge, 12-month period, £	VAT on 12-month charge, £	VAT exclusive 12-month charge, £
120 or less	570.00	95.00	475.00
125	850.00	141.67	708.33
130	850.00	141.67	708.33
135	910.00	151.67	758.33
140	965.00	160.83	804.17
145	1,020.00	170.00	850.00
150	1,080.00	180.00	900.00
155	1,135.00	189.17	945.83
160	1,190.00	198.33	991.67
165	1,250.00	208.33	1,041.67
170	1,305.00	217.50	1,087.50
175	1,360.00	226.67	1,133.33
180	1,420.00	236.67	1,183.33
185	1,475.00	245.83	1,229.17
190	1,530.00	255.00	1,275.00
195	1,590.00	265.00	1,325.00
200	1,645.00	274.17	1,370.83
205	1,705.00	284.17	1,420.83
210	1,760.00	293.33	1,466.67
215	1,815.00	302.50	1,512.50
220	1,875.00	312.50	1,562.50
225	1,930.00	321.67	1,608.33
230 or more	1,985.00	330.83	1,654.17

Fuel scale charges for 3-month period

CO_2 band	VAT fuel scale charge, 3-month period, £	VAT on 3-month charge, £	VAT exclusive 3-month charge, £
120 or less	141.00	23.50	117.50
125	212.00	35.33	176.67
130	212.00	35.33	176.67

CO_2 band	VAT fuel scale charge, 3-month period, £	VAT on 3-month charge, £	VAT exclusive 3-month charge, £
135	227.00	37.83	189.17
140	241.00	40.17	200.83
145	255.00	42.50	212.50
150	269.00	44.83	224.17
155	283.00	47.17	235.83
160	297.00	49.50	247.50
165	312.00	52.00	260.00
170	326.00	54.33	271.67
175	340.00	56.67	283.33
180	354.00	59.00	295.00
185	368.00	61.33	306.67
190	383.00	63.83	319.17
195	397.00	66.17	330.83
200	411.00	68.50	342.50
205	425.00	70.83	354.17
210	439.00	73.17	365.83
215	454.00	75.67	378.33
220	468.00	78.00	390.00
225	482.00	80.33	401.67
230 or more	496.00	82.67	413.33

Fuel scale charges for 1-month period

CO_2 band	VAT fuel scale charge, 1-month period, £	VAT on 1-month charge, £	VAT exclusive 1-month charge, £
120 or less	47.00	7.83	39.17
125	70.00	11.67	58.33
130	70.00	11.67	58.33
135	75.00	12.50	62.50
140	80.00	13.33	66.67
145	85.00	14.17	70.83
150	89.00	14.83	74.17
155	94.00	15.67	78.33
160	99.00	16.50	82.50
165	104.00	17.33	86.67
170	108.00	18.00	90.00

Value Added Tax

CO_2 band	VAT fuel scale charge, 1-month period, £	VAT on 1-month charge, £	VAT exclusive 1-month charge, £
175	113.00	18.83	94.17
180	118.00	19.67	98.33
185	122.00	20.33	101.67
190	127.00	21.17	105.83
195	132.00	22.00	110.00
200	137.00	22.83	114.17
205	141.00	23.50	117.50
210	146.00	24.33	121.67
215	151.00	25.17	125.83
220	156.00	26.00	130.00
225	160.00	26.67	133.33
230 or more	165.00	27.50	137.50

1 MAY 2010 – 3 JANUARY 2011 (17.5 per cent VAT rate)

Fuel scale charges for 12-month period

CO_2 band	VAT fuel scale charge, 12-month period, £	VAT on 12-month charge, £	VAT exclusive 12-month charge, £
120 or less	570.00	84.89	485.11
125	850.00	126.60	723.40
130	850.00	126.60	723.40
135	910.00	135.53	774.47
140	965.00	143.72	821.28
145	1,020.00	151.91	868.09
150	1,080.00	160.85	919.15
155	1,135.00	169.04	965.96
160	1,190.00	177.23	1,012.77
165	1,250.00	186.17	1,063.83
170	1,305.00	194.36	1,110.64
175	1,360.00	202.55	1,157.45
180	1,420.00	211.49	1,208.51
185	1,475.00	219.68	1,255.32
190	1,530.00	227.87	1,302.13
195	1,590.00	236.81	1,353.19
200	1,645.00	245.00	1,400.00
205	1,705.00	253.94	1,451.06
210	1,760.00	262.13	1,497.87

CO₂ band	VAT fuel scale charge, 12-month period, £	VAT on 12-month charge, £	VAT exclusive 12-month charge, £
215	1,815.00	270.32	1,544.68
220	1,875.00	279.26	1,595.74
225	1,930.00	287.45	1,642.55
230 or more	1,985.00	295.64	1,689.36

Fuel scale charges for 3-month period

CO₂ band	VAT fuel scale charge, 3-month period, £	VAT on 3-month charge, £	VAT exclusive 3-month charge, £
120 or less	141.00	21.00	120.00
125	212.00	31.57	180.43
130	212.00	31.57	180.43
135	227.00	33.81	193.19
140	241.00	35.89	205.11
145	255.00	37.98	217.02
150	269.00	40.06	228.94
155	283.00	42.15	240.85
160	297.00	44.23	252.77
165	312.00	46.47	265.53
170	326.00	48.55	277.45
175	340.00	50.64	289.36
180	354.00	52.72	301.28
185	368.00	54.81	313.19
190	383.00	57.04	325.96
195	397.00	59.13	337.87
200	411.00	61.21	349.79
205	425.00	63.30	361.70
210	439.00	65.38	373.62
215	454.00	67.62	386.38
220	468.00	69.70	398.30
225	482.00	71.79	410.21
230 or more	496.00	73.87	422.13

Value Added Tax

Fuel scale charges for 1-month period

CO$_2$ band	VAT fuel scale charge, 1-month period, £	VAT on 1-month charge, £	VAT exclusive 1-month charge, £
120 or less	47.00	7.00	40.00
125	70.00	10.43	59.57
130	70.00	10.43	59.57
135	75.00	11.17	63.83
140	80.00	11.91	68.09
145	85.00	12.66	72.34
150	89.00	13.26	75.74
155	94.00	14.00	80.00
160	99.00	14.74	84.26
165	104.00	15.49	88.51
170	108.00	16.08	91.92
175	113.00	16.83	96.17
180	118.00	17.57	100.43
185	122.00	18.17	103.83
190	127.00	18.91	108.09
195	132.00	19.66	112.34
200	137.00	20.40	116.60
205	141.00	21.00	120.00
210	146.00	21.74	124.26
215	151.00	22.49	128.51
220	156.00	23.23	132.77
225	160.00	23.83	136.17
230 or more	165.00	24.57	140.43

1 JANUARY 2010 – 30 APRIL 2010 (17.5 per cent VAT rate)

Fuel scale charges for 12-month period

CO$_2$ band, g/km	VAT fuel scale charge, 12-month period, £	VAT on 12-month charge, £	VAT exclusive 12-month charge, £
120 or less	505.00	75.21	429.79
125	755.00	112.45	642.55
130	755.00	112.45	642.55
135	755.00	112.45	642.55
140	805.00	119.89	685.11
145	855.00	127.34	727.66
150	905.00	134.79	770.21

CO$_2$ band, g/km	VAT fuel scale charge, 12-month period, £	VAT on 12-month charge, £	VAT exclusive 12-month charge, £
155	960.00	142.98	817.02
160	1,010.00	150.43	859.57
165	1,060.00	157.87	902.13
170	1,110.00	165.32	944.68
175	1,160.00	172.77	987.23
180	1,210.00	180.21	1,029.79
185	1,260.00	187.66	1,072.34
190	1,310.00	195.11	1,114.89
195	1,360.00	202.55	1,157.45
200	1,410.00	210.00	1,200.00
205	1,465.00	218.19	1,246.81
210	1,515.00	225.64	1,289.36
215	1,565.00	233.09	1,331.91
220	1,615.00	240.53	1,374.47
225	1,665.00	247.98	1,417.02
230	1,715.00	255.43	1,459.57
235 or more	1,765.00	262.87	1,502.13

Fuel scale charges for 3-month period

CO$_2$ band, g/km	VAT fuel scale charge, 3-month period, £	VAT on 3-month charge, £	VAT exclusive 3-month charge, £
120 or less	126.00	18.77	107.23
125	189.00	28.15	160.85
130	189.00	28.15	160.85
135	189.00	28.15	160.85
140	201.00	29.24	171.76
145	214.00	31.87	182.13
150	226.00	33.66	192.34
155	239.00	35.60	203.40
160	251.00	37.38	213.62
165	264.00	39.32	224.68
170	276.00	41.11	234.89
175	289.00	43.04	245.96
180	302.00	44.98	257.02
185	314.00	46.77	267.23
190	327.00	48.70	278.30
195	339.00	50.49	288.51
200	352.00	52.43	299.57
205	365.00	54.36	310.64
210	378.00	56.30	321.70

Value Added Tax

CO₂ band, g/km	VAT fuel scale charge, 3-month period, £	VAT on 3-month charge, £	VAT exclusive 3-month charge, £
215	390.00	58.09	331.91
220	403.00	60.02	342.98
225	416.00	61.96	354.04
230	428.00	63.74	364.26
235 or more	441.00	65.68	375.32

Fuel scale charges for 1-month period

CO₂ band, g/km	VAT fuel scale charge, 1-month period, £	VAT on 1-month charge, £	VAT exclusive 1-month charge, £
120 or less	42.00	6.26	35.74
125	63.00	9.38	53.62
130	63.00	9.38	53.62
135	63.00	9.38	53.62
140	67.00	9.98	57.02
145	71.00	10.57	60.43
150	75.00	11.17	63.83
155	79.00	11.77	67.23
160	83.00	12.36	70.64
165	88.00	13.11	74.89
170	92.00	13.70	78.30
175	96.00	14.30	81.70
180	100.00	14.89	85.11
185	104.00	15.49	88.51
190	109.00	16.23	92.77
195	113.00	16.83	96.17
200	117.00	17.43	99.57
205	121.00	18.02	102.98
210	126.00	18.77	107.23
215	130.00	19.36	110.64
220	134.00	19.96	114.04
225	138.00	20.55	117.45
230	142.00	21.15	120.85
235 or more	147.00	21.89	125.11

1 MAY 2009 – 31 DECEMBER 2009 (15 per cent VAT rate)

Fuel scale charges for 12-month period

CO$_2$ band, g/km	VAT fuel scale charge, 12-month period, £	VAT on 12-month charge, £	VAT exclusive 12-month charge, £
120 or less	505.00	65.87	439.13
125	755.00	98.48	656.52
130	755.00	98.48	656.52
135	755.00	98.48	656.52
140	805.00	105.00	700.00
145	855.00	111.52	743.48
150	905.00	118.04	786.96
155	960.00	125.22	834.78
160	1,010.00	131.74	878.26
165	1,060.00	138.26	921.74
170	1,110.00	144.78	965.22
175	1,160.00	151.30	1,008.70
180	1,210.00	157.83	1,052.17
185	1,260.00	164.35	1.095.65
190	1,310.00	170.87	1,139.13
195	1,360.00	177.39	1,182.61
200	1,410.00	183.91	1,226.09
205	1,465.00	191.09	1,273.91
210	1,515.00	197.61	1,317.39
215	1,565.00	204.13	1,360.87
220	1,615.00	210.65	1,404.35
225	1,665.00	217.17	1,447.83
230	1,715.00	223.70	1,491.30
235 or more	1,765.00	230.22	1,534.78

Fuel scale charges for 3-month period

CO$_2$ band, g/km	VAT fuel scale charge, 3-month period, £	VAT on 3-month charge, £	VAT exclusive 3-month charge, £
120 or less	126.00	16.43	109.57
125	189.00	24.65	164.35
130	189.00	24.65	164.35
135	189.00	24.65	164.35
140	201.00	26.22	174.78
145	214.00	27.91	186.09
150	226.00	29.48	196.52

Value Added Tax

CO$_2$ band, g/km	VAT fuel scale charge, 3-month period, £	VAT on 3-month charge, £	VAT exclusive 3-month charge, £
155	239.00	31.17	207.83
160	251.00	32.74	218.26
165	264.00	34.43	229.57
170	276.00	36.00	240.00
175	289.00	37.70	251.30
180	302.00	39.39	262.61
185	314.00	40.96	273.04
190	327.00	42.65	284.35
195	339.00	44.22	294.78
200	352.00	45.91	306.09
205	365.00	47.61	317.39
210	378.00	49.30	328.70
215	390.00	50.87	339.13
220	403.00	52.57	350.43
225	416.00	54.26	361.74
230	428.00	55.83	372.17
235 or more	441.00	57.52	383.48

Fuel scale charges for 1-month period

CO$_2$ band, g/km	VAT fuel scale charge, 1-month period, £	VAT on 1-month charge, £	VAT exclusive 1-month charge, £
120 or less	42.00	5.48	36.52
125	63.00	8.22	54.78
130	63.00	8.22	54.78
135	63.00	8.22	54.78
140	67.00	8.74	58.26
145	71.00	9.26	61.74
150	75.00	9.78	65.22
155	79.00	10.30	68.70
160	83.00	10.83	72.17
165	88.00	11.48	76.52
170	92.00	12.00	80.00
175	96.00	12.52	83.48
180	100.00	13.04	86.96
185	104.00	13.57	90.43
190	109.00	14.22	94.78
195	113.00	14.74	98.26
200	117.00	15.26	101.74
205	121.00	15.78	105.22
210	126.00	16.43	109.57

CO$_2$ band, g/km	VAT fuel scale charge, 1-month period, £	VAT on 1-month charge, £	VAT exclusive 1-month charge, £
215	130.00	16.96	113.04
220	134.00	17.48	116.52
225	138.00	18.00	120.00
230	142.00	18.52	123.48
235 or more	147.00	19.17	127.83

[¶19-320]   VAT publications having legal force

(VAT Reporter: ¶4-200)

The VAT publications that have legal force in whole or part are listed in Notice 747.

[¶19-340]   VAT registration numbers: country code prefix

(*Value Added Tax Regulations* 1995 (SI 1995/2518), reg. 2(1); Notice 725, para. 16.17 (2007 edn))

(VAT Reporter: ¶63-160)

Certain invoices should show the invoicer's registration number prefixed by the country code (also known as the alphabetical code).

Member state	Country code
Austria	AT
Belgium	BE
Bulgaria[2]	BG
Cyprus[1]	CY
Czech Republic[1]	CZ
Denmark	DK
Estonia[1]	EE
Finland	FI
France	FR
Germany	DE
Greece	EL
Hungary[1]	HU
Ireland	IE
Italy	IT
Latvia[1]	LV
Lithuania[1]	LT
Luxembourg	LU
Malta[1]	MT
Netherlands	NL

Value Added Tax

Member state	Country code
Poland[1]	PL
Portugal	PT
Romania[2]	RO
Slovakia[1]	SK
Slovenia[1]	SI
Spain	ES
Sweden	SE
United Kingdom	GB

[1] This country joined the European Union on 1 May 2004.
[2] Bulgaria and Romania joined the EU on 1 January 2007.
[3] Turkey may join the EU in the near future.

[¶19-344]   Territory of the European Community

(Directive 2006/112, art. 5; Notice 60, para. 2.5 (2010 edn); Notice 725, para. 1.3 (2002 edn); Notice 741A, para. 21 (2010 edn))

Member states

The territory of the European Community for VAT purposes consists of the following member states:

(1)   Austria;

(2)   Belgium;

(3)   Bulgaria (from 1 January 2007);

(4)   Cyprus (from 1 May 2004);

(5)   Czech Republic (from 1 May 2004);

(6)   Denmark (excluding Greenland);

(7)   Estonia (from 1 May 2004);

(8)   Finland (excluding the Aland Islands);

(9)   France (including Monaco, but excluding France's overseas departments: Martinique, French Guiana, Guadeloupe, Réunion and St Pierre and Miquelon);

(10)   Germany (excluding the territory of Büsingen and the Island of Heligoland);

(11)   Greece (excluding Mount Athos, which is also known as Agion Poros);

(12)   Hungary (from 1 May 2004);

(13)   Ireland (the Republic of) (also known as Eire);

(14)   Italy (excluding Livigno, Campione d'Italia and the Italian waters of Lake Lugano). San Marino and the Vatican City are not part of the territory of the EC for VAT purposes;

(15)   Latvia (from 1 May 2004);

(16)   Lithuania (from 1 May 2004);

(17)   Luxembourg;

(18)   Malta (from 1 May 2004);

(19)   Netherlands (also known as Holland);

(20)   Poland (from 1 May 2004);

(21)   Portugal (including the Azores and Madeira);

(22)   Romania (from 1 January 2007);

(23)   Slovakia (from 1 May 2004);

(24)   Slovenia (from 1 May 2004).

(25)   Spain (including the Balearic Islands, but excluding the Canary Islands, Ceuta and Melilla);

(26)   Sweden; and

(27)   UK (including the Isle of Man and (from 1 May 2004) the Sovereign base areas in Cyprus (Akrotiri and Dhekelia), but excluding the Channel Islands and Gibraltar).

Excluded territories

The following territories of member states are excluded from the 'territory of the country':

(1)   re Finland: the Aland Islands;

(2)   re France: the overseas departments (Martinique, French Guiana, Guadeloupe, Reunion and St Pierre and Miquelon); and

(3)   re Germany:

    (a)   the Island of Heligoland; and

    (b)   the territory of Büsingen,

(4)   re Greece: Mount Athos (also known as Agion Poros);

(5)   re Italy:

    (a)   Livigno,

    (b)   Campione d'Italia; and

    (c)   the Italian waters of Lake Lugano;

(6)   re Spain:

    (a)   the Canary Islands

    (b)   Ceuta; and

    (c)   Melilla; and

(7)   re UK:

    (a)   the Channel Islands; and

    (b)   Gibraltar.

(8)   re Cyprus the United Nations buffer zone and the part of Cyprus to the north of the buffer zone where the Republic of Cyprus does not have control;

(9)   re Denmark the Faroe Islands and Greenland.

(10) re Netherlands, Antilles.

Included areas: Monaco and the Isle of Man

Monaco and the Isle of Man are not treated as 'third territories'. They are part of France and the UK respectively. Thus, transactions originating in or intended for:

(1)   Monaco are treated as transactions originating in or intended for France; and

Value Added Tax

(2)   the Isle of Man are treated as transactions originating in or intended for the UK.

Areas not within the EC

Andorra, San Marino, the Vatican City and Liechtenstein are not within the EC for VAT purposes.

ADMINISTRATION

[¶19-500]   Civil penalties and default surcharge

(VATA 1994, s. 59ff.; FA 2007, Sch. 24; FA 2008, Sch. 41; Notices 700/41 (Late registration penalty) and 700/50 (Default surcharge); HMRC 'Compliance handbook' manual; HMRC 'VAT – Civil penalties' manual)

(VAT Reporter: ¶59-600ff.)

Offence	Civil penalty or surcharge
• Failure of a company to notify HMRC of the name of its **senior accounting officer** for a financial year beginning after 20 July 2009 (FA 2009, s. 93 and Sch. 46, para. 7).	Penalty of £5,000
• Failure of a senior accounting officer (1) to take reasonable steps to ensure that the company establishes and maintains **appropriate tax accounting arrangements** or (2) to provide an accurate **certificate** to HMRC (FA 2009, s. 93 and Sch. 46, para. 4 and 5 in relation to financial years beginning after 20 July 2009).	Penalty of £5,000
• Failure of a third party to comply with a notice from HMRC requiring **contact details for a debtor** for the purpose of collecting VAT (FA 2009, Sch. 49, para. 5).	Penalty of £300
• Deliberately **obstructing an officer** in the course of an inspection that has been pre-approved by the Tribunal	• a fixed £300 penalty (FA 2008, Sch. 36, para. 39); and • daily penalties of up to £60 for continuing default (Sch. 36, para. 40)

Offence	Civil penalty or surcharge	
• Failure to notify liability for **registration** or change in nature of supplies by person exempted from registration or certain acquisitions of goods in the UK from another member state (FA 2008, Sch. 41, para. 1, in relation to an obligation arising after 31 March 2010)	**Type of failure**	**Percentage of the tax unpaid**
	Non-deliberate failure	30%
	Deliberate but not concealed	70%
	Deliberate and concealed	100%
• Unauthorised issue of VAT **invoice** (FA 2008, Sch. 41, para. 2, in relation to an unauthorised issue of an invoice taking place after 31 March 2010)	Penalty is the same as for the late notification penalty under Sch. 41, para. 1	
• **Error** in taxpayer's document sent to HMRC[1][2]	Maximum penalty, i.e. without disclosure, under FA 2007, Sch. 24, para. 1: • for careless action, 30% of the 'potential lost revenue' (PLR); • for deliberate but not concealed action, 70% of the PLR; and • for deliberate and concealed action, 100% of the PLR.	
• **Failure to notify** HMRC within 30 days of an **underassessment** (FA 2007, Sch. 24, para. 2)[1]	30% of the potential lost revenue [2]	
• Evasion of VAT due on **imports** (FA 2003, s. 25)	Amount of import VAT evaded after 26 November 2003	
• Contravention of HMRC rules relating to **exports** after 22 December 2003 (FA 2003, s. 26; *Customs (Contravention of a Relevant Rule) Regulations* 2003 (SI 2003/3113))	Penalty of up to £2,500	
• Default **surcharge** (VATA 1994, s. 59)	1st default in surcharge period	2%
	2nd	5%
	3rd	10%
	4th or later	15%
	If a return is late, but either no VAT is due or the VAT is paid on time, although a default is recorded, no surcharge is assessed.	

Value Added Tax

Offence	Civil penalty or surcharge
	HMRC generally only issue a surcharge assessment at the 2% or 5% rate if the assessment is at least £400. The surcharge may be suspended while there is an agreement for deferred payment (FA 2009, s. 108).
	There is no automatic default surcharge for persons with an annual turnover of up to £150,000. Generally, by concession, such persons are first offered help and advice when they are late with a VAT payment. Small businesses are often allowed two defaults before a default surcharge is assessed: a first default should trigger a letter and a second default should trigger a surcharge liability notice.
	A revised penalty regime is due to replace the default surcharge and apply to taxpayers who fail to file their VAT returns on time or pay their VAT liabilities in full and on time (Budget Note BN67 (24 March 2010)). The revised penalties will treat late payment of VAT and late-filed returns separately and try to encourage filing and payment by the correct dates by imposing an escalating series of penalties, depending on the number of failures within a penalty period. Further penalties arise if there is a prolonged delay in filing returns or paying the VAT due. A late payment penalty may be avoided where the taxpayer has agreed a 'time to pay' arrangement with HMRC.
• Incorrect **certificates** as to zero-rating and reduced-rate certificates re fuel and power etc. (VATA 1994, s. 62)	VAT chargeable if certificate had been correct minus any VAT actually charged.
• Inaccurate **EC sales statement** or **reverse charge sales statement** (VATA 1994, s. 65)	£100 for a material inaccuracy on a statement submitted within 2 years of a penalty notice (itself issued after a 2nd materially inaccurate statement)

Offence	Civil penalty or surcharge	
• **Failure to submit** EC sales statement or reverse charge sales statement (VATA 1994, s. 66)	1st default including that to which the default notice relates	£5 per day
	2nd	£10 per day
	3rd	£15 per day
	(Maximum: 100 days – minimum: £50)	

• Failure to notify liability for **registration** or change in nature of supplies by person exempted from registration (VATA 1994, s. 67(1)(a) but replaced by FA 2008, Sch. 41, para. 1, in relation to an obligation arising after 31 March 2010)	**Period of failure**	**Percentage of relevant VAT**
	9 months or less	5%
	Over 9, but not over 18 months	10%
	Over 18 months	15%
	Minimum penalty: £50	

• Unauthorised issue of VAT **invoice** (VATA 1994, s. 67(1)(c) but replaced by FA 2008, Sch. 41, para. 2, in relation to an unauthorised issue of an invoice taking place after 31 March 2010)	15% of the 'VAT' shown or amount attributable to VAT (minimum penalty: £50)	

• Breach of **walking possession agreement** (VATA 1994, s. 68)	50% of the VAT due or amount recoverable	

• Breach of **regulatory provision** (VATA 1994, s. 69) (The penalty cannot be imposed without a prior written warning (VATA 1994, s. 76(2)).	• Failure to preserve records: £500	
	• Submission of return or payment is late	

Number of relevant failures in 2 years before the failure	**Greater of:**
0	£5 or 1/6 of 1% of VAT due
1	£10 or 1/3 of 1% of VAT due
2 or more	£15 or 1/2 of 1% of VAT due
• Other breaches	

Value Added Tax

Offence	Civil penalty or surcharge	
	Number of relevant failures in 2 years before the failure	**Prescribed daily rate**
	0 1 2 or more	£5 £10 £15
	Penalty: the number of days of failure (100 maximum) multiplied by above prescribed daily rate (minimum penalty £50)	
• Failure to comply with requirements of scheme for **investment gold** (VATA 1994, s. 69A)	17.5% of the value of the transaction concerned	
• Breach of **record-keeping requirements** imposed by a direction (VATA 1994, s. 69B)	Penalty: the number of days of failure (30 maximum) multiplied by £200 daily rate	
• Failure to notify acquisition of **excise duty goods** or **new means of transport** (VATA 1994, s. 75)	**Period of failure**	**Percentage of relevant VAT**
	3 months or less	5%
	Over 3 months but not over 6 months	10%
	Over 6 months	15%
• Failure for VAT periods starting after 31 July 2004 by certain persons to disclose to HMRC within the 30-day time-limit the use of a designated **(listed) avoidance scheme** (unless the scheme's promoter has already notified HMRC) or a notifiable **(hallmarked) scheme** that is not a designated scheme (Notice 700/8; VATA 1994, Sch. 11A, para. 10).	Penalty of 15% of VAT saving in relation to a designated scheme or £5,000 in relation to a notifiable scheme that is not a designated scheme	
• **Failure to pay** on time correct amount of a relevant tax (such as VAT) (*Distress for Customs and Excise Duties and Other Indirect Taxes Regulations 1997* (SI 1997/1431), reg. 4)	Distress (in Scotland: diligence, i.e. attachment or arrestment)	

Offence	Civil penalty or surcharge	
• Failure of a 'specified person' with annual turnover of at least £100,000 or with an effective date of registration after 31 March 2010 to use an **electronic return system** to make a VAT return for an accounting period which starts after 31 March 2011 (*Value Added Tax Regulations* 1995 (SI 1995/2518), reg. 25A). The turnover is calculated as at 31 December 2009 or any later date whether or not the person's turnover subsequently falls below the threshold.	**Annual VAT-exclusive turnover**	**Penalty**
	£22,800,001 or more	£400
	£5,600,001 to £22,800,000	£300
	£100,001 to £5,600,000	£200
	£100,000 and under	£100

Notes

(1) The penalty under FA 2007, Sch. 24, para. 1 and 2 is calculated on the 'potential lost revenue' (PLR) by reference to:

(a)   the amount of VAT understated;

(b)   the nature of the behaviour giving rise to the understatement; and

(c)   the extent of the taxpayer's disclosure.

Penalised behaviour	Maximum penalty, without disclosure, based on PLR	Minimum penalty, with prompted disclosure, based on PLR	Minimum penalty, with unprompted disclosure, based on PLR
Careless	30%	15%	Nil
Deliberate but not concealed	70%	35%	20%
Deliberate and concealed	100%	50%	30%

If HMRC think it right, because of special circumstances, they may reduce a penalty. 'Special circumstances' excludes:

(a)   ability to pay, or

(b)   the fact that the PLR from one taxpayer is balanced by a potential over-payment by another.

The penalty regime includes the concept of suspended penalties for careless (not deliberate) action for up to two years where the taxpayer shows that his compliance has improved. In due course, any such suspended penalty is cancelled or becomes payable. Apparently, suspension will only be used for weaknesses in the system for accounting for VAT and not for a one-off error.

The 'potential lost revenue' (PLR) in respect of an inaccuracy in a VAT return is the additional amount due or payable in respect of VAT as a result of correcting the inaccuracy or assessment. If an inaccuracy resulted in VAT being declared later than it should have been ('the delayed tax'), the PLR is:

(a)   5 per cent of the delayed tax for each year of the delay; or

(b)   a percentage of the delayed tax, for each separate period of delay of less than a year, equating to five per cent per year, i.e. the five per cent is calculated pro rata for part-years.

(2) The penalty under FA 2007, Sch. 24 for incorrect returns, etc. applies from the appointed date which, subject to the transitional provisions in SI 2008/568 (C. 20), art. 3, is:

•   1 April 2008 in relation to relevant documents relating to tax periods commencing on or after 1 April 2008;

•   1 April 2008 in relation to assessments falling within FA 2007, Sch. 24, para. 2 for tax periods commencing on or after 1 April 2008;

Value Added Tax

- 1 July 2008 in relation to relevant documents relating to claims under the thirteenth VAT directive for years commencing on or after 1 July 2008;
- 1 January 2009 in relation to relevant documents relating to claims under the eighth VAT directive for years commencing on or after 1 January 2009;
- 1 April 2009 in relation to documents relating to all other claims for repayments of relevant tax made on or after 1 April 2009 which are not related to a tax period;
- 1 April 2009 in relation to documents given where a person's liability to pay relevant tax arises on or after 1 April 2009.

The penalty for under-assessment by HMRC applies from 1 April 2008 in relation to assessments under FA 2007, Sch. 24, para. 2 for tax periods commencing on or after that date, but no person is liable to the penalty in respect of a tax period for which a return is required to be made before 1 April 2009.

[3] HMRC may waive certain interest and surcharges on VAT that was paid late and was payable by those who were adversely affected by designated national disasters, e.g. certain severe flooding (FA 2008, s. 135).

[4] HMRC may publish certain details of deliberate tax defaulters as regards return periods starting after 31 March 2010 and for failing to meet obligations that arise after 31 March 2010 (FA 2009, s. 94).

However, there is no publication of the details of an offender who made a full disclosure, either unprompted or prompted in a time considered appropriate by HMRC.

Criminal offences relating to VAT

Knowingly engaged in fraudulent evasion

If a person is knowingly concerned in, or in the taking of steps with a view to, the fraudulent evasion of VAT by him or another person, he is liable:

(1)   on summary conviction, to a penalty of the statutory maximum (£5,000) or of three times the amount of the VAT, whichever is the greater, or to imprisonment for a term not exceeding six months or to both; or

(2)   on conviction on indictment, to a penalty of any amount or to imprisonment for a term not exceeding seven years or to both

(VATA 1994, s. 72).

HMRC must prove fraud to criminal standards of proof, i.e. beyond reasonable doubt, rather than on a balance of probabilities.

The circumstances in which HMRC consider prosecution under the criminal law are described in Notice 700, para. 27.4.3 (2002 edn).

A tax evader may be charged with 'false accounting' or the common law offence of cheating the Public Revenue (*Theft Act* 1968, s. 32(1)).

Supplementary declarations (Intrastats)

As regards supplementary declarations, a failure to submit a declaration under the Intrastat system can result on summary conviction in a fine up to £2,500 (level 4 on the standard scale) (*Statistics of Trade (Customs and Excise) Regulations* 1992 (SI 1992/2790), reg. 6).

Impersonating an officer

It is a criminal offence to impersonate a HMRC officer with a view to obtaining:

- admission to premises;
- information; or
- any other benefit.

On summary conviction the penalty is imprisonment for up to 51 weeks, a fine not exceeding level 5 on the standard scale (£5,000), or both (CRCA 2005, s. 30).

[¶19-530] Reckonable dates

(VATA 1994, s. 74; FA 2009, s. 101; Notice 700/43)

(VAT Reporter: ¶60-630)

The reckonable dates for VAT are:

- *interest on overdue VAT*: due date for submission of return (usually last day of month following end of return period);
- *interest on VAT incorrectly repaid*: seven days after issue of instruction directing payment of amount incorrectly repaid.

From 1 September 2008, HMRC may charge interest on a voluntary disclosure of underdeclared VAT even if the underdeclaration error is below the disclosure threshold. However, underdeclaration errors properly corrected on a return still avoid an interest charge.

Proposed harmonisation of interest charge

From a date to be appointed, interest charged on late paid VAT and certain other taxes is to be harmonised (FA 2009, s. 101 and Sch. 53).

[¶19-560] Interest on underpaid VAT (default interest)

(VATA 1994, s. 74; Notice 700/43)

(VAT Reporter: ¶60-630)

Period of application	Days in period	Interest %
From 29/9/09	–	3.0
24/3/09–28/9/09	189	2.5
27/1/09–23/3/09	56	3.5
6/1/09–26/1/09	21	4.5
6/12/08–5/1/09	31	5.5
6/11/08–5/12/08	30	6.5
6/1/08–5/11/08	305	7.5
6/8/07–5/1/08	153	8.5
6/9/06–5/8/07	334	7.5
6/9/05–5/9/06	365	6.5
6/9/04–5/9/05	365	7.5
6/12/03–5/9/04	275	6.5
6/8/03–5/12/03	91	5.5
6/11/01–5/8/03	669	6.5
6/5/01–5/11/01	184	7.5
6/2/00–5/5/01	455	8.5
6/3/99–5/2/00	337	7.5
6/1/99–5/3/99	59	8.5
6/7/98–5/1/99	184	9.5

Value Added Tax

Period of application	Days in period	Interest %
6/2/96–5/7/98	881	6.25
6/3/95–5/2/96	337	7
6/10/94–5/3/95	151	6.25
6/1/94–5/10/94	273	5.5
6/3/93–5/1/94	306	6.25
6/12/92–5/3/93	90	7
6/11/92–5/12/92	30	7.75
6/10/91–5/11/92	397	9.25
6/7/91–5/10/91	92	10
6/5/91–5/7/91	61	10.75
6/3/91–5/5/91	61	11.5
6/11/90–5/3/91	120	12.25
1/4/90–5/11/90	219	13

[¶19-590]   Interest on overpaid VAT (statutory interest)

(VATA 1994, s. 78)

(VAT Reporter: ¶60-680)

Interest on overpaid VAT (statutory interest) arises in certain cases of official error. Such interest is not free of income or corporation tax.

Period of application	Interest rate %
From 29/9/09	0.5
27/1/09–28/9/09	0
6/1/09–26/1/09	1
6/12/08–5/1/09	2
6/11/08 – 5/12/08	3
6/1/08–5/11/08	4
6/8/07–5/1/08	5
6/9/06–5/8/07	4
6/9/05–5/9/06	3
6/9/04–5/9/05	4
6/12/03–5/9/04	3
6/8/03–5/12/03	2
6/11/01–5/8/03	3
6/5/01–5/11/01	4
6/2/00–5/5/01	5
6/3/99–5/2/00	4
6/1/99–5/3/99	5
1/4/97–5/1/99	6
6/2/93–31/3/97	8

INSURANCE PREMIUM TAX

[¶20-000] Rates

(FA 1994, Pt. III; Notice IPT 1; HMRC 'Insurance premium tax' manual)

Insurance premium tax (IPT) is imposed on certain insurance premiums where the risk is located in the UK.

Period of application	Standard rate %	Higher rate %
From 4 January 2011	6	20
1 July 1999 to 3 January 2011	5	17.5
1 April 1997 to 30 June 1999	4	17.5
1 October 1994 to 31 March 1997	2.5	n/a

Note

[1] From 1 August 1998, the higher rate applies to all travel insurance.

[¶20-100] Error correction

(*Insurance Premium Tax Regulations 1994* (SI 1994/1774), reg. 13)

If the underdeclarations or overdeclarations on previous returns do not exceed a limit, such errors may be corrected on the return for the period in which the errors are discovered.

For accounting periods starting after 30 June 2008, the limit is the greater of £10,000 and one per cent of the net IPT turnover as per Box 10 on the IPT return. However, this is subject to an upper limit of £50,000.

The previous limit was a single figure of £2,000.

LANDFILL TAX

[¶21-000]   Rates

(FA 1996, s. 42; Notices LFT 1 and 2; HMRC 'Landfill tax' manual)

Landfill tax was introduced on 1 October 1996 and is collected from landfill site operators. Landfill tax aims to encourage diversion of waste disposal from landfill sites.

Type of waste	Rate (per tonne) £
Inactive waste	
From 1 April 2008	2.50
1 October 1996 to 31 March 2008	2
Active waste:	
From 1 April 2011	56
1 April 2010 to 31 March 2011	48
1 April 2009 to 31 March 2010	40
1 April 2008 to 31 March 2009	32
1 April 2007 to 31 March 2008	24
1 April 2006 to 31 March 2007	21
1 April 2005 to 31 March 2006	18
1 April 2004 to 31 March 2005	15
1 April 2003 to 31 March 2004	14
1 April 2002 to 31 March 2003	13
1 April 2001 to 31 March 2002	12

[¶21-150]   Error correction

(*Landfill Tax Regulations 1996* (SI 1996/1527), reg. 13)

If the underdeclarations on previous returns do not exceed a limit, such errors may be corrected on the return for the period in which the errors are discovered.

For accounting periods starting after 30 June 2008, the limit is the greater of £10,000 and one per cent of net VAT turnover as per Box 6 on the VAT return for the return period. However, this is subject to an upper limit of £50,000. If the person is not required to be VAT-registered, there is a single limit of £10,000.

The previous limit was a single figure of £2,000.

AGGREGATES LEVY

[¶22-000]   Rates

(FA 2001, s. 16; Notices AGL 1 and AGL 2; HMRC 'Aggregates levy' manual)

Aggregates levy seeks to incorporate the environmental costs imposed by aggregates extraction into the price of virgin aggregate, and to encourage the use of alternative materials such as wastes from construction and demolition.

Generally, 'aggregate' is rock, gravel or sand and whatever occurs or is mixed with it as well as, in certain circumstances, spoil, offcuts and by-products.

Period of application	Rate (per tonne) £
From 1 April 2011	2.10
1 April 2009 to 31 March 2011	2.00
1 April 2008 to 31 March 2009	1.95
1 April 2002 to 31 March 2008	1.60

[¶22-100]   Error correction

(*Aggregates Levy (General) Regulations 2002* (SI 2002/761), reg. 29)

If the undercalculations or overcalculations on previous returns do not exceed a limit, such errors may be corrected on the return for the period in which the errors are discovered.

For accounting periods starting after 30 June 2008, the limit is the greater of £10,000 and one per cent of net VAT turnover as per Box 6 on the VAT return for the return period. However, this is subject to an upper limit of £50,000. If the person is not required to be VAT-registered, there is a single limit of £10,000.

The previous limit was a single figure of £2,000.

Aggregates Levy

INDEX

References are to paragraph numbers.

240

Index

Index

Index

Index

Index